The Hampstead Clinic Psychoanalytic Library
(Concept Research Group)

VOLUME IV
BASIC PSYCHOANALYTIC CONCEPTS ON
METAPSYCHOLOGY, CONFLICTS, ANXIETY
and other subjects

BASIC PSYCHOANALYTIC CONCEPTS ON METAPSYCHOLOGY CONFLICTS ANXIETY

and other subjects

by

HUMBERTO NAGERA

and

A. COLONNA, E. DANSKY, E. FIRST
A. GAVSHON, A. HOLDER, L. KEARNEY
P. RADFORD

MARESFIELD REPRINTS
LONDON

First published in 1970.
Reprinted 1981, with permission
of George Allen & Unwin, Ltd. by
H. Karnac (Books) Limited
56-58 Gloucester Road
London, S.W. 7, England

ISBN 0 950146 6 6

ACKNOWLEDGEMENTS AND COPYRIGHT NOTICES

The editor and publishers wish to thank the following publishers for their kind permission to use the material noted:

The Hogarth Press and the London Institute of Psychoanalysis for permission to quote from all volumes of the Standard Edition of *The Complete Psychological Works of Sigmund Freud*.

Routledge & Kegan Paul Ltd. for permission to quote from the following publications of Freud:

Jokes and their Relation to the Unconscious
Totem and Taboo

W. W. Norton for permission to quote from the following publications of Freud:

The Psychopathology of Everyday Life
Civilization and its Discontents
Totem and Taboo
Jokes and their Relation to the Unconscious
A Seventeenth-Century Demonological Neurosis
The Claims of Psycho-Analysis to Scientific Interest
The Question of Lay Analysis
An Outline of Psycho-Analysis
The Ego and the Id
Analysis Terminable and Interminable
An Autobiographical Study
The Psycho-Analytic View of Psychogenic Disturbances of Vision

Liveright for permission to quote from the following publications of Freud:

Introductory Lectures on Psycho-Analysis
Beyond the Pleasure Principle
Five Lectures on Psycho-Analysis
The Future of an Illusion
Dostoevsky and Parricide

International Universities Press for permission to quote from the following publication of Freud:

On Psycho-Analysis

Encyclopaedia Britannica for permission to quote from the following publication of Freud:

Psycho-Analysis

Thanks are due to the Sigmund Freud Copyrights for their permission and generous co-operation.

FOREWORD TO
THE HAMPSTEAD CLINIC LIBRARY

The series of publications of which the present volume forms a part, will be welcomed by all those readers who are concerned with the history of psychoanalytic concepts and interested to follow the vicissitudes of their fate through the theoretical, clinical and technical writings of psychoanalytic authors. On the one hand, these fates may strike us as being very different from each other. On the other hand, it proves not too difficult to single out some common trends and to explore the reasons for them.

There are some terms and concepts which served an important function for psychoanalysis in its earliest years because of their being simple and all-embracing such as for example the notion of a 'complex'. Even the lay public understood more or less easily that what was meant thereby was any cluster of impulses, emotions, thoughts, etc. which have their roots in the unconscious and, exerting their influence from there, give rise to anxiety, defences and symptom formation in the conscious mind. Accordingly, the term was used widely as a form of psychological short-hand. 'Father-Complex', 'Mother-Complex', 'Guilt-Complex', 'Inferiority-Complex', etc. became familiar notions. Nevertheless, in due course, added psychoanalytical findings about the child's relationship to his parents, about the early mother-infant tie and its consequences about the complexities of lacking self-esteem and feelings of insufficiency and inferiority demanded more precise conceptualization. The very omnibus nature of the term could not lead to its, at least partial, abandonment. All that remained from it were the terms 'Oedipus-Complex' to designate the experiences centred around the triangular relationships of the phallic phase, and 'Castration Complex' for the anxieties, repressed wishes, etc. concerning the loss or lack of the male sexual organ.

If, in the former instance, a general concept was split up to make room for more specific meanings, in other instances concepts took turns in the opposite direction. After starting out as concrete, well-defined descriptions of circumscribed psychic events, they were applied by many authors to an ever-widening circle of phenomena until their connotation became increasingly vague and imprecise and until finally special efforts had to be made to re-define them, to restrict their sphere of application and to invest them once more with precision and significance. This is what happened, for example, to the concepts of *Transference* and of *Trauma*.

The concept and term 'transference' was designed originally to establish the fact that the realistic relationship between analyst and patient is invariably distorted by fantasies and object-relations which stem from the patient's past and that these very distortions can be turned into a technical tool to reveal the patient's past pathogenic history. In present days, the meaning of the term has been widened to the extent that it comprises whatever happens between analyst and patient regardless of its derivation and of the reasons for its happening.

A 'trauma' or 'traumatic happening' meant originally an (external or internal) event of a magnitude with which the individual's ego is unable to deal, i.e. a sudden influx of excitation, massive enough to break through the ego's normal stimulus barrier. To this purely quantitative meaning of the term were added in time all sorts of qualifications (such as cumulative, retrospective, silent, beneficial), until the concept ended up as more or less synonymous with the notion of a pathogenic event in general.

Psychoanalytic concepts may be overtaken also by a further fate, which is perhaps of even greater significance. Most of them owe their origin to a particular era of psychoanalytic theory, or to a particular field of clinical application, or to a particular mode of technique. Since any of the backgrounds in which they are rooted, are open to change, this should lead either to a corresponding change in the concepts or to their abandonment. But, most frequently, this has failed to happen. Many concepts are carried forward through the changing scene of psychoanalytic theory and practice without sufficient thought being given to their necessary alteration or re-definition.

A case in kind is the concept of *acting out*. It was created at the very outset of technical thinking and teaching, tied to the treatment of neurotic patients, and it characterized originally a specific reaction of these patients to the psychoanalytic technique, namely that certain items of their past, when retrieved from the unconscious, did not return to conscious memory but revealed themselves instead in behaviour, were 'acted on', or 'acted out' instead of being remembered. By now, this clear distinction between remembering the recovered past and re-living it has been obscured;

the term 'acting out' is used out of this context, notably for patients such as adolescents, delinquents or psychotics whose impulse-ridden behaviour is part of their original pathology and not the direct consequence of analytic work done on the ego's defences against the repressed unconscious.

It was in this state of affairs that Dr H. Nagera initiated his enquiry into the history of psychoanalytic thinking. Assisted by a team of analytic workers, trained in the Hampstead Child-Therapy Course and Clinic, he set out to trace the course of basic psycho-analytic concepts from their first appearance through their changes in the twenty-three volumes of the Standard Edition of *The Complete Psychological Works of Sigmund Freud*, i.e. to a point from where they are meant to be taken further to include the writings of the most important authors of the post-Freudian era.

Dr Nagera's aim in this venture was a fourfold one:

to facilitate for readers of psychoanalytic literature the under-standing of psychoanalytic thought and of the terminology in which it is expressed;

to understand and define concepts, not only according to their individual significance, but also according to their relevance for the particular historical phase of psychoanalytic theory within which they have arisen;

to induce psychoanalytic authors to use their terms and con-cepts more precisely with regard for the theoretical framework to which they owe their origin, and to reduce thereby the many sources of misunderstanding and confusion which govern the psychoanalytic literature at present;

finally, to create for students of psychoanalysis the opportunity to embark on a course of independent reading and study, linked to a scholarly aim and designed to promote their critical and constructive thinking on matters of theory-formation.

Anna Freud, London

CONTENTS

INTRODUCTION

This volume is a sample of scholastic research work carried out at the Hampstead Child Therapy Clinic and Course relating to the study of a large number of pre-selected psychoanalytic concepts postulated and developed by Freud in his psychoanalytic writings, spanning the time from his earliest to his latest conceptualizations.

This research work has been carried out during the last six years by the Concept Research Group. These drafts on basic concepts are in no way meant to replace the study of Freud's works themselves. On the contrary, they are intended as a guide to help the student in that very aim.

The group's method has been to assign to each of its members one pre-selected concept at a time. This member's task then is to extract all the relevant material from Freud's published papers, books, correspondence, Minutes of the Meetings of the Vienna Psychoanalytic Society, etc., and to prepare a written summary of a given concept for discussion. This first draft is referred to as the 'personal draft' and is circulated among members some time before it is due for discussion.

As far as possible the draft makes use of 'literal quotations', giving at the same time the source of the quotations. This facilitates the study of the drafts by the group members who meet weekly to discuss the personal drafts. On the basis of the general discussion by the Group a second draft is produced which we designate as the 'group draft'.

Our aims are multiple and are very much in accordance with the views expressed by Hartmann, Kris and Loewenstein in their paper 'The Function of Theory in Psychoanalysis'[1] and in other publications.

Like these authors, we believe that Freud's views are often misrepresented in a considerable number of the vast amount of psychoanalytic writings due to the fact that certain of Freud's statements are not always evaluated within their proper context.

[1] Hartmann, H., Kris, E., Loewenstein, R.M., 'The Function of Theory in Psychoanalysis', *Drives, Affects and Behaviour*, International Universities Press, Inc., New York, 1953.

Thus, not infrequently, specific aspects are torn out of a long historical line of theoretical development and isolated from the rest, and similarly one or the other phase of psychoanalytic thinking is given undue emphasis out of context. Such misrepresentations are apt to convey the erroneous impression that whatever aspect has been singled out embraces all that Freud or psychoanalysis had ever to say on some specific topic. In this sense we very much endorse the statement made by Hartmann, Kris and Loewenstein that 'quoting Freud is, as a rule, meaningful only if it is part of a laborious but unavoidable attempt to gain insight into the position of the quoted passage within the development of Freud's thought'.[1] This is precisely one of the major aims of the Concept Research Group.

We were similarly prompted for what we felt with Hartmann, Kris and Loewenstein, to be 'the disregard for the psychoanalytic theory as a coherent set of assumptions'.[2] 'Freud's hypotheses are interrelated in a systematic way: there is a hierarchy of hypothesis in their relevance, their closeness to observation, their degree of verification. It is none the less true that there exists no comprehensive presentation of analysis from this angle. Here again recourse to the historical approach seems imperative . . . by showing the actual problems in their right proportions and in their right perspective.'[3]

Another important factor is the realization that Freud made many statements in the course of developing his theories which he withdrew or modified in subsequent works. This in itself constitutes a major source of frequent misrepresentation of Freud's views. One of the aims of this work, in which we try to evaluate Freud's basic psychoanalytic concepts in their historical context, is precisely to avoid such pitfalls and misrepresentations.

We further agree with Hartmann, Kris and Loewenstein that a serious danger of misrepresentation exists when there is an insufficient understanding of the hierarchy of psychoanalytic propositions. It is therefore essential to have a clear understanding of

---

[1] Hartmann, H., 'The Development of the Ego Concept in Freud's Work', I.J.P., Vol. XXXVII, Part VI, 1956. (Paper read at the Freud Centenary Meeting of the British Psycho-Analytical Society, May 5, 1956.)

[2] Hartmann, H., Kris, E., Loewenstein, R. M., 'The Function of Theory in Psychoanalysis', *Drives, Affects and Behaviour*, International Universities Press, Inc., New York, 1953, p. 23.

[3] Hartmann, H., 'The Development of the Ego Concept in Freud's Work', I.J.P., Vol. XXXVII, Part VI, London 1956, p. 425.

how the different parts of psychoanalytic theoretical propositions fit together, both when quoting and when attempting new formulations.

We are planning to publish the remainder of the work of the Concept Research Group up to the present moment in the near future in order to make it available to teachers and students in the psychoanalytic and related fields. We think that this contribution will be of special value and interest to any student of Freud, especially students in training who will have an encyclopaedic review of basic psychoanalytic concepts in an extremely condensed but meaningful way. From these summaries of concepts the student can readily find his way back to Freud's work in order to pursue and become more fully acquainted with his formulations. In this way he can study specific aspects in the development of the theory while being able, at the same time, to get a more comprehensive and over-all view of the particular topic and its relations with other aspects of the theory. We believe that our work will be similarly useful to lecturers and seminar leaders, to research workers in the field of psychoanalysis and related fields and to those writing papers which require a review of Freud's statements with regard to a specific topic. Altogether this form of scholastic research may help to avoid confusion, constant reformulations and the introduction of new terms when authors in fact refer to 'concepts' already clearly described by Freud in the past. This work may well help to open the way to standardize and find some measure of agreement as to the precise meaning of terms used in psychoanalysis today.

Although we have taken as much care as possible to be comprehensive and to avoid misrepresentations, experience has taught us that we can have no claim to perfection or completeness. It is practically impossible, within a vast and complex volume of theory such as Freud's life output represents, not to overlook or even slightly to misrepresent one or another aspect or set of factors. Furthermore, the capacity to comprehend and the level of insight possible for any given person or group of persons engaged in such work increases as the work proceeds. Thus certain formulations become more meaningful, are suddenly understood in a new light, assume a different significance, etc. Because of our realization of potential shortcomings we hope that future readers of these concepts will contribute to complete and clarify the work which the Concept Group has started, by drawing our attention to relevant material which has been either overlooked, misrepresented or not understood in its full significance.

It is hoped that in this way the concepts will become more and more representative and complete in the course of time.

Dr Humberto Nagera

METAPSYCHOLOGY

Metapsychology is defined by Freud as an approach 'according to which every mental process is considered in relation to three co-ordinates', namely the *dynamic, topographical,* and *economic* respectively'.[1] Freud considered this as 'the consummation of psychoanalytic research' and it seemed to him 'to represent the furthest goal that psychology could attain'.[2] The purpose of a metapsychological approach to mental phenomena was described as an endeavour 'to clarify and carry deeper the theoretical assumptions on which a psychoanalytic system could be founded'.[3] Furthermore Freud thought it 'impossible to define health except in metapsychological terms'.[4]

As to the *genetic point of view* it may be assumed with considerable certainty that it was never explicitly mentioned as a metapsychological criterion because genetic assumptions and propositions are inherent in most psychoanalytic formulations. This is stated clearly in the following passage:

'Not every analysis of psychological phenomena deserves the name of psychoanalysis. The latter implies more than the mere analysis of composite phenomena into simpler ones. It consists in tracing back one psychical structure to another which preceded it in time and out of which it developed. Medical psychoanalytic procedure was not able to eliminate a symptom until it had traced that symptom's origin and development. Thus from the very first psychoanalysis was directed towards tracing developmental processes. It began by discovering the genesis of neurotic symptoms, and was led, as time went on, to turn its attention to other psychical structures and to construct a genetic psychology which would apply to them too.'[5]

[1] (1925d) *An Autobiographical Study*, S.E., Vol. 20, p. 58 f.
[2] (1915e) 'The Unconscious', S.E., Vol. 14, p. 181.
[3] (1917d) 'A Metapsychological Supplement to the Theory of Dreams', S.E., Vol. 14, p. 222 n.
[4] (1937c) 'Analysis Terminable and Interminable', S.E., Vol. 23, p. 226 n.
[5] (1913j) 'The Claims of Psycho-Analysis to Scientific Interest', S.E., Vol. 13, p. 182 f.

Dynamic, economic, genetic and even topographic considerations and assumptions are to be found in Freud's psychoanalytic formulations since the beginning of his work. Thus, we think it essential to emphasize that the essence of the metapsychological approach which he proposed in 1915 is based on the *simultaneous* study and description of the phenomena from all these different angles (dynamic, economic, genetic and topographic).

A more detailed exposition of the three essential metapsychological points of view is to be found in the paper on 'Psycho-Analysis' where we read:

'Psychoanalysis, in its character of depth-psychology, considers mental life from three points of view: the dynamic, the economic and the topographical.

From the first of these standpoints, the *dynamic* one, psycho-analysis derives all mental processes (apart from the reception of external stimuli) from the interplay of forces, which assist or inhibit one another, combine with one another, enter into compromises with one another, etc. All of these forces are originally in the nature of *instincts*; thus they have an organic origin. They are characterized by possessing an immense (somatic) persistence and reserve of power (*'repetition-compulsion'*); and they are represented mentally as images or ideas with an affective charge ('cathexis'). . . .

From the *economic* standpoint psychoanalysis supposes that the mental representations of the instincts have a *cathexis* of definite quantities of energy, and that it is the purpose of the mental apparatus to hinder any damming-up of these energies and to keep as low as possible the total amount of the excitations to which it is subject. The course of mental processes is automatically regulated by the *'pleasure-pain principle'*; and pain is thus in some way related to an increase of excitation and pleasure to a decrease. In the course of development the original pleasure principle undergoes a modification with reference to the external world, giving place to the *'reality principle'*, whereby the mental apparatus learns to postpone the pleasure of satisfaction and to tolerate temporarily feelings of pain.

Topographically, psychoanalysis regards the mental apparatus as a composite instrument, and endeavours to determine at what points in it the various mental processes take place. According to the most recent psychoanalytic views, the mental apparatus is composed of an '*id*', which is the reservoir of the instinctive impulses, of an '*ego*', which is the most superficial portion of the id and one which is modified by the influence of the external world, and of a '*super-ego*', which develops out of the id, dominates the ego and represents the inhibitions of instinct characteristic of man. Further, the property of consciousness has a topographical reference; for processes in the id are entirely unconscious, while consciousness is the function of the ego's outermost layer, which is concerned with the perception of the external world.'[1]

Freud's reply (1915) to Abraham's comments on the paper on 'Mourning and Melancholia' contains an important reference to metapsychology:

'You do not emphasize enough the essential part of my hypothesis, i.e. the topographical consideration in it, the regression of the libido and the abandoning of the unconscious cathexis . . . instead you put sadism and anal-erotism in the foreground as the final explanation. Although you are correct in that, you pass by the real explanation. Anal-erotism, castration complexes, etc. are ubiquitous sources of excitation which must have their share in *every* clinical picture. One time this is made from them, another time that. Naturally we have the task of ascertaining what is made from them, but the explanation of the disorder can only be found in the mechanism—considered dynamically, topographically and economically.'[2]

His paper on 'The Unconscious' contains one of the clearest and most concise expositions of his metapsychology. He proposes in this paper that 'when we have succeeded in describing a psychical process in its dynamic, topographical and economic aspects, we should speak of it as a *metapsychological* presentation. We must say at once that in the present state of our knowledge there are only a few points at which we shall succeed in this'.[3] In the same paper

---

[1] (1926f) 'Psycho-Analysis', S.E., Vol. 20, p. 265 f. The text of the quotation used above is from the original publication in the *Encyclopaedia Britannica* and not from the *Standard Edition*. There are only very minor differences in the wording.

[2] Jones, E., *Sigmund Freud, Life and Work*, The Hogarth Press, Vol. 2, London, 1958, p. 368.

[3] (1915e) 'The Unconscious', S.E., Vol. 14, p. 181.

he proceeds to 'make a tentative effort to give a metapsychological description of the process of repression in the three transference neuroses which are familiar to us', i.e. anxiety hysteria, conversion hysteria, and obsessional neurosis. We restrict ourselves here to Freud's description of the first phase of a phobia, with some comments on what is implicit in it: 'It consists in anxiety appearing without the subject knowing what he is afraid of.' This statement implies the existence of forces in conflict (dynamic point of view) which, due perhaps to an increase in their magnitude, has led to the development of anxiety (economic point of view.)

Freud continues: 'We must suppose that there was present in the *Ucs* some love-impulses demanding to be transposed into the system *Pcs*.' This sentence contains both the dynamic and the topographical points of view. The postulation of an unconscious love-impulse states the existence of a dynamic force and its direction, i.e. the demand for transposition into a different system. From the topographical point of view we see that the systems *Ucs* and *Pcs* are involved in the conflict.

Freud's metapsychological description continues: 'but the cathexis directed to it from the latter system (*Pcs*) had drawn back from the impulse (as though in an attempt at flight) and the unconscious libidinal cathexis of the rejected idea has been discharged in the form of anxiety'.[1] This statement is concerned mainly with the economic point of view, i.e. an economic principle is involved in the withdrawal of the preconscious cathexis which bars the progression of the unconscious love-impulse to preconsciousness and possibly to consciousness and motility. Instead the affect of anxiety appears which also serves an economic function.

The above illustration not only shows the application of the metapsychological approach to clinical phenomena but also highlights the basic assumption of an existing conflict between different mental forces which can only be better understood by this type of description.

The concept of 'metapsychology' appears as early as 1896, in Freud's correspondence with Fliess[2] and it recurs frequently in this correspondence and is there simply defined as the 'psychology

[1] (1915e) 'The Unconscious', S.E., Vol. 14, p. 182.
[2] (1950a[1887–1902]) *The Origins of Psycho-Analysis*, Imago, London, 1954, p. 157, Letter 41, 1896; cf. also pp. 161, 218, 246, 260, 287.

which leads behind consciousness'.[1] The term made its first published appearance in 1901 in *The Psychopathology of Everyday Life* where Freud uses it to exemplify the attempt of psychoanalysis "to transform *metaphysics* into *metapsychology*".[2]

The metapsychological approach to mental phenomena has enabled psychoanalysts to depart 'from the descriptive "psychology of consciousness" and has raised new problems and acquired a new content. Up till now it has differed from that psychology mainly by reason of its *dynamic* view of mental processes; now in addition it seems to take account of psychical *topography* as well, and to indicate in respect of any given mental act within what system or between what systems it takes place. On account of this attempt, too, it has been given the name of "depth psychology". We shall hear that it can be further enriched by taking yet another point of view into account'.[3] The reference in the last sentence of the above quotation is obviously to the economic point of view which, historically, was the last which Freud explicitly added as an essential part of a complete metapsychological presentation of mental phenomena, in particular of conflictual situations.

Attention must be drawn to the fact that in all of Freud's explicit definitions of metapsychology he makes reference only to the dynamic, topographical and economic points of view. Neither the structural nor the genetic point of view was explicitly included in his definitions. With regard to the structural point of view, it is clear that the structural superseded the topographical theory. It is nevertheless to be noted that Freud kept referring to the 'topographical point of view' even after the introduction of the structural theory.

From a passage in *The Ego and the Id* (1923)—the paper which introduced the structural concepts—we can infer that descriptions in structural terms were largely to supersede topographical ones in view of the latter's shortcomings in explaining clinical phenomena:

'We have come upon something in the ego itself which is also unconscious . . . the consequence of this discovery is that we land in endless obscurities and difficulties if we keep to our habitual forms of expression and try, for instance, to derive neuroses from a

[1] ibid., p. 246, Letter 84, 1898.
[2] (1901b) *The Psychopathology of Everyday Life*, S.E., Vol. 6, p. 259.
[3] (1915e) 'The Unconscious', S.E., Vol. 14, p. 173.

conflict between the conscious and the unconscious. We shall have to substitute for this antithesis another, taken from our insight into the structural conditions of the mind—the antithesis between the coherent ego and the repressed which is split off from it.'[1]

We have already pointed out that although it was not until 1915 that Freud stated that a complete metapsychological description has to take account simultaneously of the dynamic, the topographical, and the economic points of view,[2] he applied them separately on many previous occasions. The fact that, in the years preceding 1915, metapsychology was not yet clearly conceptualized in its post-1915 sense, explains why some of the earlier statements do not yet show the later conceptual clarity and frequently deal with one or another aspect of the conflict only. Freud himself referred in *An Autobiographical Study* to how dynamic and economic considerations were at the basis of his formulations in *Studies on Hysteria*: 'It [the theory put forward in the *Studies on Hysteria*] introduced a dynamic factor, by supposing that a symptom arises through the damming-up of an affect, and an economic factor, by regarding that same symptom as the product of the transformation of an amount of energy which would otherwise have been employed in another way.'[3] Thus he had written: 'The patient's ego had been approached by an idea which proved to be incompatible, which provoked on the part of the ego a repelling force of which the purpose was defence against this incompatible idea. This defence was in fact successful. The idea in question was forced out of consciousness and out of memory.' A few lines later he continued: 'Thus a psychical force, aversion on the part of the ego, had originally driven the pathogenic idea out of association and was now opposing its return to memory.'[4]

It is convenient to point out that in earlier papers 'dynamic' was occasionally used in more than one sense and not necessarily with the one that will best characterize the metapsychological use of it.

Similarly, terms like 'unconscious' have more than the topographical connotations and are frequently used descriptively to refer to a quality.

---

[1] (1923b) *The Ego and the Id*, S.E., Vol. 19, p. 17.
[2] (1915e) 'The Unconscious', S.E., Vol. 14, p. 181.
[3] (1925d [1924]) *An Autobiographical Study*, S.E., Vol. 20, p. 22.
[4] (1895d) *Studies on Hysteria*, S.E., Vol. 2, p. 269.

'Topographical' propositions are of course to be found before 1915 though they do not necessarily form part of a systematic metapsychological approach to mental phenomena.

The early model of the mind described in Chapter VII of *The Interpretation of Dreams* is already based on spatial and topographical propositions. The mental apparatus is there likened to a 'compound microscope or a photographic apparatus'. On the basis of this comparison 'psychical locality will correspond to a point inside the apparatus at which one of the preliminary stages of an image comes into being'. These images occur 'in part at ideal points, regions in which no tangible component of the apparatus is situated'. Thus 'psychical locality' has nothing to do with 'anatomical locality'.[1] Further assumptions of the 'mental apparatus as a compound instrument' state that it is composed of components which are called 'systems' and that 'in a given psychical process the excitation passes through the systems in a particular *temporal* sequence'.[2] In the same work Freud distinguishes between the system *Ucs* whose excitations are *"inadmissible to consciousness"*, and the system *Pcs* whose 'excitations . . . are able to reach consciousness. . . . We have described the relations of the two systems to each other and to consciousness by saying that the system *Pcs* stands like a screen between the system *Ucs* and consciousness'.[3]

As has been pointed out earlier already, the economic point of view was the last one explicitly to be recognized by Freud as an essential component of any metapsychological formulation. However, he was concerned with economic considerations long before the formulation of the metapsychological point of view in 1915. An economic principle is implied when Freud, in *The Interpretation of Dreams*, speaks of the necessity 'to arrive at a more efficient expenditure of psychical force'.[4] In the same work he states that 'for the sake of efficiency the second system succeeds in retaining the major part of its cathexes of energy in a state of quiescence and in employing only a small part on displacement'.[5] This also deals with economics.

[1] (1900a) *The Interpretation of Dreams*, S.E., Vol. 5, p. 536.
[2] ibid., p. 536 f.
[3] ibid., p. 614 f.; cf. also (1912g) 'A Note on the Unconscious in Psycho-Analysis', S.E., Vol. 12, p. 262.
[4] ibid., p. 568.
[5] ibid., p. 599; cf. also ibid., pp. 565, 616.

The whole work on *Jokes and their Relation to the Unconscious*[1] is very much concerned with economic considerations involved in jokes, laughter, humour, and the comic in general. All these phenomena are characterized by an economy in the expenditure of psychical energy, either a saving of or a relief from psychical expenditure.

Thus we see that the foundations of all three points of view subsumed under metapsychology in 1915 were laid down long before, enabling Freud eventually to formulate the elements which had to form part of a metapsychological presentation.

[1] (1905c) *Jokes and their Relation to the Unconscious*, S.E., Vol. 8.

THE DYNAMIC POINT OF VIEW

The term 'dynamic', as used throughout Freud's works, does not always carry metapsychological implications with it. This does not only apply to its use preceding the formulation of the meta-psychological point of view in 1915, but also to formulations in subsequent works, as the following quotation from *An Outline of Psycho-Analysis* illustrates: The ego's 'psychological function consists in raising the passage [of events] in the id to a higher dynamic level (perhaps by transforming freely mobile energy into bound energy, such as corresponds to the preconscious state)'.[1] This state of affairs is a frequent source of confusion and misinterpretation, and it is indeed sometimes difficult to distinguish between Freud's use of the concept 'dynamic' in a metapsychological and in a purely physical sense.

Dymanic propositions are present all the way through in Freud's formulations.

Already in his *Studies on Hysteria* in 1895 his formulation was a dynamic one, assuming the existence of forces that were engaged in conflict: 'Thus a psychical force, aversion on the part of the ego, had originally driven the pathogenic idea out of association and was now opposing its return to memory.'[2] In a letter to Fliess he said: '*Conflict* coincides with my concept of defence [fending off].'[3]

This assumption remains a corner-stone of psychoanalysis and the whole theory of the neuroses is based on the existence of these mental forces in conflict. In what follows only a few quotations have been selected as representative of the dynamic propositions.

Dynamically, psychoanalytic metapsychology 'derives all mental processes (apart from the reception of external stimuli) from the interplay of forces, which assist or inhibit one another, enter into compromises with one another, etc. All of these forces are originally in the nature of *instincts*; thus they have an organic origin. They are characterized by possessing an immense (somatic) store of power ('*the compulsion to repeat*'); and they are represented mentally

---

[1] (1940a [1938]) *An Outline of Psycho-Analysis*, S.E., Vol. 23, p. 199.
[2] (1895d) *Studies on Hysteria*, S.E., Vol. 2, p. 269.
[3] (1950a[1887–1902]) *The Origins of Psycho-Analysis*, S.E., Vol. I, p. 188.

as images or ideas with an affective charge'.[1] It is by means of their mental representations that we are enabled to study and make inferences about these forces. As the quotation suggests, affects have to be conceived of as one form of representation of these dynamic forces which operate within and between psychic structures.

It is very important to notice in this definition of the dynamic point of view of metapsychology that Freud emphasized the 'interplay of forces'. As he points out further, they may be forces which have the same direction, i.e. 'assist' or 'combine with one another'. But there can be no doubt that metapsychology was in the first instance developed out of a need to understand and explain the interplay of forces which are in conflict with each other, i.e. those which 'inhibit one another' or 'enter into compromises with one another'. As Freud points out elsewhere conflicts 'are certainly always present' so that the question is how individuals 'succeed in emerging from such conflicts . . . without falling ill'. He stresses that this outcome depends 'on the relative magnitudes of the trends which are struggling with one another'.[2] In other words, conflicts only become pathogenic when there is an imbalance between the dynamic forces opposing each other, causing the overthrow of the psychic equilibrium. In *An Outline of Psycho-Analysis* Freud poses the question as to why neurotics 'live so much worse and with so much greater difficulty and, in the process, suffer more feelings of unpleasure, anxiety and pain?' And he answers it by saying, 'Quantitative *disharmonies* are what must be held responsible for the inadequacy and sufferings of neurotics.'[3]

Freud is quite explicit about the fact that the dynamic forces on both sides of any conflict are initially derived from one and the same source, namely the driving force of the instincts: '. . . We assume that the forces which drive the mental apparatus into activity are produced in the bodily organs as an expression of the major somatic needs. . . . We give those bodily needs, in so far as they represent an instigation to mental activity, the name of *"Triebe"* . . . these instincts fill the id: all the energy in the id . . . originates from them. Nor have the forces in the ego any other origin.'[4] But in spite of their common origin they may enter into conflict and

---

[1] (1926f) 'Psycho-Analysis', S.E., Vol. 20, p. 265.
[2] (1924b) 'Neurosis and Psychosis', S.E., Vol. 19, p. 152.
[3] (1940a [1938]) *An Outline of Psycho-Analysis*, S.E., Vol. 23, p. 183.
[4] (1926e) *The Question of Lay Analysis*, S.E., Vol. 20, p. 200.

oppose each other, an outcome which is usually the result of mental economics, particularly in the case of interstructural conflicts.

Dynamic forces, whether they are opposing one another in conflict or combine and add up their striving for a common goal, are characterized by two major qualities, namely their magnitude and their direction. Their magnitude has already been referred to in this paper as 'possessing an immense (somatic) store of power' and when he stated that 'by the pressure of an instinct we understand its motor factor, the amount of force or the measure of the demand for work which it represents. The characteristic of exercising pressure is common to all instincts; it is in fact their very essence'.[1]

The second major quality of dynamic forces, namely that they always have a direction, can be seen in his referring to them as 'a manifestation of purposeful intentions'.[2] Most generally the goal or 'ultimate aim of mental activity' can be qualitatively described as 'an endeavour to obtain pleasure and avoid unpleasure'.[3] Freud enlarges on this principle in more specifically dynamic terms when he states in *The Ego and the Id*: 'Sensations of a pleasurable nature have not anything inherently impelling about them, whereas unpleasurable ones have it in the highest degree. The latter impel towards change, towards discharge, and that is why we interpret unpleasure as implying a heightening and pleasure a lowering of energic cathexis.'[4] But in this, there is already an economic principle involved which will be dealt with at length under the economic point of view.

From a passage in the *Introductory Lectures on Psycho-Analysis* it can be seen quite clearly that quantitative considerations are involved in both the dynamic and economic points of view: 'I have introduced a fresh factor into the structure of the aetiological chain —namely, the quantity, the magnitude, of the energies concerned. We have still to take this factor into account everywhere. A purely qualitative analysis of the aetiological determinants is not enough. Or, to put it in another way, a merely *dynamic* view of these mental processes is insufficient; an *economic* line of approach is also needed. We must tell ourselves that the conflict between two trends does not break out till certain intensities of cathexis have been

[1] (1915c) 'Instincts and their Vicissitudes', S.E., Vol. 14, p. 122.
[2] (1916–17) *Introductory Lectures on Psycho-Analysis*, S.E., Vol. 15, p. 67.
[3] ibid., p. 375.
[4] (1923b) *The Ego and the Id*, S.E., Vol. 19, p. 22.

reached, even though the determinants for it have long been present so far as their subject-matter is concerned.'[1] How closely the dynamic and economic points of view were linked in Freud's mind can also be seen from a passage in *The Ego and the Id*, where he states that 'we have arrived at the term or concept of the unconscious along another path, by considering certain experiences in which mental *dynamics* play a part. We have found . . . that very powerful mental processes or ideas exist (and here a quantitative or *economic* factor comes into question for the first time) which can produce all the effects in mental life that ordinary ideas do . . . though they themselves do not become conscious'.[2]

Dynamic considerations are implied in many formulations dealing with the topic of repression, or of defence and conflict in general. The concepts of repressed and repressing forces imply the assumption of dynamic forces in opposition, and Freud speaks of 'repression in the *dynamic* sense, when a psychical act is held back at the lower, unconscious, stage. The fact is that repression is a topographico-dynamic concept'.[3]

Still in the *Introductory Lectures on Psycho-Analysis* Freud concerned himself with the dynamics involved in symptom-formation. He states that 'this experience of ours with the resistance of neurotics to the removal of their symptoms became the basis of our dynamic view of the neuroses'. He goes on to say that these dynamics remained hidden as long as hypnosis was employed. From the patient's struggle against relief of his symptoms we can infer 'powerful forces here which oppose any alteration of the patient's condition . . . there is a precondition for the existence of a symptom: some mental process must not have been brought to an end normally—so that it could become conscious. The symptom is a substitute for what did not happen at that point'.[4]

When in his paper on 'Psycho-Analysis', Freud spoke of the possibility that the 'interplay of forces' can result in their entering 'into compromises', it is very likely that he was thinking of symptom formation.[5]

---

[1] (1916–17) *Introductory Lectures on Psycho-Analysis*, S.E., Vol. 15, p. 374.
[2] (1923b) *The Ego and the Id*, S.E., Vol. 19, p. 14.
[3] (1916–17) *Introductory Lectures on Psycho-Analysis*, S.E., Vol. 15, p. 342.
[4] ibid., p. 292 ff.
[5] (1926f) An article in the *Encyclopaedia Britannica* [published as 'Psycho-Analysis: Freudian School'] *Encyclopaedia Britannica*, 13th edn., New Vol. 3, p. 253; S.E., Vol. 20, p. 265.

THE ECONOMIC POINT OF VIEW

The economic point of view 'endeavours to follow out the vicissi-tudes of amounts of excitation and to arrive at least at some *relative* estimate of their magnitude'.[1] A more detailed exposition of the economic point of view is to be found in the paper on 'Psycho-Analysis': 'From the *economic* standpoint psycho-analysis supposes that the mental representatives of the instincts have a charge (*cathexis*) of definite quantities of energy, and that it is the purpose of the mental apparatus to hinder any damming-up of these energies and to keep as low as possible the total amount of the excitations with which it is loaded. The course of mental processes is auto-matically regulated by the *"pleasure-unpleasure principle"* . . . In the course of development the original pleasure principle under-goes a modification with reference to the external world, giving place to the *"reality principle"*, in accordance with which the mental apparatus learns to postpone the pleasure of satisfaction and to tolerate temporarily feelings of unpleasure.'[2] Seen from a structural point of view, it is the task of the ego to find the most adequate economic solution in any conflict between the various structures of the mind and the external world; 'Thus the ego, driven by the id, confined by the super-ego, repulsed by reality, struggles to master its economic task of bringing about harmony among the forces and influences working in and upon it . . .'.[3] Whereas the economics of the ego are—or ought to be—governed by the reality principle, in regard to the id, 'The economic, or . . . the quantitative factor, which is intimately linked to the pleasure-principle, dominates all its processes. Instinctual cathexes seeking discharge—that, in our view, is all there is in the id.'[4]

Mental health or illness will largely depend on the ego's capacity to deal successfully with the 'conflicts with its various ruling agencies'. Whether and how the ego 'can succeed in emerging from

---

[1] (1915e) 'The Unconscious', S.E., Vol. 14, p. 181.
[2] (1926f) 'Psycho-Analysis' S.E., Vol. 20, p. 265 f.; cf. (1916–17) *Introductory Lectures on Psycho-Analysis*, S.E., Vol. 16, p. 356 f.
[3] (1933a) *New Introductory Lectures on Psycho-Analysis*, S.E., Vol. 22, p. 78.
[4] ibid., p. 74.

such conflicts, which are certainly always present, without falling ill . . . will undoubtedly depend on economic considerations—on the relative magnitudes of the trends which are struggling with one another'.[1] Thus, from an economic point of view, mental activity has the task of 'mastering the amounts of excitation (mass of stimuli) operating in the mental apparatus, and of keeping down their accumulation which creates unpleasure'.[2] In *An Outline of Psycho-Analysis* Freud describes the kind of economic conflicts which arise out of inter-structural disharmonies. He says that the 'severest demand on the ego is probably the keeping down of the instinctual claims of the id, to accomplish which it is obliged to maintain large expenditures of energy on anticathexes. But the demands made by the super-ego too may become so powerful and so relentless that the ego may be paralysed, as it were, in the face of its other tasks. We may suspect that, in the economic conflicts which arise at this point, the id and the super-ego often make common cause against the hard-pressed ego which tries to cling to reality in order to retain its normal state. If the other two become too strong, they succeed in loosening and altering the ego's organization, so that its proper relation to reality is disturbed or even brought to an end'.[3]

It is in *The Ego and the Id* that Freud makes a reference to the fact that 'sensations and feelings' yielded by internal perception 'are more primordial, more elementary, than perceptions arising externally' and that they have a 'greater economic significance'.[4] Freud had given the reasons for this view in *Beyond the Pleasure Principle*: Towards the outside the mental apparatus 'is shielded against stimuli, and the amounts of excitation impinging on it have only a reduced effect. Towards the inside there can be no such shield; the excitations in the deeper layers extend into the system [*Pcpt-Cs*] directly and in undiminished amount, in so far as certain of their characteristics give rise to feelings in the pleasure · unpleasure series'.[5]

Economic considerations are essential for an understanding of repression. Already in 1900 Freud had emphasized the fact that a preconscious (or conscious) cathexis of an unpleasurable memory

[1] (1924b) 'Neurosis and Psychosis' S.E., Vol. 19, p. 152.
[2] (1916–17) *Introductory Lectures on Psycho-Analysis*, S.E., Vol. 16, p. 375.
[3] (1940a [1938]) *An Outline of Psycho-Analysis*, S.E., Vol. 23, p. 172 f.
[4] (1923b) *The Ego and the Id*, S.E., Vol. 19, p. 22.
[5] (1920g) *Beyond the Pleasure Principle*, S.E., Vol. 18, p. 29.

implied 'a simultaneous inhibition of the discharge of excitation', and that it was the 'key of the whole theory of repression' that the system preconscious *can only cathect an idea if it is in a position to inhibit any development of unpleasure that may proceed from it*.[1] In his paper on 'Repression' he expressed the same point of view in similar terms when he said that 'it has consequently become a condition for repression that the motive force of unpleasure shall have acquired more strength than the pleasure obtained from satisfaction'.[2] From an economic point of view, repression is not a very efficient solution because it 'demands a persistent expenditure of force . . . the repressed exercises a continuous pressure in the direction of the conscious, so that this pressure must be balanced by an unceasing counter-pressure. Thus the maintenance of a repression involves an uninterrupted expenditure of force, while its removal results in a saving from an economic point of view'.[3]

In the *Introductory Lectures on Psycho-Analysis*, he defines the term 'traumatic' in economic terms: 'the term "traumatic" has no other sense than an economic one. We apply it to an experience which within a short period of time presents the mind with an increase of stimulus too powerful to be dealt with or worked off in the normal way, and this must result in permanent disturbances of the manner in which the energy operates'.[4]

In Inhibitions, Symptoms and Anxiety Freud points out that it was for economic reasons that the mechanism of signal anxiety was developed. The experience of birth and situations in infancy when stimulation is excessive and cannot be mastered psychically lead to an 'economic disturbance caused by an accumulation of amounts of stimulation which require to be disposed of'. A reaction of anxiety sets in, and only when the infant has learned that an external object can put an end to the dangerous situation is it capable of displacing 'the content of the dangers it fears . . . from the economic situation on to the condition which determined that situation, *viz.*, the loss of object. It is the absence of the mother that is now the danger; and as soon as the danger arises the infant gives the signal of anxiety, before the dreaded economic situation

[1] (1900a) *The Interpretation of Dreams*, S.E., Vol. 5., p. 601.
[2] (1915d) 'Repression', S.E., Vol. 14, p. 147.
[3] ibid., p. 151; cf. (1916–17) *Introductory Lectures on Psycho-Analysis*, S.E., Vol. 16, p. 356 f.
[4] (1916–17) *Introductory Lectures on Psycho-Analysis*, S.E., Vol. 16, p. 275.

has set in'.[1] This fact led to a change in Freud's views about the economics involved in anxiety. Whereas he formerly believed 'that anxiety invariably arose automatically by an economic process', he now felt that the 'conception of anxiety as a signal given by the ego in order to affect the pleasure-unpleasure agency does away with the necessity of considering the economic factor'.[2] However, Freud did not abandon the earlier view that one form of anxiety in later life was 'involuntary, automatic and always justified on economic grounds, and arose whenever a danger-situation analogous to birth had established itself'.[3] Anxiety, thus, 'occupies a unique position in the economy of the mind' in so far as it has 'something to do with the essential nature of danger'.[4]

Clinical experience led to the formulation of economic factors involved in various neurotic illnesses. In the following quotation, referring to dreams, neuroses and war neuroses, the pleasure principle as a determining factor is emphasized: 'dreams of recovery very frequently occur, for instance, when the patient is about to enter upon a new and disagreeable phase of the transference. He is behaving in this just like some neurotics who after a few hours of analysis declare they have been cured—because they want to escape all the unpleasantness that is bound to come up for discussion in the analysis. Sufferers from war neuroses, too, who gave up their symptoms because the therapy adopted by the army doctors succeeded in making being ill even more uncomfortable than serving at the front—these sufferers, too, were following the same economic laws'.[5]

Light is thrown on the perversions from an economic point of view when Freud states that the 'feeling of happiness derived from the satisfaction of a wild instinctual impulse untamed by the ego is incomparably more intense than that derived from sating an instinct that has been tamed. The irresistibility of perverse instincts, and perhaps the attraction in general of forbidden things finds an economic explanation here'.[6]

Freud has concerned himself with the economics of many other

[1] (1926d) *Inhibitions, Symptoms and Anxiety*, S.E., Vol. 20, p. 137 f.

[2] ibid., p. 140; cf. ibid., p. 161.

[3] ibid., p. 162.

[4] ibid., p. 150.

[5] (1923c) 'Remarks on the Theory and Practice of Dream-Interpretation', S.E., Vol. 19, p. 112.

[6] (1930a) *Civilization and its Discontents*, S.E., Vol. 21, p. 79.

phenomena, such as dreaming, jokes, happiness, work, etc. Here we can only give illustrations with regard to a few of these. Thus, for instance, in 'Mourning and Melancholia', he deals with some economic aspects of these two conditions. He wonders, for instance, why, in the case of mourning, there is no hint 'of the economic condition for a phase of triumph'. Following his statement that 'we do not even know the economic means by which mourning carries out its task', he makes the following conjecture: 'Each single one of the memories and situations of expectancy which demonstrate the libido's attachment to the lost object is met by the verdict of reality that the object no longer exists; and the ego, confronted as it were with the question whether it shall share this fate, is persuaded by the sum of the narcissistic satisfactions it derives from being alive to sever its attachment to the object that has been abolished. We may perhaps suppose that this work of severance is so slow and gradual that by the time it has been finished the expenditure of energy necessary for it is also dissipated.'[1] As to the 'economic condition for the emergence of mania after the melancholia has run its course', Freud argues that neither the loss of the object nor the ambivalance are relevant for this outcome, as both these factors are also involved in mourning. Therefore, 'the third factor', i.e. the 'regression of libido into the ego' is 'the only one responsible for the result'.[2]

With the introduction of the structural point of view Freud was able to see several economic phenomena from a new angle. He realized, for instance, that 'in a great number of neuroses an unconscious sense of guilt . . . plays a decisive economic part and puts the most powerful obstacles in the way of recovery.'[3] This unconscious sense of guilt is a consequence of the morality functioning in the super-ego. Of this Freud says that 'In suffering under the attacks of the super-ego or perhaps even succumbing to them, the ego is meeting with a fate like that of the *protista* which are destroyed by the products of decomposition that they themselves have created. From the economic point of view the morality that functions in the super-ego seems to be a similar product of decomposition.'[4]

[1] (1917e) 'Mourning and Melancholia', S.E., Vol. 14, p. 255; cf. (1926d) *Inhibitions, Symptoms, and Anxiety*, S.E., Vol. 20, p. 171.
[2] ibid., p. 258.
[3] (1923b) *The Ego and the Id*, S.E., Vol. 19, p. 27.
[4] ibid., p. 56 f.

The realization that psychical energies can be transformed led Freud to the assumption of the existence of neutralized energy in the mind. He came to formulate this view—which is essential to an understanding of the economic functioning of the mental apparatus—when he dealt with the problem of the transformation of hate into love.[1]

In Civilization and its Discontents Freud dealt at length with various aspects of human happiness which, according to him, is largely concerned with the economics of the individual's libido, i.e. it is closely connected with the pleasure principle. Although we can never attain complete happiness, we must never give up our efforts in that direction. We can do this by giving 'priority either to the positive aspect of the aim, that of gaining pleasure, or to its negative one, that of avoiding unpleasure. By none of these paths can we attain all that we desire. Happiness, in the reduced sense in which we recognize it as possible, is a problem of the economics of the individual's libido'.[2] And in a footnote added a year later Freud continues by saying that 'No discussion of the possibilities of human happiness should omit to take into consideration the relation between narcissism and object libido. We require to know what being essentially self-dependent signifies for the economics of the libido.'[3] Freud sees the function of intoxicating media in this light. The service rendered by them 'in the struggle for happiness and in keeping misery at a distance is so highly prized as a benefit that individuals and peoples alike have given them an established place in the economics of their libido. We owe to such media not merely the immediate yield of pleasure, but also a greatly desired degree of independence from the external world'.[4] Whereas intoxication—with regard to the economics of the libido— leads to independence from the external world, work on the other hand has the opposite aim, namely to give the individual 'a secure place in a portion of reality, in the human community. The possibility it offers of displacing a large amount of libidinal components, whether narcissistic, aggressive or even erotic, on to professional work and on to the human relations connected with it lends it a value by no means second to what it enjoys as something indispensible to the preservation and justification of existence in

[1] (1923b) *The Ego and the Id*, S.E., Vol. 19, p. 44.
[2] (1930a) *Civilization and its Discontents*, S.E., Vol. 21, p. 83.
[3] ibid., p. 84.   [4] ibid., p. 78.

society'.[1] The possibility of displacing libidinal components on to work again implies the assumption of neutral or neutralized energies. This also applies to Freud's remarks about the connection between civilization and libidinal economy, in that 'civilization is obeying the laws of economic necessity, since a large amount of the psychical energy which it uses for its own purposes has to be withdrawn from sexuality'.[2] Freud makes it quite clear, in a later passage, that in his view 'this struggle between the individual and society is not a derivative of the contradiction . . . between the primal instincts of Eros and death. It is a dispute within the economics of the libido, comparable to the contest concerning the distribution of libido between ego and objects; and it does admit of an eventual accommodation in the individual, as it may be hoped, it will also do in the future of civilization'.[3]

[1] ibid., p. 80 n.   [2] ibid., p. 104.   [3] ibid., p. 141.

THE TOPOGRAPHICAL POINT OF VIEW

The topographical point of view of metapsychology indicates 'in respect of any given mental act within what system or between what systems it takes place. On account of this attempt, too, it has been given the name of "depth psychology"'.[1] In *An Outline of Psycho-Analysis* Freud points out that the division of the mind into three systems (*Ucs, Pcs, Cs*) 'is not a theory at all but a first stock-taking of the facts of our observations, that it keeps as close to those facts as possible and does not attempt to explain them'.[2]

Whereas the genetic, dynamic, and the economic points of view of metapsychology remained essentially the same throughout Freud's works, the topographical theory and the topographical metapsychological point of view were eventually superseded by the structural theory, even though descriptions in topographical terms were never completely abandoned. Freud often referred to the structures of ego, id and super-ego in these topographical terms.

It is well to remember at this point that though the topographical theory was specially formulated in 1915 in the paper on 'The Unconscious', topographical propositions were already at the basis of the model of the mind Freud proposed in Chapter VII of *The Interpretation of Dreams*.

With the topographical hypothesis 'is bound up that of a topographical separation of the systems *Ucs* and *Cs* and also the possibility that an idea may exist simultaneously in two places in the mental apparatus—indeed, that if it is not inhibited by the censorship it regularly advances from one position to the other, possibly without losing its first location or registration'.[3]

In the *Introductory Lectures on Psycho-Analysis*, Freud uses a spatial analogy to characterize and describe the two systems and the censorship between them. He compares the unconscious system to 'a large entrance hall, in which the mental impulses jostle one another, like separate individuals. Adjoining this entrance hall there is a second, narrower room—a kind of drawing-room—in

---

[1] (1915e) 'The Unconscious', S.E., Vol. 14, p. 173.
[2] (1940a [1938]) *An Outline of Psycho-Analysis*, S.E., Vol. 23, p. 161.
[3] (1915e) 'The Unconscious', S.E., Vol. 14, p. 175.

which consciousness, too, resides. But on the threshold between these two rooms a watchman performs his function: he examines the different mental impulses, acts as a censor, and will not admit them into the drawing-room if they displease him'.[1]

In the paper on 'The Unconscious' Freud further added that 'the system Pcs shares the characteristics of the system Cs and that the rigorous censorship exercises its office at the point of transition from the Ucs to the Pcs (or Cs)'.[2]

In the 'Metapsychological Supplement' Freud ascribes to the system Cs the function of 'conscious perception', and it is the system 'on whose activity becoming conscious usually depends'. But he adds here—and this is already an indication of dissatisfaction with the topographical formulations—that 'the fact of a thing's becoming conscious still does not wholly coincide with its belonging to a system, for we have learnt that it is possible to be aware of sensory mnemic images to which we cannot possibly allow a psychical location in the systems Cs or $Pcpt$'.[3]

Before the introduction of the structural division of the mind, the topographical point of view enabled Freud to gain a deeper insight into certain clinical phenomena than what is called 'normal psychology' could do. To psychoanalysis the explanation of 'The strange behaviour of patients, in being able to combine a conscious knowing with not knowing . . . presents no difficulty. The phenomenon we have described, moreover, provides some of the best support for a view which approaches mental processes from the angle of topographical differentiation. The patients now know of the repressed experience in their conscious thought, but this thought lacks any connection with the place where the repressed recollection is in some way or other contained. No change is possible until the conscious thought-process has penetrated to that place and has overcome the resistances of repression there.'[4]

With the help of a topographical understanding of the process of repression it was also possible to throw light 'on the mechanism of mental disturbances. In dreams the withdrawal of cathexis (libido

[1] (1916–17) *Introductory Lectures on Psycho-Analysis*, S.E., Vol. 16, p. 295; cf. also (1940a [1938] *An Outline of Psycho-Analysis*, S.E., Vol. 23, p. 144 f.

[2] (1915c) 'The Unconscious', S.E., Vol. 14, 173; cf. also (1940a [1938]) *An Outline of Psycho-Analysis*, p. 232.

[3] (1917d [1915]) 'A Metapsychological Supplement to the Theory of Dreams', S.E., Vol. 14, p. 232.

[4] (1913c) 'On Beginning the Treatment' S.E., Vol. 12, p. 142.

or interest) affects all systems equally; in the transference neuroses, the *Pcs* cathexis is withdrawn; in schizophrenia, the cathexis of the *Ucs*; in amentia, that of the *Cs*.'[1] Repression as such could be characterized very adequately by means of topographical considerations: It 'interferes only with the relation of the instinctual representative to *one* psychical system, namely, to that of the conscious'[2] or: '*Our* knowledge about the unconscious material is not equivalent to *his* knowledge; if we communicate our knowledge to him, he does not receive it *instead of* his unconscious material, but *beside* it; and that makes very little change in it. We must rather picture this unconscious material topographically, we must look for it in his memory at the place where it became unconscious owing to a repression.'[3]

The realization of the insufficiency of the division of the mind into an Unconscious, Preconscious, and Conscious paved the way to the division of the mind into the structures of the id, ego, and super-ego. In *The Ego and the Id* Freud pointed out that the discovery of an unconscious part of the ego has the consequence 'that we land in endless obscurities and difficulties if we keep to our habitual forms of expression and try, for instance, to derive neuroses from a conflict between the conscious and the unconscious. We shall have to substitute for this antithesis another, taken from our insight into the structural conditions of the mind—the antithesis between the coherent ego and the repressed which is split off from it'.[4] He goes on to say that structural considerations lead to the recognition 'that the *Ucs*. does not coincide with the repressed; it is still true that all that is repressed is *Ucs*., but not all that is *Ucs* is repressed. A part of the ego, too . . . may be *Ucs*., undoubtedly is *Ucs*. And this *Ucs*. belonging to the ego is not latent like the *Pcs*; for if it were, it could not be activated without becoming *Cs*, and the process of making it conscious would not encounter such great difficulties.'[5]

There are many instances to show that Freud considered the structural point of view as an extension of the topographical one.

[1] (1917d) 'A Metapsychological Supplement to the Theory of Dreams', S.E., Vol. 14, p. 235.
[2] (1915d) 'Repression', S.E., Vol. 14, p. 149.
[3] (1916–17) *Introductory Lectures on Psycho-Analysis*, S.E., Vol. 16, p. 436; cf. ibid., p. 341 f.
[4] (1923b) *The Ego and the Id*, S.E., Vol. 19, p. 17.
[5] ibid., p. 17 f.

In *An Outline of Psycho-Analysis*, Freud equates the two terms 'topographical' and 'structural'.[1] In his paper on 'Psycho-Analysis' the two points of view are combined in his definition of the topographical point of view of metapsychology: '*Topographically*, psychoanalysis regards the mental apparatus as a compound instrument, and endeavours to determine at what points in it the various processes take place. According to the most recent psychoanalytic views, the mental apparatus is composed of an "*id*", . . . of an "*ego*" . . . and of a "*super-ego*".'[2] 'Having now decided upon the topographical dissection of the psychical apparatus into an ego and an id, with which the difference in quality between preconscious and unconscious runs parallel. . . .'[3]

When the topographical theory was superseded by the structural theory psychoanalysis was in a better position to supplement the genetic, dynamic and economic points of view of metapsychology. The underlying conflict characteristic of some pathological processes could best be described sometimes as an inter-systemic conflict, at others as an intrasystemic one.

'Transference neuroses correspond to a conflict between the ego and the id; narcissistic neuroses, to a conflict between the ego and the super-ego; and psychoses, to one between the ego and the external world.'[4]

Freud could now, for instance, describe 'the essence of a neurosis' by stating, in structural terms, 'that the ego . . . is not able to fulfil its function of mediating between the id and reality, that in its feebleness it draws back from some instinctual portions of the id and, to make up for this, has to put up with the consequences of its renunciation in the form of restrictions, symptoms and unsuccessful reaction-formations'. Our ego may take 'refuge in repression' in childhood, and if 'the process of repression' is repeated in later life, 'the instincts tear themselves away from the ego's domination, find their substitute satisfactions along the paths of regression, and the poor ego has become helplessly neurotic'.[5] Similarly, the interaction between the three structures and the

---

[1] (1940a [1938]) *An Outline of Psycho-Analysis*, S.E., Vol. 23, p. 204.
[2] (1926f) 'Psycho-Analysis', S.E., Vol. 20, p. 266.
[3] (1940a [1938]) *An Outline of Psycho-Analysis*, S.E., Vol. 23, p. 163.
[4] (1924b) 'Neurosis and Psychosis', S.E., Vol. 19, p. 152.
[5] (1926e) *The Question of Lay Analysis*, S.E., Vol. 23, p. 241 f.

potential for neurotic conflicts could now be described very lucidly: 'It is the ego's task to meet the demands raised by its three dependent relations—to reality, to the id and to the super-ego—and nevertheless at the same time to preserve its own organization and maintain its own autonomy. The necessary precondition of the pathological states . . . can only be a relative or absolute weakening of the ego which makes the fulfilment of its tasks impossible. The severest demand on the ego is probably the keeping down of the instinctual claims of the id, to accomplish which it is obliged to maintain large expenditures of energy on anticathexes. But the demands made by the super-ego too may become so powerful and so relentless that the ego may be paralysed, as it were, in the face of its other tasks. We may suspect that, in the economic conflicts which arise at this point, the id and the super-ego often make common cause against the hard-pressed ego which tries to cling to reality in order to retain its normal state. If the other two become too strong, they succeed in loosening and altering the ego's organization, so that its proper relation to reality is disturbed or even brought to an end.'[1]

[1] (1940a [1938]) *An Outline of Psycho-Analysis*, S.E., Vol. 23, p. 172 f.

THE GENETIC POINT OF VIEW

The fact that genetic considerations underlie all psychoanalytic formulations makes it difficult to find concise formulations of this point of view in Freud's works. He never himself explicitly included the genetic point of view in his definitions of metapsychology. However, the whole theory of infantile sexuality, the postulation of specific phases of libidinal development, the assumption of fixation points and the possibility of regression to these, and many further analytic concepts emphasize the genetic roots in any disturbance. Freud points to this fact when he states that when 'an adult neurotic patient comes to us for psychoanalytic treatment . . . we find regularly that his neurosis has as its point of departure an infantile anxiety . . . and is in fact a continuation of it; so that, as it were, a continuous and undisturbed thread of psychical activity, taking its start from the conflicts of his childhood, has been spun through his life'.[1] A similar view is expressed in a later paper where Freud states that 'in spite of all the later development that occurs in the adult, none of the infantile mental formations perish. All the wishes, instinctual impulses, modes of reaction and attitudes of childhood are still demonstrably present in maturity and in appropriate circumstances can emerge once more. They are not destroyed but merely overlaid—to use the spatial mode of description which psycho-analytic psychology has been obliged to adopt'.[2]

A little earlier in the same paper, Freud draws attention to the phenomena of regression and fixation, processes which emphasize the importance of genetic considerations for the understanding of adult neuroses: 'The normal sexuality of adults emerges from infantile sexuality by a series of developments, combinations, divisions and suppressions, which are scarcely ever achieved with ideal perfection and consequently leave behind predispositions to a retrogression of the function in the form of illness.'[3] In the *Three*

[1] (1909b) 'Analysis of a Phobia in a Five-Year-Old Boy', S.E., Vol. 10, p. 143.
[2] (1913j) 'The Claims of Psycho-Analysis to Scientific Interest', S.E., Vol. 13, p. 184 ff.
[3] ibid., p. 180 f.

Essays on the Theory of Sexuality he elaborates on these predisposing factors when he states that 'The importance of all early sexual manifestations is increased by a psychical factor . . . these early impressions of sexual life are characterized by an increased pertinacity or susceptibility to fixation in persons who are later to become neurotics or perverts. . . . Part of the explanation of this pertinacity of early impressions may perhaps lie in another psychical factor which we must not overlook in the causation of neuroses, namely the preponderance attaching in mental life to memory-traces in comparison with recent impressions. A good proportion of the deviations from normal sexual life which are later observed both in neurotics and in perverts are thus established from the very first by the impressions of childhood.'[1]

The analysis of little Hans confirmed Freud in views developed by inference from the treatment of adult neurotics: 'the neuroses of these other patients could in every instance be traced back to the same infantile complexes that were revealed behind Hans's phobia. I am therefore tempted to claim for this neurosis of childhood the significance of being a type and a model, and to suppose that the multiplicity of the phenomena of repression exhibited by neuroses and the abundance of their pathogenic material do not prevent their being derived from a very limited number of processes concerned with identical ideational complexes'.[2]

There are many instances where Freud elaborates in greater detail on the reasons why the genetic foundations of later neurotic illnesses are laid down in childhood and its experiences. One of the most lucid expositions of this point of view is to be found in *The Question of Lay Analysis* where Freud writes that the 'essence of a neurosis' is to be found in the fact 'that the ego . . . is not able to fulfil its function of mediating between the id and reality. . . .

A feebleness of the ego of this sort is to be found in all of us in childhood; and that is why the experiences of the earliest years of childhood are of such great importance for later life. Under the extraordinary burden of this period of childhood . . . our ego takes refuge in repression and lays itself open to a childhood neurosis, the precipitate of which it carries with it into maturity as a disposition to a later nervous illness.'[3] In the same context Freud argues

---

[1] (1905d) *Three Essays on the Theory of Sexuality*, S.E., Vol. 7, p. 242.
[2] (1909b) 'Analysis of a Phobia in a Five-Year-Old Boy', S.E., Vol. 10, p. 147.
[3] (1926e) *The Question of Lay Analysis*, S.E., Vol. 20, p. 261.

that 'if the relative feebleness of the ego is the decisive factor for the genesis of a neurosis' then even a later illness can produce it, 'provided that it can bring about an enfeeblement of the ego'.[1]

The same state of affairs is described from a somewhat different angle in *An Outline of Psycho-Analysis* (1938) where Freud states that 'from a biological standpoint . . . the ego comes to grief over the task of mastering the excitations of the early sexual period, at a time when its immaturity makes it incompetent to do so. It is in this lagging of ego development behind libidinal development that we see the essential precondition of neurosis; it may be that the aetiology of neurotic illnesses is more complicated than we have here described it; if so, we have at least brought out one essential part of the aetiological complex'.[2]

Another factor which has to be borne in mind in the genetic assessment of a neurosis is the possibility of early traumas. In *Moses and Monotheism* Freud points out that the change 'with which the definitive neurosis becomes manifest as a belated effect of the trauma' often only appears at a later stage, after a period of 'latency' and 'undisturbed development'. He goes on to say that 'The phenomenon of a latency of the neurosis between the first reactions to the trauma and the later outbreak of the illness must be regarded as typical.'[3]

Throughout his works Freud maintained the emphasis on the importance of early childhood, and in particular of infantile sexuality, for an understanding of later neuroses. In *An Outline of Psycho-Analysis* he pointed out again that 'our views on the aetiology of the neuroses and our technique of analytic therapy' are derived from our knowledge that 'the onset of sexual life is diphasic, that it occurs in two waves', that 'the events of this early period . . . fall a victim to *infantile amnesia*', and from the insight gained from this knowledge.[4] The study of the sexual functions led Freud to the conviction that 'the aetiology of the disorders which we study is to be looked for in the individual's developmental history—that is to say, in his early life'[5] and that 'neuroses are acquired only in early childhood . . . even though their symptoms may not make their

---

[1] ibid., p. 242.
[2] (1940a [1938]) *An Outline of Psycho-Analysis*, S.E., Vol. 23, p. 200 f.
[3] (1939a) *Moses and Monotheism*, S.E., Vol. 23, p. 77.
[4] (1940a [1938]) *An Outline of Psycho-Analysis*, S.E., Vol. 23, p. 153.
[5] ibid., p. 156.

appearance till much later. . . . In every case the later neurotic illness links up with the prelude in childhood'.[1]

In the same work, Freud also draws attention to the 'influence of civilization among the determinants of neurosis'. He points out that 'in the space of a few years the little primitive creature must turn into a civilized human being; he must pass through an immensely long stretch of human cultural development in an almost uncannily abbreviated form. This is made possible by hereditary disposition; but it can almost never be achieved without the additional help of upbringing, of parental influence'. For these reasons it is necessary to 'bear in mind the part played by this biological characteristic of the human species—the prolonged period of its childhood dependence—in the aetiology of the neuroses'.[2] The above quotation makes the important point that the genetic point of view has to take into account two fundamental factors, namely on the one hand the experiences of early childhood as possible predisposing influences, and on the other the quality of the hereditary disposition and its pathogenic potential.

A basically genetic approach is implied in the correlation between certain neurotic disturbances (e.g. hysteria, obsessional neurosis, etc.) and specific fixation points. From another point of view the genesis is conceived of in terms of conflicts between structures of the mind or between one of them and the external world: 'We now see that we have been able to make our simple genetic formula more complete, without dropping it. Transference neuroses correspond to a conflict between the ego and the id; narcissistic neuroses, to a conflict between the ego and the superego; and psychoses, to one between the ego and the external world.'[3]

Here again we see the emphasis which Freud puts on the factor of conflict for a metapsychological understanding of pathological phenomena.

[1] (1940a [1938]) *An Outline of Psycho-Analysis*, S.E., Vol. 23, p. 184.
[2] ibid., p. 185.
[3] (1924b) 'Neurosis and Psychosis', S.E., Vol. 19, p. 152.

PRINCIPLES OF MENTAL FUNCTIONING

Freud established from the beginning of his clinical work a framework of principles of mental functioning, the adequate application of which would be a determining factor in an individual's psychopathology. These are (1) pleasure-unpleasure principle with its variations in the principles of constancy, neuronic inertia and nirvana (2) its modification, the reality principle and (3) the principle of the compulsion to repeat. He saw the application of these principles in terms of the amounts of tension in the mental apparatus, arising out of external and internal stimuli; and the purpose of the apparatus—to get rid of stimuli or of reducing them to the lowest possible level; or if it were feasible, maintaining itself in an altogether unstimulated condition—unpleasure being related to an increase in excitation and pleasure to a decrease. The means by which the apparatus accomplishes this is its use of mobile and bound cathexis by which it can repress, inhibit or allow partial or complete satisfaction to the mental representatives of the instinct. As the repetition compulsion is the manifestation of the repressed which is outlawed from the ego, its cathexis cannot be bound and it is not dominated by the pleasure principle.

1. *Principle of Constancy*

The mental apparatus endeavours to keep the quantity of excitation present in it as low as possible or at least to keep it constant.[1] This presupposes that the apparatus carries a charge of energy (cathexis) emanating from the instinctual needs which varies in quantity and quality.

This principle originally stated in 1892 was redefined as 'the principle of neuronic inertia' in 'The Project'. In neurological terms: 'neurones tend to divest themselves of quantity' i.e. of charges of excitation.

As he returned, however, to attempt formulations in psychological terms, he reverted to the earlier terminology: principle of constancy. It was then developed in the form of the 'pleasure principle' 'which follows from the principle of constancy: actually

[1] (1920g) *Beyond the Pleasure Principle*, S.E., Vol. 18, p. 9.

the latter principle was inferred from the facts which forced us to adopt the pleasure principle'.[1] (It was named the unpleasure principle in *The Interpretation of Dreams*.) A programme of finding the satisfaction of happiness is imposed by it on the individual as his main aim. This may be a positive one of experiencing strong feelings of pleasure, or, a negative one of avoiding pain and unpleasure. Pleasure and unpleasure are related to the quantity of excitation that is present in the mind but not in any way bound; unpleasure corresponds to an increase in the quantity of excitation and pleasure to a diminution, in a given period of time. 'Sensations of a pleasurable nature have not anything inherently impelling about them, whereas unpleasurable ones have it in the highest degree. The latter impel towards change, towards discharge, and that is why we interpret unpleasure as implying a heightening and pleasure a lowering of energic cathexis. Let us call what becomes conscious as pleasure and unpleasure, a quantitative and qualitative "something" in the course of mental events . . .'[2] The pleasure principle enforces, therefore, that the work of the mental apparatus shall be to avoid unpleasure by keeping the quantity of excitation low and constant.

Freud identified the 'nirvana principle' with the pleasure principle until his formulation of the two primal instincts in 1920g. He then defined 'nirvana principle' as the tendency of the mental apparatus to reduce its tension to zero in direct relationship with the death instinct. The pleasure principle in direct relationship with Eros, attempts to keep tension as low and as constant as possible.

2. *The Reality Principle*

'Under the influence of the ego's instinct of self-preservation, the pleasure principle is replaced by the *reality principle*. This latter principle does not abandon the intention of ultimately obtaining pleasure, but it nevertheless demands and carries into effect the postponement of satisfaction, the abandonment of a number of possibilities of gaining satisfaction and the temporary toleration of unpleasure as a step on the long indirect road to pleasure.'[3] This modification of the pleasure principle retains the aim of satisfaction; but a certain amount of protection against suffering (which

---

[1] (1920g) *Beyond the Pleasure Principle*, S.E., Vol. 18, p. 9.
[2] (1923b) *The Ego and the Id*, S.E., Vol. 19, p. 22.
[3] (1920g) *Beyond the Pleasure Principle*, S.E., Vol. 18, pp. 10–11.

might be the consequence of the unfettered application of the pleasure principle) is secured in that the immediate non-satisfaction of pleasure is not so painfully felt in the case of instincts kept in dependence (by the higher psychical agencies) as in the case of uninhibited ones totally under the domination of the pleasure principle.[1]

3. *Principle of the Compulsion to Repeat*
Freud defined this as the manifestation of the power of the repressed; the attraction exerted by the unconscious prototypes upon the repressed instinctual process and having the strength of an instinctual striving.

HISTORICAL SURVEY

From 1893–1900 Freud began to explore fully his lifelong interest in the mental apparatus and the principles by which it functioned particularly in relation to pathology. On January 11, 1893, he was lecturing that 'if a person experiences a psychical impression, something in his nervous system which we will for the moment call "the sum of excitation", is increased. Now in every individual there exists a tendency to diminish this sum of excitation once more, in order to preserve his health'. In the 'Mechanism of Hysterical Phenomena' (1893) he outlined further this tentative statement which he later called the principle of constancy (a principle which he was still regarding as fundamental in his later speculations in 1920): 'The increase of the sum of excitation takes place along sensory paths, and its diminution along motor ones. So we may say that if anything impinges on someone he reacts in a motor fashion. We can now safely assert that it depends on this reaction how much of the initial psychical impression is left.'[2]

The *Studies on Hysteria* (1895d) attempted theoretically to connect this general tendency (the principle of constancy) of mental functioning with the causation of hysteria. Quantities of excitation which the hysteria produces cannot be discharged in the normal way and the sum of excitation reduced. There is, therefore, the clinical necessity of abreaction of affect to restore the balance. 'In our patients we find a large complex of ideas that are admissible to consciousness existing side by side with a smaller complex of ideas

---

[1] (1930a) *Civilization and its Discontents*, S.E., Vol. 21, p. 79.
[2] (1893h) 'On the Psychical Mechanism of Hysterical Phenomena', S.E., Vol. 3, p. 36.

that are not. Thus in them the field of ideational psychical activity does not coincide with potential consciousness. The latter is more restricted than the former. Their psychical ideational activity is divided into a conscious and an unconscious part, and their ideas are divided into some that are admissible and some that are inadmissible to consciousness.'[1] Freud thought the capacity to be admitted to consciousness is determined by the feeling of pleasure or unpleasure which is aroused. To this conception, Breuer linked the theory of bound and mobile cathexis which Freud made a corner stone of all his later formulations. In 1894, in connection with the 'Neuro-Psychoses of Defence', he referred to 'the concept that in mental functions something is to be distinguished—a quota of affect or sum of excitation—which possesses all the characteristics of a quantity (though we have no means of measuring it), which is capable of increase, diminution, displacement and discharge, and which is spread over the memory traces of ideas . . .? He considered this hypothesis was 'provisionally justified by its utility in co-ordinating and explaining a great variety of psychical states'.[2]

Freud attempted in his posthumously published work, 'The Project' written in 1895, to formulate and carry further these theories of mental functioning in physiological terms. Many of his later psychological concepts were here outlined but on the basis of neurological findings. He stated in 1915, although 'research has afforded irrefutable proof that mental activity is bound up with the function of the brain as it is with no other organ', but every attempt to deduce from these facts a localization of mental processes, every endeavour to think of ideas as stored up in nerve cells and of excitations as travelling along nerve fibres, has completely miscarried.[3] However, as many of his later formulations are directly related to his thinking in 'The Project' and help to clarify them, a summary of its concepts is justified.

Freud attempted to explain the principle of constancy in greater detail giving it a new name as the principle of neuronic inertia. He viewed the excitations of the neuronic system as quantities in a condition of flow which aim towards inertia (i.e. reducing the level

[1] (1893a) 'On the Psychical Mechanism of Hysterical Phenomena', S.E., Vol. 2, p. 225.
[2] (1894a) 'The Neuro-Psychoses of Defence', S.E., Vol. 3, pp. 60 and 61.
[3] (1915e) 'The Unconscious', S.E., Vol. 14, p. 174.

of tension to zero) but the system, however, has to maintain a sufficient store of quantities to meet demands for specific action but its trend, persists 'to keep the quantity down, at least, so far as possible and avoid any increase in it' (that is, to keep the level of tension constant). All the performances of the neuronic system are to be comprised under the headings of (1) the primary function (i.e. the process of discharge of acquired quantities of excitation through muscular mechanism) or of (2) the secondary function imposed by exigencies of life.[1] (This is the forerunner of the differentiation made in *Beyond the Pleasure Principle* (1920g) and in 'The Economic Problem of Masochism' (1924c) between the nirvana principle related to the death instinct—reducing the level of tension to zero—and the pleasure principle related to Eros—keeping the level of tension as low as possible.) He saw the task of the *structure* of the neuronic system as that of holding back quantity (cathexis) from the neurones, while its *function* served the purpose of discharging quantity; facilitations are set up as if to protect the system by allowing easy flow of cathexis. This in turn is related to the trend in psychical life towards avoiding unpleasure which 'we are tempted to identify with the primary trend towards inertia'.[2] Unpleasure would coincide with a rise in the level of quality or with a quantitative increase of pressure; pleasure would be the sensation of discharge.

The system is subject to internal and external stimuli and the interplay between them. The infant is probably dependent on an alteration in the external world to discharge its internal tension: 'It is brought about by extraneous help, when the attention of an experienced person has been drawn to the child's condition by a discharge taking place along the path of internal discharge (e.g. crying) which thus acquires an extremely important secondary function—*viz.*, of bring about an understanding with other peoples; and the original helplessness of human beings is thus the primal source of all moral motives.'[3] 'An experience of satisfaction' is constituted and this leads to the establishment of a facilitation between the two memory images (the wished for object and the reflex movement) and the cathected neurones, so that when a similar state of urgency, e.g. of hunger reoccurs, the cathexis can

[1] (1950a [1887–1902]) *The Origins of Psycho-Analysis*, Imago, London, 1954, p. 358.
[2] ibid., p. 373.   [3] ibid., p. 379.

pass to the memory and bring about a wishful activation of the experience of satisfaction. As the infant finds the hallucination un-fulfilled, disappointment occurs and unpleasure is released from the interior of the body. To avoid this, 'the ego organization is formed whose presence interferes with the passage of quantities (cathexis) which would lead to unpleasure and repress the wish. While it must be the ego's endeavour to get rid of its cathexes by the method of satisfaction, it must inevitably influence the repetition of experiences of pain and affects; and it must do so in the . . . manner which is generally called "inhibition"'.[1] It is this inhibition that 'makes possible a criterion for distinguishing between a perception and a memory'[2] i.e. of reality testing. Freud stresses that this correct exploitation of the indications of reality is a *sine qua non* of a secondary psychical process, which is a modification of the original primary processes. [This theory he extended considerably in *The Interpretation of Dreams* but 'the characteristics of the ego organization' had to await the full formulation of the structural theory (*The Ego and the Id* 1923b).]

He deduced that judgement, thought and attention, all secondary process aspects of the ego, developed and are used to enable the subject to get back to 'its original first satisfying (and hostile) object'[3] in order that it may attain a 'state of identity'.[4] (Freud later explained this in *The Interpretation of Dreams* as a 'perceptual identity'—i.e. a repetition of the perception which was linked via the cathexis with the satisfaction of its needs.) As however, 'originally a perceptual cathexis, being the heir to an experience of pain, released unpleasure', the ego must as far as it can restrict this affect through using memory traces as a signal.[5] (In *Inhibitions, Symptoms and Anxiety* (1926d) this idea was applied to the problem of anxiety.) The fundamental concept of bound and free cathexis enables us to understand how the ego can then regulate the effect and so defend itself against unpleasure.[6]

In the 'Principle of the Insusceptibility to Excitation of Un-cathected Systems' he had stated that a quantity passes more easily from a neurone to a cathected neurone than to an uncathected one; (He returned briefly to this concept in 'A Metapsychological

[1] (1950a [1887–1902]) *The Origins of Psycho-Analysis*, Imago, London, 1954, p. 384.
[2] ibid., p. 386.   [3] ibid., p. 393.   [4] ibid., pp. 417 and 435.
[5] ibid., p. 415.   [6] ibid., p. 429.

Supplement to the Theory of Dreams' (1917d [1915]), in *Beyond The Pleasure Principle* (1920g) and in 'A Note Upon the "Mystic Writing-Pad"' (1925a)). The primary defence, therefore, against release of unpleasure is for the ego not to cathect neurones which would lead to such a release. If this defence should fail, if '*an indication of reality appears, the perceptual cathexis which is simultaneously present, must be hypercathected*. This is the second biological rule [of defence]'.[1] Quantitatively large and repeated binding from the ego is needed to counterbalance the strong cathexis of unpleasurable, painful experiences.[2]

1900. Freud translated his principles of mental functioning back into psychological terms with no attachment to anatomical and physiological concepts; the principles of constancy (*Studies in Hysteria*) and of neuronic inertia ('The Project') were related directly to the psychic apparatus and were not named as such in Chapter VII of *The Interpretation of Dreams* (1900a) but their functioning was linked to that of the unpleasure-pleasure principle which was recognized as the overriding law dominating the mental apparatus in both its primary and secondary systems. Freud met the need of the developing apparatus for refinements of the grosser automatism of the unpleasure-pleasure regulation by a tentative approach to the principle of reality as a necessary development of the dominant principle. The more sophisticated needs of the mind were noted in his application of the principle of the minimal expenditure of innervation and of the appropriate excitation of the psychical apparatus in the ways most economical for the prevention of unpleasure and obtaining of pleasure.

The principles were explicitly defined:

Principle of Constancy

Freud considered that the activities of the primitive, psychical apparatus are regulated by an effort to avoid an accumulation of excitation and to maintain itself so far as possible without excitation i.e. free from stimuli.[3] He was here bringing together the principles of neuronic inertia by which the apparatus attempts to rid itself of all tension (quantities) and return to a state of zero, and of constancy by which having accepted that some excitations (stimuli) are necessary for living, the apparatus aims at keeping the

[1] ibid., p. 429.   [2] ibid., p. 437.
[3] (1900a) *The Interpretation of Dreams*, S.E., Vol. 5, p. 598.

sum of excitation as low and as constant as possible, thus avoiding unpleasure and obtaining pleasure.

The Unpleasure Principle

It does this through the application of the unpleasure principle (in his later works Freud calls this the pleasure principle) which in the first instance automatically regulates the displacement of cathexis which will relieve the unpleasure.[1] 'Pleasure and unpleasure . . . prove to be almost the only psychical quality attaching to the transpositions of energy inside of the apparatus . . . *these releases of pleasure-unpleasure automatically regulate the course of the cathectic processes.*'[2] The structure of the primitive apparatus is built upon a plan of 'a reflex apparatus, so that any sensory excitation impinging upon it could be promptly discharged along a motor path'.[3] As, however, internal stimuli in the form of major somatic needs cannot be satisfied by movement—the hungry baby kicks but remains hungry and finds the excitations from the hunger an unpleasurable feeling which the unpleasure principle will not tolerate—a change can only come about if in some other way (for the baby, through outside help) 'an "experience of satisfaction" can be achieved which puts an end to the internal stimulus. An essential component of this experience of satisfaction is a particular perception, the mnemic image of which remains associated thenceforward with the memory trace of the excitation produced by the need'.[4] This experience, then, involved a diminution of excitation and was felt as pleasure. A current of this kind starting from unpleasure, i.e. an accumulation of excitation (tension) which cannot be relieved by motor discharge, and aiming at pleasure, 'we have termed a "wish"; and we have asserted that only a wish is able to set the apparatus in motion and that the course of excitation in it is automatically regulated by feelings of pleasure and unpleasure'.[5]

In the first instance, the wish is fulfilled if the perception of the experience of satisfaction reappears and 'the shortest path to the fulfilment of the wish is a path leading direct from the excitation produced by the need to a complete cathexis of the perception. . . . Thus the aim of this first psychical activity was to produce a "perceptual identity"—a repetition of the perception which was

[1] (1900a) *The Interpretation of Dreams*, S.E., Vol. 5, p. 616.
[2] ibid., p. 574. [3] ibid., p. 565. [4] ibid., p. 565. [5] ibid., p. 598.

linked with the satisfaction of the need'.[1] But this hallucinatory cathecting of the memory of satisfaction does not conform to the principle of unpleasure-pleasure as it neither ends the need nor, therefore, provides the satisfaction. The apparatus automatically regulated by the principle has therefore to find a second activity; a second system diverts the excitation arising from the need from its path towards perceptual identity, to a 'roundabout path which ultimately, by means of voluntary movement, altered the external world in such a way that it became possible to arrive at a real perception of the object of satisfaction'[2] and thus to conform to the unpleasure-pleasure principle.

Principle of Least Expenditure of Innervation
Freud stressed the importance of the second system finding a way which would not exhaust psychic energy in seeking for the experience of satisfaction in an unsatisfactory hallucinatory mnemic image, but in seeking and obtaining it from the external world. It must constantly feel its way, and alternately send out and withdraw cathexes both to have the whole of the material of memory freely at its command; but also not to expend energy unnecessarily, 'if it sent out large quantities of cathexis along the various paths of thought and thus caused them to drain away to no useful purpose and diminish the quantity available for altering the external world. I therefore postulate that for the sake of efficiency the second system succeeds in retaining the major part of its cathexis of energy in a state of quiescence and in employing only a small part on displacement'.[3] Thus the second system in the service of the unpleasure-pleasure adopts the principle of the least expenditure of innervation in cathecting those ideas which will end unpleasure and bring pleasure.

This development is essential in that the first system directed towards securing the free discharge of the quantities of excitation, is, as a result of the unpleasure principle, totally incapable of bringing anything disagreeable into the context of its thoughts. Essential memories which when cathected might be unpleasurable are therefore excluded, and, it is left to the second system to find a method of cathecting them but in such a way as to inhibit this discharge in the direction of the development of unpleasure and thus conform to the principle of unpleasure. Freud considered that this

[1] ibid., p. 566.　　[2] ibid., p. 599.　　[3] ibid., p. 599.

cathexis of an idea by the second system which simultaneously inhibited discharge of unpleasurable excitation might be the key to
the theory of repression brought about by this inhibition of the
mobile cathexis of the first system.

Principle of Excitation of Psychical Apparatus
It is presumed that under the dominion of the second system the
discharge of excitation is governed by quite different mechanical
conditions from those in force in the primary system under the
automatic domination of the primary unpleasure principle. 'The
consequent restrictions imposed upon efficiency are interrupted by
the processes of sensory regulation, which are themselves in turn
automatic in action'[1] and an advance comes when the perception
by the psychical sense organs, *Pcpt* and *Cs* has 'the result of directing
a cathexis of attention to the paths along which the incoming sensory excitation is spreading; the qualitative excitation of the *Pcpt*
system acts as a regulator of the discharge of the mobile quantity in
the psychical apparatus'.[2]

To make more delicately adjusted performances possible, therefore, the course of ideas becomes less dependent upon the presence
or absence of unpleasure. The system *Pcs* acquires a quality of its
own—by linking itself with the mnemic system of indications of
speech[3]—which attracts consciousness. This enables the latter to
become a sense organ for a portion of our thought processes as well
as for being susceptible to excitation by qualities. It still, however,
has no memory. Greater delicacy in functioning can then be obtained by means of a further hypercathexis brought about by consciousness. The value of this can be seen 'by the fact of its creation
of a new series of qualities and consequently of a new process of
regulation which constitutes the superiority of men over animals.
. . . In order that thought-processes may acquire quality, they are
associated in human beings with verbal memories, whose residues
of quality are sufficient to draw the attention of consciousness to
them and to endow the process of thinking with a new mobile
cathexis from consciousness'.[4]

Excitatory material flows into consciousness from two directions:
'from the *Pcpt* system, whose excitation, determined by qualities,
is probably submitted to a fresh revision before it becomes a

[1] (1900a) *The Interpretation of Dreams*, S.E., Vol. 5, p. 617.
[2] ibid., p. 616.   [3] ibid., p. 574.   [4] ibid., p. 617.

conscious sensation, and from the interior of the apparatus itself, whose quantitative processes are felt qualitatively in the pleasure-unpleasure series when, subject to certain modifications, they make their way to consciousness'.[1] By perceiving new qualities this then makes a new contribution to 'directing the mobile quantities of cathexis and distributing them in an expedient fashion. By the help of its perception of pleasure and unpleasure it influences the discharge of the cathexes within what is otherwise an unconscious apparatus operating by means of the displacement of quantities'.[2] This then introduces a more discriminating regulation than the unpleasure principle, one 'which is even able to oppose the former one, and which perfects the efficiency of the apparatus by enabling it, in contradiction to the original plan, to cathect and work over even what is associated with the release of unpleasure'.[3] (This formulation in 'Two Principles of Mental Functioning', 1911, Freud later called the reality principle.) Freud warns us, however, that this last aim is seldom attained completely even in normal mental life and 'our thinking always remains exposed to falsification by interference from the unpleasure principle'.[4]

Freud had, therefore, in *The Interpretation of Dreams* applied his principles of mental functioning to the fiction of a primitive psychical apparatus. Its activities are regulated by efforts to avoid an accumulation of excitation and to maintain itself so far as possible without excitation. As more sophisticated demands are made on the apparatus, a second system evolves. The primary process is directed towards freeing itself from tension and unpleasure by securing the free discharge of the quantities of excitation. The second process, also dominated by the unpleasure principle, inhibits the discharge and transforms the cathexis into a quiescent one until it has assured itself unpleasure will not ensue.[5] It is able to do this by freeing itself from exclusive regulation by the unpleasure principle and being ruled by the reality principle, making full use of repression to do so.[6]

1901–16

Freud expanded these ideas further in the period following *The Interpretation of Dreams*. His views on the principles which regulate mental functioning did not undergo any fundamental change

---

[1] ibid., pp. 615–16.   [2] ibid., p. 616.   [3] ibid., p. 616.
[4] ibid., p. 600.   [5] ibid., p. 600.   [6] ibid., p. 604.

when he applied them to the topographical model of the mind which he used between 1901 and 1916. The basic laws which he had outlined in 'The Project' and in Chapter VII in *The Interpretation of Dreams*, 1900, could be clearly recognized in his stocktaking *Introductory Lectures on Psycho-Analysis*, in 1916–17. 'Our total mental activity is directed towards achieving pleasure and avoiding unpleasure—it is automatically regulated by the *pleasure principle* . . . pleasure *is in some* way connected with the diminution . . . of stimulus prevailing in the mental apparatus and similarly unpleasure is connected with their increase' [the principles of constancy and of physical inertia]. 'The ego instincts . . . learn to replace this pleasure principle by a modification of it. For them the task of avoiding unpleasure turns out to be almost as important as that of obtaining pleasure. . . . . it no longer lets itself be governed by the pleasure principle, but obeys the *reality principle*, which also at bottom seeks to obtain pleasure, but pleasure which is assured by taking account of reality.'[1]

The principle of the repetition compulsion is tentatively introduced; a possible differentiation of the pleasure principle and the principle of constancy looks back to the two differing principles of constancy and physical inertia as outlined in *Studies in Hysteria* and in 'The Project' and forward to the pleasure and nirvana principles separated in *Beyond the Pleasure Principle* (1920g) and 'The Economic Problem of Masochism' (1924c).

Anticipation of his later formulation (1920) of the nirvana and pleasure principles in the instincts of life and death is indicated in his chapter on The General Theory of Neurosis in the *Introductory Lectures on Psycho-Analysis* (1916–17): 'Sexual instincts from beginning to end of their development, work towards obtaining pleasure, they retain their original function unaltered. The . . . ego [self-preservative] instincts, have the same aim to start with. But under the influence of the instructress Necessity, they soon learn to replace the pleasure principle. . . .'[2] Later, in 1924, he was to attribute the nirvana principle (originally the principle of psychical inertia) to the death instinct, and its modification the pleasure principle which contains the principles of constancy and of reality, to the life instinct.

There is, however, during the period, a shift of emphasis in the

---

[1] (1916–17) *Introductory Lectures on Psycho-Analysis*, S.E., Vol .16, pp. 356-7.
[2] ibid., p. 357.

relative importance attached to the pleasure principle and the reality principle in the development of psychical life. This probably reflects Freud's increased preoccupation with the role of instincts during this time. In 'Formulations on the Two Principles of Mental Functioning' in 1911, he noted the need to investigate the relation of mankind to reality and so 'to bring the psychological significance of the real external world into the structure of our theories'. He considered that 'the psychical apparatus had to decide to form a conception of the real circumstances in the external world and to endeavour to make a real alteration in them'[1] and this brought about the development of thinking, judgement and purposeful action. But in 1915, in 'Instincts and their Vicissitudes' he stressed that: 'External stimuli impose only the single task of withdrawing from them; this is accomplished by muscular movements. . . . Instinctual stimuli, which originate from within the organism, cannot be dealt with by this mechanism. Thus they make for higher demands on the nervous system and cause it to undertake involved and interconnected activities. . . . We may therefore well conclude that instincts and not external stimuli are the true motive forces behind the advances that have led the nervous system with its unlimited capacities, to its present high level of development.'[2] In his discussion on the vicissitudes the instincts undergo arising out of their subjection to the three great polarities which dominate mental life, *viz:* subject-object, pleasure-unpleasure, activity-passivity, Freud may, however, have been indicating the strong link between the relative influence of inner and external reality on each other.

Principle of Constancy
Freud did not explicitly name this principle as one by which his topographical model was regulated; it was, however, implicit in his description of the functioning of the mental apparatus. A guiding postulate in the field of psychological phenomena is 'of a biological nature, and makes use of the concept of "purpose" (or perhaps of expediency) and runs as follows: the nervous system is an apparatus which has the function of getting rid of stimuli that reach it, or of reducing them to the lowest possible level; or which, if it were

---

[1] (1911b) 'Formulations on the Two Principles of Mental Functioning', S.E., Vol. 12, p. 219.
[2] (1914d) 'On the History of the Psycho-Analytic Movement', S.E., Vol. 14, p. 120.

feasible, would maintain itself in an altogether unstimulated condition'.[1]

This formulation correlates the principle of constancy, i.e. keeping the quantity of excitation as low and as constant as possible (1893) with that of the principle of physical inertia (1893), i.e. to reduce tension to zero. However, there is a hint of doubt about this correlation in this same paper as well as in the chapter on 'The General Theory of the Neurosis' in the *Introductory Lectures on Psycho-Analysis* (1916–17). Freud noted that this mastering of stimuli is demanded by the pleasure principle since unpleasure feelings create an increase in tension and pleasurable feelings a decrease. But in the sexual instincts an increase of tension is pleasurable. He therefore decided there were many varied relations between pleasure and unpleasure and the fluctuations in the stimulus affecting mental life of which he still had insufficient knowledge.[2] His later investigations relating to the developments in his 'instinct theory' led to more precise definitions of these principles in *Beyond the Pleasure Principle* (1920g).

The Pleasure Principle

Freud never changes in his view of the importance of the pleasure principle as the chief regulator of the mental apparatus. He re-named it in 1911 from the unpleasure principle of *The Interpretation of Dreams* to the pleasure principle but this did not alter his formulation in any way. He accepted that its substitution by the reality principle was only a way of safeguarding it more fully; in 1915 he was still stating specifically that the pleasure principle automatically regulated even the most highly developed mental apparatus. As indicated in the previous section, the pleasure principle was correlated with the principle of constancy during this period except for the doubt Freud expressed in 'Instincts and Their Vicissitudes' (1915c).

The close link between the Unconscious System and the pleasure principle is defined more precisely as Freud restated this theory in metapsychological terms. In the 'Two Principles of Mental Functioning', it was specified how the primary processes are governed totally by the pleasure principle. 'The strangest characteristic of unconscious (repressed) processes . . . is due to their entire

[1] (1915c) 'Instincts and their Vicissitudes', S.E., Vol. 14, p. 120.
[2] (1916–17) *Introductory Lectures on Psycho-Analysis*, S.E., Vol. 15, p. 121.

disregard of reality-testing; they equate reality of thought with external actuality, and wishes with their fulfilment—with the event—just as happens automatically under the dominance of the ancient pleasure principle'.[1] The fate of unconscious processes depends only on how strong they are and whether they fulfil the demands of the pleasure-unpleasure regulation ('The Unconscious' 1915).

The strength and force which Freud assigned to the principle was outlined in relation to hate; this formulation in 'Instincts and Their Vicissitudes' can be seen as a possible link with the loving and hating (destructiveness) inherent in the Eros and Thanatos instinct theory. 'The relation of *unpleasure* seems to be the sole decisive one. The ego [here meaning self] hates, abhors, and pursues with intent to destroy all objects which are a source of unpleasurable feeling for it, without taking into account whether they mean a frustration of sexual satisfaction or of the satisfaction of self-preservative needs. Indeed, it may be asserted that the prototypes of the relation of hate are derived not from sexual life, but from the ego's struggle to preserve and maintain itself.'[2]

Freud's original concept of the relationship of pleasure (unpleasure) feelings to the quantities of mental excitation and energy arising from internal and external stimuli remained unchanged in this period. The need of the apparatus to regulate the flow of the excitations (cathexis) in order to maximize pleasure and diminish unpleasure led him to a greater clarification of the reality principle in 1911b, and then in 1915c to a further attempt to trace the sequence of pleasure and reality in relation to internal and external needs. Just as the pleasure-ego can do nothing but *wish*, work for a yield of pleasure, and avoid unpleasure, so the reality-ego need do nothing but strive for what is useful and guard itself against damage.[3] He considers that an individual has reached maturity when he can renounce the pleasure principle, adjust himself to reality and turns to the external world for the object of his desires.[4]

The Reality Principle

The existence of a reality principle was inherent in the formulation

[1] (1911b) 'Formulations on the Two Principles of Mental Functioning', S.E., Vol. 12, p. 225.

[2] (1915c) 'Instincts and their Vicissitudes', S.E., Vol. 14, p. 138.

[3] (1911b) 'Formulations on the Two Principles of Mental Functioning', S.E., Vol. 12, p. 223.

[4] (1912–13) *Totem and Taboo*, S.E., Vol. 13, p. 90.

of primary and secondary processes with differing energic system of mobile and bound cathexis regulated automatically by the pleasure principle. Freud had indicated this in both 'The Project' and *The Interpretation of Dreams*; he gave fuller definition to it in his stock-taking review in 1911b, of the principles regulating the apparatus. The reality principle is a necessary institution arising out of situations of frustration in which originally the internal stimuli cannot be satisfied, tension lessened and unpleasure removed except through external intervention. 'The psychical apparatus had to decide to form a conception of the real circumstances in the external world and to endeavour to make a real alteration in them. A new principle of mental functioning was thus introduced; what was presented in the mind was no longer what was agreeable but what was real, even if it happened to be disagreeable.'[1] The dissatisfaction caused by the renunciation of direct instinctual satisfaction through the replacement of the pleasure principle by the reality principle then itself becomes part of reality. However, 'actually the substitution of the reality principle for the pleasure principle implies no deposing of the pleasure principle, but only a safeguarding of it. A momentary pleasure, uncertain in its results, is given up, but only in order to gain along the new path an assured pleasure at a later time'.[2]

Freud saw the transition from the pleasure principle to the reality principle as one of the most important, momentous steps in the ego's development. In the primary psychical processes dominated by the pleasure principle, the apparatus does not distinguish between an idea or a wish and a perception; but if the primary process working on this lack of differentiation used its mobile, free energy to push forward to discharge, unpleasure might result. Therefore, its process had to be inhibited, its cathexis bound at least temporarily by a secondary psychical process to allow indications of reality to arrive from the perceptual apparatus, the ego directing its attention cathexis to the external world so as to observe these indications. This delay enables the reality consequences to be assessed and cathexis can then be allowed to continue into action or blocked (repressed) as appropriate to the circumstances in the external world.

Freud described this reality testing, the instrument of the reality

[1] (1911b) 'Formulations on the Two Principles of Mental Functioning', S.E., Vol. 12, p. 219.   [2] ibid., p. 223.

principle, as the function of orientating the individual in the world by discriminating between what is internal and what is external. It was always recognized as a function of the secondary system; in 1911, the increased significance of external reality heightened the importance of the sense organs and of *consciousness* attached to them. 'Consciousness now learned to comprehend sensory qualities in addition to the qualities of pleasure and unpleasure which hitherto alone have been of interest to it.'[1] In the paper 'The Unconscious' (1915e), Freud considered that the system *Pcs* in which processes are conscious or capable of becoming conscious, had reality testing in its province.[2] He placed it more precisely in 'A Metapsychological Supplement to the Theory of Dreams', (1917d [1915]), when he put reality-testing in the third of the psychical systems, *Cs* which he considered coincided with the system *Pcpt* described in *The Interpretation of Dreams* (1900a). He thus was beginning to move towards his structural theory where reality testing is in the domain of the ego. The system *Cs* had at its disposal 'a motor innervation which determines whether the perception can be made to disappear or whether it proves resistent. Reality testing need be nothing more than this contrivance'.[3]

With the development of the recognition of an external world which could be changed, the system 'conscious' develops special functions 'A special function was instituted which had periodically to search the external world, in order that its data might be familiar already if an urgent internal need should arise—the function of *attention*. Its activity meets the sense-impressions half-way instead of waiting their appearance.'[4] A system of notation of these impressions then formed part of memory which in turn facilitated reality testing.

Motor discharge which had been used under the pleasure principle to unburden the apparatus of stimuli by sending 'innervations into the interior of the body leading to expressive movements and the play of features and to manifestations of affect', could now be converted into purposeful action to alter the external world. Thinking in turn could restrain action; this having been made possible

[1] ibid., p. 220.

[2] (1915e) 'The Unconscious', S.E., Vol. 14, p. 188.

[3] (1917d [1915]) 'A Metapsychological Supplement to the Theory of Dreams', S.E., Vol. 14, p. 232.

[4] (1911b) 'Formulations on the Two Principles of Mental Functioning', S.E., Vol. 12, p. 220.

by the binding of cathexis by the secondary process. Judgement became a facet of the system and could enable it to distinguish realities from ideas and wishes, however intense they may be and thus avoid unpleasure in the external world.

However, two aspects of the apparatus do not come under the regulation of the reality principle and because of this Freud considered they were the two danger areas for mental health—the sexual instincts and phantasy, i.e. making the obtaining of pleasure free from the assent of reality. Because the sexual instincts can obtain satisfaction auto-erotically, they are not placed in situations of frustration which are the mainspring for the development of the reality principle. They remain far longer under the domination of the pleasure principle and in many people they are never withdrawn from its domination.

Because men have always found it hard to renounce pleasure, they find some compensation in fantasying. This is a 'mental activity in which all the abandoned sources of pleasure and methods of achieving pleasure are granted a further existence—a form of existence in which they are left free from the claims of reality and of what we call "reality testing" . . . in the activity of fantasy human beings continue to enjoy the freedom from external compulsion which they have long since renounced in reality. They have contrived to alternate between remaining an animal of pleasure and being once more a creature of reason'.[1]

In *The Interpretation of Dreams* (1900a) Freud had described the gradual development of the reality principle as arising out of the baby's inability to get rid of unpleasurable feelings caused by unsatisfied internal stimuli (needs) without the help of the external world whose attention he manages to obtain by some form of motor discharge. He described this in 1911 in terms of a pleasure ego having gradually to be transformed into a reality ego since the pleasure ego only wishes and works for a yield of pleasure while the reality ego strives for what is useful and guards itself against damage.

However, in 'Instincts and their Vicissitudes' (1915c) he postulated that there is an original 'reality ego' which by means of its perceptions distinguishes between internal and external according to the efficacy of its muscular activity whose task is to remove external stimuli.[2] This would seem to be using the same apparatus

[1] (1916–17) *Introductory Lectures on Psycho-Analysis*, S.E., Vol. 16, pp. 371–2.
[2] (1915c) 'Instincts and their Vicissitudes', S.E., Vol. 14, pp. 118–19.

as the reality ego which supersedes the pleasure ego according to the formulation in 1917 in 'A Metapsychological Supplement to the Theory of Dreams' (1917d [1915]), where, having given up hallucinatory satisfaction of our wishes we set up a kind of reality testing. This need be nothing more than a motor innervation at the disposal of the system Cs (Pcpt) which determines whether the perception can be made to disappear or whether it proves resistant.[1] The still helpless organism finds out through its perceptions what is internal and external through use of movement—if he can move away from something he knows it is outside of himself and real: where such action makes no difference, the perceptions originate from within and are not real. But, because of the strength of the auto-erotic libidinal instincts, there is a pull away and a diversion of this original reality ego into a pleasure ego which is dominated only by the pleasure principle and need not test out what is internal and what is external. If this diversion is supported by adequate parental care of the helpless infant, this state of narcissism is prolonged and the non-erotic, self-preservative instincts which would have maintained the original reality ego are temporarily overruled.

This original 'reality ego' having discovered that the device of muscular activity is insufficient to relieve it of tension arising out of the internal demands of the instincts, uses projection '. . . the external world is divided into a part that is pleasurable, which it has incorporated into itself, and a remainder that is extraneous to it. It has separated off a part of its own self, which it projects into the external world and feels as hostile. After this new arrangement, the two polarities coincide once more: the ego-subject coincides with pleasure, and the external world with unpleasure'.[2] When the purely narcissistic stage has given place to the object stage, out of its needs to relieve tension, the ego establishes a pure-pleasure relation to the satisfying object while pursuing 'with intent to destroy all objects which are a source of unpleasurable feeling to it'.[3] But it discovers that this may cause further unpleasure and a second reality ego must develop. This makes use of repression, whose motive and purpose is avoidance of unpleasure, to relieve the tension caused by the instincts non-attainment of its aim where its

---

[1] (1917d [1915]) 'A Metapsychological Supplement to the Theory of Dreams', S.E., Vol. 14, pp. 231–2.

[2] (1915c) 'Instincts and their Vicissitudes', S.E., Vol. 14, p. 136.

[3] ibid., p. 138.

attainment would cause greater unpleasure in other parts of the apparatus.[1] The importance of adequate external objects is thus stressed as vital in the possible degrees of pleasure allowable by the self-preservative instincts.

Principle of Inertia

Freud had stated in 'The Project' that the neurones of the nervous system aimed at divesting themselves of quantity and eventually reaching a state of inertia. In the topographical model, he seemed to use this concept more precisely as if foreshadowing his death instinct theory. He considered inertia itself as the most universal characteristic of all matter, animate and inanimate.[2] He disagreed with Jung's theory that 'a "psychical inertia" which opposes change and progress is a fundamental pre-condition of neurosis', preferring to describe this special inertia as a fixation, a manifestation of very early linkages between instincts and impressions and the objects involved in those impressions.[3] But he later attributed the phenomena of this resistance to recovery to the power of the compulsion to repeat (1926). The latter principle was used as evidence to postulate a death instinct, of the need of all matter to return to a state of inertia.

Principle of the Repetition

The formulation of this principle as the manifestation of the power of the repressed was begun in 1914. Freud wrote in 'Remembering, Repeating and Working Through' (1914g) of the clinical significance of the patients' compulsion to repeat in action what has been repressed, correlating it with the abreacting of the quotas of affect strangulated by repression.[4] In his metapsychological paper 'Repression' he tried to explain the strength of the compulsion. 'The instinctual representative develops with less interference and more profusely if it is withdrawn by repression from conscious influence.' Repression does not hinder the instinctual representative from continuing to exist in the unconscious, from organizing itself

[1] (1915d) 'Repression', S.E., Vol. 14, pp. 146–9.
[2] (1914d) 'On the History of the Psycho-Analytic Movement', S.E., Vol. 14, p. 63.
[3] (1915f) 'A Case of Paranoia Running Counter to the Psycho-Analytic Theory of the Disease', S.E., Vol. 14, p. 219.
[4] (1914g) 'Remembering, Repeating and Working Through (Further Recommendations on the Technique of Psycho-Analysis, II)', S.E., Vol. 12, p. 155.

further, putting out derivatives and establishing connections.[1] The neurotic thus fears the seemingly extraordinary and dangerous strength of the instinct which, Freud later explained having its representatives outlawed by the ego, is left independent of the ego's inhibiting control.

Principle of the Least Expenditure of Innervation
Freud had outlined this principle in *The Interpretation of Dreams* in relation to the second system when he postulated that as small a part as possible of all its energy is employed to function at one time. In 'Formulation on the Two Principles of Mental Functioning' (1911b) Freud employed the principle in relation to the secondary system and also to the domination of the pleasure principle on the whole apparatus.

He traced the effects of the adoption of the reality principle on the mental apparatus in terms of the increase and definition of functions resulting from the secondary system's ability to inhibit discharge. Of these *thinking*, developed from the presentation of ideas, 'is essentially an experimental kind of acting, accompanied by displacement of relatively small quantities of cathexis together with less expenditure (discharge) of them'.[2] The economic aspect of the principle is explicitly applied in 1915 to the functioning of the *Pcs* system: 'the processes of the system *Pcs* display . . . an inhibition of the tendency of cathected ideas towards discharge. When a process passes from one idea to another, the first idea retains part of its cathexis and only a small portion undergoes displacement'.[3]

Freud related the 'splitting off' of one species of thought-activity, fantasying, from the reality principle to the specific application of the economic principle of saving expenditure of energy. 'A general tendency of our mental apparatus [i.e. this principle] . . . seems to find expression in the tenacity with which we hold on to the sources of pleasure at our disposal, and in the difficulty with which we renounce them. With the introduction of the reality principle one species of thought-activity was split off; it was kept free from reality-testing and was subordinated to the pleasure principle alone. This activity is *fantasying* . . .'[4]

[1] (1915d) 'Repression', S.E., Vol. 14, p. 149.
[2] (1911b) 'Formulations on the Two Principles of Mental Functioning', S.E., Vol. 12, p. 221.
[3] (1915e) 'The Unconscious', S.E., Vol. 14, p. 153.
[4] (1911b) 'Formulations on the Two Principles of Mental Functioning', S.E., Vol. 12, p. 222.

The Principle of the Insusceptibility to Excitation of Uncathected Systems

This principle had had a significant place in Freud's physiologically orientated explanation of the mental apparatus in 'The Project' in 1895. There he had laid down that a quantity of excitation passes more easily to a cathected neurone than to an uncathected one; he used as an example how dreams are devoid of motor elements because there is no spinal pre-cathexis and the neurones cannot pass to these uncathected neurones.

In 'A Metapsychological Supplement to the Theory of Dreams' (1917d [1915]) he applied the principle in psychological terms to mental processes in general but he queried how completely validly it can be applied to the system Cs (Pcpt). He explained how the complete emptying of the system Pcs of its cathexis renders it little susceptible to initiation and thus prevents a dream wish, (a wish fulfilling fantasy) becoming a delusion or finding direct motor discharge. However, the state of sleep 'withdraws cathexis from the system Cs as well as from the other systems, the Pcs and the Ucs, in so far as the cathexes in them obey the wish to sleep. With the system Cs thus uncathected, the possibility of reality testing is abandoned; and the excitations which, independently of the state of sleep, have entered on the path of regression will find that path clear as far as the system Cs where they will count as undisputed reality'. Freud explained in a footnote that the principle seems to be invalidated for the system Cs (Pcpt); he thought, however, that the principle might demand only a *partial* removal of cathexis, 'for the perceptual system in especial we must assume many conditions for excitation which are widely divergent from those of other systems'.[1]

1920-35 The further extension of the principles of mental functioning in *Beyond the Pleasure Principle* 1920 and 'The Economic Problem of Masochism' 1924 arose out of Freud's development of his instinct theory and his need to relate this to his basic assumptions of the dominance of the pleasure principle and its modification, the reality principle. He retained his earlier assumptions on the functioning of the mental apparatus as it is affected by external and

---

[1] (1917d [1915]) 'A Metapsychological Supplement to the Theory of Dreams', S.E., Vol. 14, p. 234 and n2.

internal stimuli, stressing the importance of tension being removed, or decreased and kept constant. The methods employed by the ego through its use of bound cathexis by which it could regulate the flow of quantities of excitation, bring about inhibition, and use repression to force the instinctual strivings to remain unconscious, were all contained in his now extended formulation. The important changes introduced into the principles of mental functioning were the inclusion of the general principle of repetition compulsion and the differentiation between the pleasure principle and the nirvana principle; both these changes were based on and arising out of the formulation of the theory of Eros and death instincts.

Principle of Repetition Compulsion
Although earlier in his technical paper on 'Remembering, Repeating and Working Through' (1914g), Freud had described a compulsion to repeat, he had not seen it as anything new but only as a more comprehensive view of how the repressed manifested itself through compulsive acting out. However, in 'The Uncanny' written in the year before *Beyond The Pleasure Principle* (1920g), he could recognize such a compulsion proceeding from instinctual impulses and probably inherent in the very nature of instincts so powerful that it could overrule the pleasure principle. Using 'his knowledge of patients' unpleasurable repetitions in the transference of infantile instinctual sexual wishes which never were nor could be satisfied and bring pleasure, Freud postulated that there must be a 'tendency' in the mental functioning more primitive than the pleasure principle and independent of it. He saw it as a manifestation of the power of the repressed which is in fact seldom seen without other motives often obscuring its compulsive, unpleasurable nature. Inquiring into its relationship with the pleasure principle and the conditions under which it emerges, he considered the vital factor was whether the regressed memory traces of the primeval unpleasurable experiences were in a sufficiently bound state for this to act as a shield against the stimulus of the strong upward drive of repressed instinctual excitation. He pointed out that it was only after binding had been accomplished by the higher strata of the mental apparatus that the dominance of the pleasure principle could proceed unhindered.

'We have found that one of the earliest and most important functions of the mental apparatus is to bind the instinctual impulses which impinge on it, to replace the primary process prevailing in them by the secondary process and convert their freely mobile cathectic energy into a mainly quiescent (tonic) cathexis. While this transformation is taking place no attention can be paid to the development of unpleasure; but this does not imply the suspension of the pleasure principle. On the contrary, the transformation occurs on *behalf* of the pleasure principle; the binding is a preparatory act which introduces and assures the dominance of the pleasure principle.'[1]

It is assumed, however, that feelings of pleasure and unpleasure can be produced equally from the unbound, primary processes and the bound, secondary processes but that all must be related to the operation of the pleasure principle to keep 'the mental apparatus entirely free from excitation or to keep the amount of excitation in it constant or to keep it as low as possible'. This must be concerned with 'the most universal endeavour of all living substance—namely to return the quiescence of the inorganic world'.[2] Thus the compulsion to repeat supports the thesis of the death instinct.

Nirvana and Pleasure Principle
In exploring this further, Freud continued with a speculation he had made in 'Instincts and their Vicissitudes' (1915) that the pleasure principle may well have two sections: (1) its need to end all tension, and (2) its need to lessen tension as far as possible and keep it constant. He hinted in *Beyond the Pleasure Principle* that he was not satisfied as formerly with the equation of the nirvana principle with the pleasure principle. It was, however, in 'The Economic Problem of Masochism' (1924) that he restated the principle differentiating between the nirvana principle attributed to the death instinct and the pleasure principle, a modification of it, due to the influence of life instinct. He noted that to identify them as the same principle would mean that every 'unpleasure ought thus to coincide with heightening, and every pleasure with a lowering, of mental tension due to stimulus; the Nirvana principle (and the pleasure principle which is supposedly identical with it) would be entirely in the service of the death instincts, whose aim is to conduct the restlessness of life into the stability of the inorganic state, and it would have the function of giving warnings against the demands

[1] (1920g) *Beyond the Pleasure Principle*, S.E., Vol. 18, pp. 62–3.
[2] ibid., p. 62.

of the life instincts—the libido—which try to disturb the intended course of life. But such a view cannot be correct. It seems that in the series of feelings of tension we have a direct sense of the increase and decrease of amounts of stimulus, and it cannot be doubted that there are pleasurable tensions and unpleasurable relaxations of tension. The state of sexual excitation is the most striking example of a pleasurable increase of stimulus of this sort, but it is certainly not the only one'.[1]

'We must perceive that the nirvana principle, belonging as it does to the death instinct, has undergone a modification in living organisms through which it has become the pleasure principle; and we shall henceforward avoid regarding the two principles as one. It is not difficult, if we care to follow up this line of thought, to guess what power was the source of the modification. It can only be the life instinct, the libido, which has thus, alongside of the death instinct, seized upon a share in the regulation of the process of life. In this way we obtain a small but interesting set of connections. The *Nirvana* principle expresses the trend of the death instinct; the *pleasure* principle represents the demand of the libido; and the modification of the latter principle, the *reality* principle, represents the influence of the external world.

'None of these three principles is actually put out of action by another. As a rule they are able to tolerate one another, although conflicts are bound to arise occasionally from the fact of the differing aims that are set for each—in one case a quantitative reduction of the load of the stimulus, in another a qualitative characteristic of the stimulus, and, lastly [in the third case], a postponement of the discharge of the stimulus and a temporary acquiescence in the unpleasure due to tension.'[2]

Freud made no significant changes to this theory in his remaining works; the development of the structural concepts helped to clarify the varying functions of the pleasure and reality principles without, however, modifying them to any appreciable extent. In looking into any 'instructive connections', between the structures—the ego, id and super-ego—the two classes of instinct and 'the pleasure principle (i.e. the perception of unpleasure) which dominated mental processes',[3] he recognized the ego as that part of the

---

[1] (1924c) 'The Economic Problem of Masochism', S.E., Vol. 19, pp. 159–60.
[2] ibid., pp. 160–1.
[3] (1923b) *The Ego and the Id*, S.E., Vol. 19, p. 42.

id modified by the external world which in trying to fulfil its task of acting as an intermediary between id and the external world, binds cathexis in order that it can substitute the reality principle for the pleasure principle. It is thus able to protect the id totally dominated by an impulsion to obtain satisfaction for its instinctual needs in accordance with the pleasure principle, and unable to take into consideration the strength of the external world, from being destroyed by an unguided and unmodified expression of its instinctual strivings. The id has achieved unified will under the domination of the need to relieve itself of tension—unpleasurable feelings. In the struggle between one group of instincts defending itself against the other, it 'would be possible to picture the id as under the domination of the mute but powerful death instincts which desire to be at peace and (prompted by the pleasure principle) to put Eros, the mischief-maker, to rest'.[1] However, the ego receiving excitation from the outside and from the inside uses sensations of pleasure and unpleasure to direct the course of mental events in accordance with the pleasure principle itself. 'We are very apt to think of the ego as powerless against the id; but when it is opposed to an instinctual process in the id it has only to give a "*signal of unpleasure*" in order to attain its object with the aid of that almost omnipotent institution, the pleasure principle.'[2]

Relationship of Pleasure Principle and Principle of Repetition Compulsion

It is then able to protect itself (and incidentally the id) by binding the excitations and thus repressing the dangerous instinctual impulse. But this repression causes the ego to renounce some of its own sovereignty. 'This is inevitable from the nature of repression, which is, fundamentally, an attempt at flight. The repressed is now, as it were, an outlaw; it is excluded from the great organization of the ego and is subject only to the laws which govern the realm of the unconscious. If, now, the danger-situation changes so that the ego has no reason for fending off a new instinctual impulse analogous to the repressed one, the consequence of the restriction of the ego which has taken place will become manifest. The new impulse will run its course under an automatic influence—or, as I should prefer to say, under the influence of the compulsion to repeat. It

[1] (1923b) *The Ego and the Id*, S.E., Vol. 19, p. 59.
[2] (1926d) *Inhibitions, Symptoms and Anxiety*, S.E., Vol. 20, p. 92.

will follow the same path as the earlier, repressed impulse, as though the danger-situation that had been overcome still existed.'[1] And it will make use of the immense (somatic) store of power ("the compulsion to repeat") which has escaped the binding process of the ego.[2] The ego's high degree of organization needed for its highest achievements thus is restricted; representatives of the instinct which became 'an outlaw' when repressed find no place in the coherent unity the ego strives to achieve and therefore are not subordinated to the reality principle, the modification of the pleasure principle.[3]

Freud did not consider, however, that he had solved the questions posed in *The Ego and The Id* (1923b) of the relationship between the instincts and the pleasure principle. In 'Analysis Terminable and Interminable' (1937c) he was convinced that the two primal instincts are not confined to a single province of the mental apparatus; and that there is a force at work which prevents the belief that mental processes are governed exclusively by a striving after pleasure. He thinks this 'a power in mental life which, according to its aim, we call the aggressive or destructive instinct' and is derived from the primal death instinct.[4] This destructive instinct is constantly opposed by Eros, the life instinct, but: How the elements of these two species of instinct combine to fulfil the various functions, under what conditions such combinations grow looser and break up, what disturbances correspond to these changes and what feelings they evoke in the perceptual scale of the pleasure principle—'these are problems whose elucidation would be the most valuable achievement of psychological research. For the moment we must bow to those superior forces which foil our efforts.'[5]

It seemed to him in *An Outline of Psycho-Analysis* (1940a [1938]), however, that the id and every other agency of the mind obeyed 'the inexorable pleasure principle'. It seems as though the activity of the other agencies of the mind is able only to modify the pleasure principle but not to nullify it; and it remains a question of the greatest theoretical importance, and one that has not yet been

---

[1] ibid., pp. 153–4.
[2] (1926f) 'Psycho-Analysis', S.E., Vol. 20, p. 265.
[3] (1933a) *New Introductory Lectures on Psycho-Analysis*, S.E., Vol. 22, pp. 98–9.
[4] (1937c) 'Analysis Terminable and Interminable', S.E., Vol. 23, p. 243.
[5] ibid., p. 243.

answered, when and how it is ever possible for the pleasure principle to be overcome. The consideration that the pleasure principle requires a reduction, or perhaps ultimately the extinction, of the tension of the instinctual needs (that is, a state of nirvana) leads to problems that are still examined in the relations between the pleasure principle and the two primal forces, Eros and the death instinct.[1]

Clinical Implications

The defining of the principles of mental functioning arose out of Freud's and Breuer's clinical work; the ideas of conflict and of repression of unpleasurable ideas were inherent in their *Studies on Hysteria* (1895). Freud saw the mental apparatus as being first and foremost a device for mastering excitations which would otherwise be felt as distressing or would have pathogenic effects. He saw the predominance of the life of fantasy and of illusion born of an unfulfilled wish as the ruling factor in the psychology of neurosis. Neurotics are guided by psychological reality and not ordinary objective reality; a 'hysterical symptom is based upon fantasy instead of upon the repetition of real experience, and the sense of guilt in an obsessional neurosis is based upon the fact of an evil intention which was never carried out.'[2]

As early as 1911 in 'Formulations on the Two Principles of Mental Functioning', it was noted that all memories turned away from reality and that the choice of neurosis might well be related to the stage of development of the ego, to the pleasure or the reality principles. The distinction between psychosis and neurosis was also related to the extent to which the reality principle was superseded by the pleasure principle. 'The aetiology common to the onset of a psychoneurosis and of a psychosis always remains the same. It consists in a frustration, a non-fulfilment, of one of those childhood wishes which are forever undefeated and which are so deeply rooted in our phylogenetically determined organization. This frustration is in the last resort always an external one; but in the individual case it may proceed from the internal agency (in the super-ego) which has taken over the representation of the demands of reality. The pathogenic effect depends on whether, in a conflictual tension of this kind, the ego remains true to its dependence

---

[1] (1940a [1938]) *An Outline of Psycho-Analysis*, S.E., Vol. 23, p. 198.
[2] (1921c) *Group Psychology and the Analysis of the Ego*, S.E., Vol. 18, p. 80.

on the external world and attempts to silence the id, or whether it lets itself be overcome by the id and thus torn away from reality. A complication is introduced into this apparently simple situation, however, by the existence of the super-ego, which, through a link that is not yet clear to us, unites in itself influences coming from the id as well as from the external world, and is to some extent an ideal model of what the whole endeavour of the ego is aiming at—a reconciliation between its various dependent relationships. The attitude of the super-ego should be taken into account—which has not hitherto been done—in every form of psychical illness.'[1]

The world of phantasy plays the same vital part in the psychosis as in the neurosis and is the storehouse from which the materials for the pattern for building the new (psychotic) reality are devised. This reality, however, attempts to take the place of external reality unlike that of the neurotic where it has a more symbolic significance. Freud noted how humour could illustrate this difference; humour itself signifies not only the triumph of the ego but also of the pleasure principle which is able to assert itself against the unkindness of the real circumstances.

'These last two features—the rejection of the claims of reality and the putting through of the pleasure principle—bring humour near to the regressive or reactionary processes which engage our attention so extensively in psychopathology. Its fending off of the possibility of suffering places it among the great series of methods which the human mind has constructed in order to evade the compulsion to suffer—a series which begins with neurosis and culminates in madness and which includes intoxication, self-absorption and ecstasy.'[2]

His stress upon the relative strengths of the reality principle and the pleasure principle as an indication of psychopathology was a vital feature of his formulations. He did, however, recognize that each one of us behaves in some respects like a paranoic and corrects some aspect of the world which is unbearable to us by the construction of a wish and introduces this delusion into reality.[3]

Freud saw the Principle of Repetition Compulsion as of utmost importance in the analytical treatment of neurosis. A patient's compulsion to repeat in the transference the acting out of repressed

---

[1] (1924b) 'Neurosis and Psychosis', S.E., Vol. 19, pp. 151–2.
[2] (1927d) 'Humour', S.E., Vol. 21, p. 163.
[3] (1930a) *Civilization and its Discontents*, S.E., Vol. 21, pp. 81–2.

instinctual strivings may if the resistances of the ego are sufficiently reduced through the analytic procedure, be used to bring about a therapeutic change in the manifest personality—the inhibitions, unserviceable attitudes and the pathological character traits. However, in some cases the inherent masochism, the negative therapeutic reaction and the neurotic's sense of guilt seems to bring about a loss of plasticity—mental processes, relations and distributions of energy are immutable, fixed rigid—which operates against the success of the analysis.

CATHEXIS

1. *Definition*

Cathexis is an energic concept, referring both to mental states and processes (dynamics), and is one of the most fundamental concepts of Freud's psychological theory. It can be defined as a charge of excitation, or an investment with energy and refers to an aspect of mental functioning 'which possesses all the characteristics of a quantity (though we have no means of measuring it), which is capable of increase, diminution, displacement and discharge, and which is spread . . . somewhat as an electric charge is spread over the surface of a body.'[1] 'Excitation' and 'psychical intensity', are two of several terms used by Freud to describe the unknown energy of cathexis.[2] He distinguished two principal forms of cathexis, namely mobile and bound cathexis; three major qualities, namely libidinal, aggressive, and neutral cathectic energy; and three main functions served by cathectic energies, namely those of cathexis, anticathexis (counter-cathexis), and hypercathexis.

The term 'cathexis' is the rendering of the German 'Besetzung', a word in ordinary use with the principal meaning of 'occupation'. Freud himself once used the term 'interest' as a translation of 'Besetzung'.[3] As Strachey points out, Freud 'was unhappy' about the term 'cathexis', but he 'may perhaps have become reconciled to it in the end, since it is to be found in his original manuscript of his *Encyclopaedia Britannica* article' of 1926.[4]

Although the only extensive theoretical discussion of cathexis is to be found in 'The Project' (1895)—where the topic is dealt with from a neurophysiological point of view—Freud was always fully aware of 'what a large contribution is made to the understanding of mental processes . . . by the dynamic changes in the *quantity* of energic cathexis'.[5] The mental apparatus receives stimuli both from the outside (by means of perceptions by the sense organs),

[1] (1894a) 'The Neuro-Psychoses of Defence', S.E., Vol. 3, p. 60.
[2] ibid., p. 66.
[3] Jones, E., *Sigmund Freud, Life and Work*, The Hogarth Press, London, 1958, Vol. 2, p. 69 f.
[4] (1894a) 'The Neuro-Psychoses of Defence', S.E., Vol. 3, p. 63 n.
[5] (1927d) 'Humour', S.E., Vol. 21, p. 165.

and from the interior of the body (i.e. endogenous stimuli) which lead to shifts in cathexis.[1]

2. *Historical survey*

Two main phases can be distinguished in Freud's use of the concept of cathexis. During the first, lasting up to *The Interpretation of Dreams*, cathexis was used—with very few exceptions—in a purely physiological sense. Thus we read in 'The Project', for instance: 'If we combine this account of the neurones with the conception of the [quantity] theory, we arrive at the idea of a cathected neurone . . . filled with a certain [quantity] while at other times it may be empty.'[2] It would be tempting to include here an exposition of Freud's detailed conceptualization of cathectic processes in neurophysiological terms as contained in his 'Project'. However, we are here concerned only with the psychological implications of the concept of cathexis. It will be seen that the roots of many of Freud's psychological formulations in regard to cathexis after the turn of the century can be found in ideas expressed in 'The Project'. But Freud himself explicitly repudiated the use of the term 'cathexis' in a neurophysiological sense when he wrote in 1905: 'what are "really psychically effective" are psychical processes which are unconscious in themselves . . . when I speak of the "cathexis of psychical paths" . . . I am making no attempt to proclaim that the cells and nerve fibres, or the systems of neurones . . . are these psychical paths.'[3]

It was *The Interpretation of Dreams* which marks the clear turning-point from the use of cathexis in a neurological to a psychological sense. Although in the theoretical seventh chapter cathexis has an entirely non-physical meaning characteristic of all later formulations, we still find passages in it which point to Freud's hope of expressing psychic phenomena in neurological terms: 'the second system succeeds in retaining the major part of its cathexes of energy in a state of quiescence and in employing only a small part on displacement. The mechanics of these processes are quite unknown to me; anyone who wished to take these ideas seriously would have to look for physical analogies to them and find a means

---

[1] (1950a [1887–1902]) *The Origins of Psycho-Analysis*, S.E., Vol. 1, p. 314 f.
[2] ibid., p. 298.
[3] (1905c) *Jokes and their Relation to the Unconscious*, S.E., Vol. 8, p. 147 f.

of picturing the movements that accompany excitation of neurones.'[1]

No theoretical discussions of cathectic processes in psychological terms can be found in Freud's works, which adds to the difficulties of a clear exposition of the meaning of cathexis and cathectic processes. Nor can a development in the use of the term be discerned. The important distinction between 'mobile' and 'bound' cathexes is already foreshadowed in 'The Project' (1895).

3. Types and characteristics of cathexes

The distinction between the two forms of mobile and bound cathexes is one of the most fundamental. Among other things it is used for the explanation of the difference between primary and secondary mental processes. Freud attributes the introduction of the distinction to Breuer on several occasions, as for instance: 'As a new factor we have taken into consideration Breuer's hypothesis that charges of energy occur in two forms; so that we have to distinguish between two kinds of cathexis of the psychical systems or their elements—a freely flowing cathexis that presses on towards discharge and a quiescent cathexis. We may perhaps suspect that the binding of the energy that streams into the mental apparatus consists in its change from a freely flowing into a quiescent state.'[2] Implicit in this formulation is the notion of cathexis as a process (mobile) and as a state (quiescent), the latter being the result of binding.

In Freud's opinion this distinction between the two forms of cathexis 'represents the deepest insight we have gained up to the present into the nature of nervous energy, and I do not see how we can avoid making it'.[3]

The idea of bound cathexis is foreshadowed in 'The Project' where Freud puts forward the notion that a 'side cathexis . . . beinds a quota of the . . . [quantity] flowing through the neurone',[4] so that only a small current can flow in spite of a high cathexis, a state of affairs seen as both characteristic of the ego and thought-processes.[5] Freud elaborates on this in *The Interpretation*

---

[1] (1900a) *The Interpretation of Dreams*, S.E., Vol. 5, p. 599.

[2] (1920g) *Beyond the Pleasure Principle*, S.E., Vol. 18, p. 31; cf. also ibid., p. 26 f. and (1915e) 'The Unconscious', S.E., Vol. 14, p. 188.

[3] (1915e) 'The Unconscious', S.E., Vol. 14, p. 188.

[4] (1950a [1887–1902]) *The Origins of Psycho-Analysis*, S.E., Vol. 1, p. 335.

[5] ibid., p. 368 f.

of Dreams when he states that 'for the sake of efficiency the second system succeeds in retaining the major part of its cathexis of energy in a state of quiescence and in employing only a small part on displacement . . . the activity of the *first* system is directed towards securing the *free discharge* of the quantities of excitation, while the *second* system, by means of the cathexes emanating from it, succeeds in *inhibiting* this discharge and in transforming the cathexis into a quiescent one, no doubt with a simultaneous raising of its level'.[1] The process of binding of mobile cathexes helps to explain the fact that dreams are usually prevented from disturbing sleep: 'The cathexis from the *Pcs* which goes half-way to meet the dream after it has become perceptual, having been directed on to it by the excitation in consciousness, binds the dream's unconscious excitation and makes it powerless to act as a disturbance.'[2]

At the end of the penultimate quotation Freud made reference to the fact that a system's cathectic level is raised by the transformation of mobile into quiescent cathexis. In his later theory this was seen as one of the characteristic functions of the ego which itself contains a high sotre of bound energy. 'Its constructive function consists in raising the passage [of events] in the id to a higher dynamic level (perhaps by transforming freely mobile into bound energy, such as corresponds to the preconscious state).'[3] The capacity of a psychic structure to bind cathectic energy depends on the height of its own level of cathexis: 'a system which is itself highly cathected is capable of taking up an additional stream of fresh inflowing energy and of converting it into quiescent cathexis, that is of binding it psychically. The higher the system's own quiescent cathexis, the greater seems to be its binding force, conversely, therefore, the lower its cathexis, the less capacity will it have for taking up inflowing energy'.[4]

Seen from a topographical point of view the process of binding is characteristic of the system preconscious and is one of its main functions. The processes of the system *Pcs* display '. . . an inhibition of the tendency of cathected ideas towards discharge'.[5] To

[1] (1900a) *The Interpretation of Dreams*, S.E., Vol, 5, p. 599.
[2] ibid., p. 578.
[3] (1940a [1938]), *An Outline of Psycho-Analysis*, S.E., Vol. 23, p. 199.
[4] (1920g) *Beyond the Pleasure Principle*, S.E., Vol. 18, p. 30; cf. also ibid., p. 31 f.
[5] (1915e) 'The Unconscious', S.E., Vol. 14, p. 188; cf. also (1900a) *The Interpretation of Dreams*, S.E., Vol. 5, p. 578.

perform this function, however, it has 'at its disposal for distribution a mobile cathectic energy, a part of which is familiar to us in the form of attention'.[1] This mobile cathexis is characterized by the fact that it can be directed purposively and its aim is the opposite of direct discharge. 'Cathexis by the second system implies a simultaneous inhibition of the discharge of excitation . . . *the second system can only cathect an idea if it is in a position to inhibit any development of unpleasure that may proceed from it.'*[2]

Whereas the system preconscious is characterized both by quiescent and mobile cathexes (both serving the purpose of binding), the system conscious is supposed to 'carry no bound energy capable of free discharge'. Freud justifies this view by stating that in the system *Cs* there is no resistance to the passage of an excitation as its exists in other parts of the mental apparatus.[3] However, these mobile energies of the system conscious are put to a different use from those of the systems preconscious or unconscious. 'By perceiving new qualities' the system conscious 'makes a new contribution to directing the mobile quantities of cathexis and distributing them in an expedient fashion. By the help of its perception of pleasure and unpleasure it influences the discharge of the cathexes within what is otherwise an unconscious apparatus operating by means of the displacement of quantities. It seems probable that in the first instance the unpleasure principle regulates the displacement of cathexes automatically. But it is quite possible that consciousness of these qualities may introduce in addition a second and more discriminating regulation, which is even able to oppose the former one, and which perfects the efficiency of the apparatus by enabling it, in contradiction to its original plan, to cathect and work over even what is associated with the release of unpleasure'.[4]

When Freud speaks of 'mobile cathexis' in connection with the 'second system' (*Pcs*) he must be referring to a type of cathectic energy which is qualitatively different from the freely mobile cathexes characteristic of processes in the first system, the unconscious. This is implicit in the following passage (even though it contrasts bound and mobile cathexis): 'the impulses arising from the instincts do not belong to the type of *bound* nervous processes

[1] (1900a) *The Interpretation of Dreams*, S.E., Vol. 5, p. 615.
[2] ibid., p. 601.
[3] (1920g) *Beyond the Pleasure Principle*, S.E., Vol. 18, p. 26 f.
[4] (1900a) *The Interpretation of Dreams*, S.E., Vol. 5, p. 616.

METAPSYCHOLOGY, CONFLICTS, ANXIETY

but of *freely mobile* processes which press towards discharge . . .
the processes in the unconscious systems [are] fundamentally
different from those in the preconscious (or conscious) systems. In
the unconscious, cathexes can easily be completely transferred, displaced and condensed'.[1] Freud expressed the same hypothesis in
structural terms, stating that 'in the unconscious id the energy is
in a freely mobile state, and that the id sets more store by the
possibility of discharging quantities of excitation than any other
consideration'.[2] Pleasure and unpleasure are related to 'the quantity of excitation that is present in the mind but is not in any way
"bound"'.[3] In dreams, the characteristic of the processes to which
the dream-thoughts are subjected by the dream-work is that 'the
whole stress is laid upon making the cathecting energy mobile and
capable of discharge; the content and the proper meaning of the
psychical elements to which the cathexes are attached are treated as
of little consequence'.[4] The displaceability of cathexis is one of the
foremost characteristics of mobile psychic energy, and is typical
of processes in the system unconscious. By way of displacement of
cathexis 'ideas which originally had only a *weak* charge of intensity
take over the charge from ideas which were originally *intensely*
cathected and at last attain enough strength to enable them to force
an entry into consciousness'.[5] In the case of dreams, this complete
transfer of cathexes from one idea to another probably 'makes
possible the cathexis of the system *Pcpt* in the reverse direction,
starting from thoughts, to the pitch of complete sensory vivid-
ness'.[6] The fact that 'the satisfaction of one instinct can take the
place of the satisfaction of others' also finds an explanation in the
possibility of the displacement of 'their libidinal cathexis to one
another'.[7]

From this discussion of the characteristics of the mobile cathectic energy in the three systems unconscious, preconscious, and
conscious, we may conclude that this energy serves different purposes in each of them, i.e. direct discharge in the case of the un-

---

[1] (1920g) *Beyond the Pleasure Principle*, S.E., Vol. 18, p. 34.
[2] (1940a [1938]) *An Outline of Psycho-Analysis*, Vol. 23, p. 168.
[3] (1920g) *Beyond the Pleasure Principle*, S.E., Vol. 23, p. 7 f.
[4] (1900a) *The Interpretation of Dreams*, S.E., Vol. 5, p. 597.
[5] ibid., Vol. 4, p. 177.
[6] ibid., p. 543; cf. also (1940a [1938]) *An Outline of Psycho-Analysis*, Vol. 23, p. 168.
[7] (1923a) 'Two Encyclopaedia Articles', S.E., Vol. 18, p. 256.

conscious, binding of unconscious excitations in the case of the preconscious, and purposive direction on the basis of perception of quality in the case of the system conscious.

The distinction between mobile and bound cathectic energy and that between thing- as opposed to word-cathexes are two of the major characteristics in the differentiation between primary and secondary mental processes. Freud states that 'it is easy to identify the primary psychical process with Breuer's freely mobile cathexis and the secondary process with changes in his bound or tonic cathexis. If so, it would be the task of the higher strata of the mental apparatus to bind the instinctual excitation reaching the primary process'.[1] The replacement of the primary by the secondary process and the conversion of the former's 'freely mobile cathectic energy into a mainly quiescent (tonic) cathexis' is considered by Freud as 'one of the earliest and most important functions of the mental apparatus'.[2] In regard to feelings of pleasure and unpleasure in connection with primary and secondary processes Freud points out that they 'can be produced equally from bound and from unbound excitatory processes', but that the former 'give rise to far more intense feelings in both directions'. On the other hand, the transformation into bound energy 'occurs on *behalf* of the pleasure principle' and the 'binding is a preparatory act which introduces and assures the dominance of the pleasure principle'.[3] The main aim of the primary psychical process is 'motor discharge or, if the path is open, hallucinatory revival of the desired perceptual identity', and primary processes 'appear wherever ideas are abandoned by the preconscious cathexis, are left to themselves and can become charged with the uninhibited energy from the unconscious which is striving to find an outlet'.[4]

A distinction between the systems Conscious and Unconscious is not only possible in terms of secondary and primary processes, but also on the basis of word- and thing-cathexes. In a letter to Abraham in 1914 Freud wrote: 'Recently I succeeded in defining a characteristic of the two systems *Bw* (consciousness) and *Ubw* (the unconscious) which almost makes both of them comprehensible. . . . All cathexes of objects make up the unconscious. The system *Bw* signifies the connecting of these unconscious ideas with

[1] (1920g) *Beyond the Pleasure Principle*, S.E., Vol. 18, p. 34 f.
[2] ibid., p. 62.   [3] ibid., p. 62.
[4] (1900a) *The Interpretation of Dreams*, S.E., Vol. 5, p. 604 f.

the concepts of *words*.'[1] Elsewhere Freud refers to the system unconscious as 'the region of the memory-traces of *things* (as contrasted with *word*-cathexes)'.[2] In the paper on 'The Unconscious'
(1915) he is quite specific about the fact that 'the transition from
the system *Ucs* to the system next to it is not effected through the
making of a new registration but through a change in its state, an
alteration in its cathexis'.[3]

From a passage in *The Ego and the Id* (1923) we can infer
that Freud theoretically distinguished between three fundamentally
different qualities of cathectic energies, i.e. libidinal, aggressive, and
neutral, when he states that we have to assume the existence of 'a
displaceable energy which, neutral in itself, can be added to a
qualitatively differentiated erotic or destructive impulse, and
augment its total cathexis'.[4] There is no difficulty in seeing the
sources of libidinal and aggressive cathexes in the two basic instinctual drives distinguished by Freud. The fact that we find in-
numerable references to 'libidinal cathexis' throughout Freud's
work but hardly any to 'aggressive cathexis' may be connected both
with the relatively late introduction of the concept of the death
instinct and the circumstance that 'erotic instincts appear to be
altogether more plastic, more readily diverted and displaced than the
destructive instincts' and are therefore of greater significance in
clinical and theoretical formulations.[5] 'Narcissistic cathexis', a
term often used by Freud, has to be regarded as a special form of
libidinal cathexis. 'Object cathexis', on the other hand, can refer
to either libidinal or aggressive qualities of cathexis, though again
the former have received far more attention in Freud's work than
the latter.

The third quality or cathectic energy, 'neutral energy', is
defined by Freud as 'desexualized Eros'. It 'proceeds from the
narcissistic store of libido' and is 'active both in the ego and in the
id'.[6] It does not seem quite clear how neutral energy, being defined
as desexualized Eros—which seems to imply an ego-process—can
be operative in the id. Such a process of neutralization is supposed
to take place at the time of the passing of the oedipus complex:

[1] Jones, E., *Sigmund Freud, Life and Work*, Vol. 2, The Hogarth Press,
London, 1958, p. 200.
[2] (1917e [1915]) 'Mourning and Melancholia', S.E., Vol. 14, p. 256 f.
[3] (1915e) 'The Unconscious', S.E., Vol. 14, p. 180.
[4] (1923b) *The Ego and the Id*, S.E., Vol. 19, p. 44.
[5] ibid., p. 44 f.   [6] ibid., p. 44.

'Its libidinal cathexes are abandoned, desexualized and in part sublimated.'[1] When Freud uses the term 'ego-cathexes' (in the sense of 'cathexes *by* the ego') he seems to have predominantly such neutral energies in mind. We infer this from a passage in the Schreber case (1911) where he poses the question whether 'the ego-cathexes which still remained in existence [would not] have been sufficient to maintain *rapport* with the external world' after the 'general detachment of the libido' from it. He continues: 'To meet this difficulty we should either have to assume that what we call libidinal cathexis . . . coincides with interest in general, or we should have to consider the possibility that a very widespread disturbance in the distribution of libido may bring about a corresponding disturbance in the ego-cathexes.'[2]

The term 'hypercathexes' is used by Freud with at least two different meanings. On the one hand it can refer to the exclusive or excessive cathexis of one single system, function, or representation. Freud uses the term in this sense in a description of the clinical picture of schizophrenic patients with their incapacity for transference, 'their characteristic repudiation of the external world, the appearance of signs of a hypercathexis of their own ego, the final outcome in complete apathy—all these clinical features seem to agree excellently with the assumption that their object-cathexes have been given up'.[3] When Freud discusses the reaction to physical pain, saying that 'cathectic energy is summoned from all sides to provide sufficiently high cathexes of energy in the environs of the breach' so that 'all the other psychical systems are impoverished', this is a similar example of this type of hypercathexis, even though Freud uses the term 'anticathexis' in this particular instance.[4]

The other meaning of the term 'hypercathexis' is probably more significant from the point of view of psychoanalytic theory. It is based on the assumption that each of the major psychic systems (*Ucs, Pcs, Cs*) has its own cathetic energies at its disposal, and that progression of an ideational representative from one system to another is dependent upon its cathexis from two systems, i.e. upon

[1] (1925j) 'Some Psychical Consequences of the Anatomical Distinction between the Sexes', S.E., Vol. 19, p. 257.
[2] (1911c) 'Psycho-Analytic Notes on an Autobiographical Account of a Case of Paranoia (Dementia Paranoides)' S.E., Vol. 14, p. 197.
[3] (1915e) 'The Unconscious', S.E., Vol. 14, p. 197.
[4] (1920g) *Beyond the Pleasure Principle*, S.E., Vol. 18, p. 30.

its receiving a hypercathexis. This idea finds clearest expression in the following passages: 'The system *Ucs* contains the thing-cathexes of the objects . . .; the system *Pcs* comes about by this thing-presentation being hypercathected through being linked with the word-presentations corresponding to it. It is these hyper-cathexes . . . that bring about a higher psychical organization and make it possible for the primary process to be succeeded by the secondary process which is dominant in the *Pcs*.'[1] A further hyper-cathexis is needed to make a preconscious idea conscious: 'the existence of the censorship between the *Pcs* and the *Cs* teaches us that becoming conscious is no mere act of perception, but is probably also a *hypercathexis*, a further advance in the psychical organization.'[2] In *The Interpretation of Dreams* (1900) Freud dis-cussed this 'further advance' in greater detail where he refers to hypercathexis as a summation of a (preconscious) 'purposive cathe-xis' and an 'attention'-cathexis from consciousness.[3] The hyper-cathexis achieved by the contribution from the system *Cs* leads to a 'greater delicacy of functioning' through the 'perception of pleas-ure and unpleasure'. The value of the hypercathexis which is set up in the mobile quantities by the regulating influence of the sense organ of the *Cs* cannot be better illustrated than by the fact of its creation of a new series of qualities and consequently of a new process of regulation.'[4]

The significance and function of anti-cathexes will be dealt with as a separate concept.

4. *Effects of cathectic processes*

Perhaps the most significant effect of cathectic processes is the laying down of permanent traces which are called 'facilitations'. Freud discussed the problem of facilitations at great length in 'The Project' (1895), and although we find only few references to this phenomenon in his later work, his views in this respect remained essentially the same. In *Beyond the Pleasure Principle* (1920) we read: 'It may be supposed that, in passing from one element to another, an excitation has to overcome a resistance, and that the diminution of resistance thus effected is what lays down a perma-

---

[1] (1915e) 'The Unconscious', S.E., Vol. 14, p. 201 f.
[2] ibid., p. 194.
[3] (1900a) *The Interpretation of Dreams*, S.E., Vol. 5, p. 594.
[4] ibid., p. 602 f., p. 616 f.

nent trace of the excitation, that is, a facilitation'.[1] We therefore think it justified to take recourse to 'The Project' for some quotations in regard to the function of facilitations. Freud there points out that facilitations help to prevent the accumulation of excessive quantities of undischarged excitations in the mental apparatus which 'avoids, to some extent at least, being filled with quantity, avoids cathexis, that is,—by setting up facilitations'. They are, therefore, in the first place, a characteristic of the primary process.[2] Facilitations also come about between two memory-traces which are simultaneously cathected because of the fact that 'two cathexes that are present simultaneously *must* . . . be brought into connection [with each other]'.[3] Facilitations are of particular importance with regard to mental economy in so far as they facilitate something akin to signal-anxiety: 'Since the release of unpleasure can be an extremely big one when there is quite a trivial cathexis of the hostile memory, we may conclude that pain leaves behind it specially abundant facilitations.'[4]

In 'A Metapsychological Supplement to the Theory of Dreams' (1915) Freud restates a principle with which he had dealt at great length already in his early 'Project', namely 'the principle of the insusceptibility to excitation of uncathected systems'. This principle mainly applies to processes during the state of sleep and refers to the fact that 'a complete emptying of a system renders it little susceptible to instigation'.[5] In regard to the system *Pcpt*, Freud had already expressed this view in 'The Project': 'with a lack of cathexis, their capacity for reception vanishes'.[6] However, in the 'Metapsychological Supplement' he points out that in the case of sleep, with the system *Cs* uncathected, 'the excitations which . . . have entered on the path of regression will find that path clear as far as the system *Cs* where they will count as undisputed reality'. In a footnote Freud states that in this instance 'the principle of the insusceptibility to excitation of uncathected systems appears to be invalidated. . . . But it may be a question of only the *partial*

---

[1] (1920g) *Beyond the Pleasure Principle*, S.E., Vol. 18, p. 26 f.

[2] (1950a [1887–1902]) *The Origins of Psycho-Analysis*, S.E., Vol. 1, p. 300 f.

[3] ibid., p. 338; cf. also ibid., p. 318 f.

[4] ibid., p. 382.

[5] (1917d [1915]) 'A Metapsychological Supplement to the Theory of Dreams', S.E., Vol. 14, pp. 227 n. and 234 n.

[6] (1950a [1887–1902]) *The Origins of Psycho-Analysis*, Imago, London, 1954, p. 312; cf. also ibid. p. 337.

removal of cathexis; and for the perceptual system in especial we must assume many conditions for excitation which are widely divergent from those of other systems'.[1]

In *Studies on Hysteria* (1895) Freud also pointed out that ideas may be insusceptible to new cathexes if they had, in the past, been associated with a strong painful affect. 'An idea whose affect is unresolved always involves a certain amount of associative inaccessibility and of incompatibility with new cathexes.'[2]

Sensations of pleasure and unpleasure are intimately connected with cathectic processes, or rather cathectic states, i.e. they are dependent on what Freud calls the 'level of cathexis'. He points out that 'sensations of a pleasurable nature have not anything inherently impelling about them whereas unpleasurable ones have it in the highest degree. The latter impel towards change, towards discharge, and that is why we interpret unpleasure as implying a heightening and pleasure a lowering of energic cathexis.'[3] We find the same notion expressed already in Freud's 'Project' where he adds that owing to the cathexis of memories unpleasure is *released* from the interior of the body and freshly conveyed up.[4]

5. Cathectic processes in the ego

In the introduction to *The Origins of Psycho-Analysis*, the editor points out that in 'The Project' 'the ego is represented as an organism distinguished by the possession of a constant cathexis of energy —a hypothesis which a quarter of a century later became the cornerstone of the psychoanalytic theory of psychic structure.'[5] Although this is true, Freud was much less explicit about this hypothesis of a 'constant cathexis' of the ego in his later writings than he was in 'The Project'. In the later works we have to infer it from things like the distinction between bound and mobile cathectic processes, from the description of thought-processes etc., and from statements like: 'The ego itself came to be regarded as a reservoir of what was described as narcissistic libido'[6] and others. In 'The Project' Freud had been much more specific. We read there that

[1] (1917d [1915]) 'A Metapsychological Supplement to the Theory of Dreams', S.E., Vol. 14, p. 234 and p. 243 n.

[2] (1895b) *Studies on Hysteria*, S.E., Vol. 2, p. 89.

[3] (1923b) *The Ego and the Id*, S.E., Vol. 19, p. 22.

[4] (1950a [1887–1902]) *The Origins of Psycho-Analysis*, S.E., Vol. 1, p. 320.

[5] (1950a [1887–1902]) *The Origins of Psycho-Analysis*, Imago, London, 1954, p. 26.

[6] (1923a) 'Two Encyclopaedia Articles', S.E., Vol. 18, p. 249.

the ego 'retains a constant cathexis and . . . constitutes the vehicle for the store of quantity required by the secondary function'.[1] In another context he speaks of 'the effects produced by a group of neurones with a *constant* cathexis (the ego) upon other neurones with *changing* cathexes.'[2] It is this constant store of cathexes which permits the ego to perform its many functions. Some of the basic cathectic mechanisms underlying the performance of these functions seem to be the following:

(a) *Turning powerful into weak cathexes*: 'It amounts to an approximate fulfilment of the task if the ego succeeds in *turning this powerful idea into a weak one*, in robbing it of the affect—the sum of excitation—with which it is loaded [cathected].'[3]

(b) *The inhibition of cathexes*: In connection with the discussion of hallucinations, Freud states that *'it is the inhibition brought about by the ego that makes possible a criterion for distinguishing between a perception and a memory'*. A *sine qua non* of the secondary process 'is a correct exploitation of the indications of reality' which is 'only possible when there is inhibition on the part of the ego'.[4] Laughter in connection with jokes is the most common phenomenon exemplifying the lifting of an 'inhibitory cathexis'.[5]

(c) *The application of purposive cathexes*: 'It lies within the choice of the ego to modify the course' of cathectic processes 'in the direction of any purposive cathexis . . . in reality our ego always entertains purposive cathexes—and often many at the same time',[6] e.g. in thinking, judgements, anticathexes etc.

(d) *The withdrawal of cathexis*: This mechanism is a characteristic of many defences (cf. the withdrawal of preconscious cathexis). It is familiar to us in its most extreme form in the state of sleep. The 'psychological characteristics of sleep are to be looked for essentially in modifications in the cathexis of this particular system—a system that is also in control of access to the power of movement,

[1] (1950a [1887–1902]) *The Origins of Psycho-Analysis*, Imago, London, 1954, p. 384.
[2] ibid., p. 417; cf. also ibid., pp. 426 f.
[3] (1894a) 'The Neuro-Psychoses of Defence', S.E., Vol. 3, p. 48.
[4] (1950a [1887–1902]), *The Origins of Psycho-Analysis*, Imago, London, 1954, pp. 387–9; cf. also ibid., pp. 390 f. and 394–6.
[5] (1905c) *Jokes and their Relation to the Unconscious*, S.E., Vol. 8, pp. 147–52.
[6] (1950a [1887–1902]) *The Origins of Psycho-Analysis*, Imago, London, 1954, p. 434.

which is paralysed during sleep'.[1] In sleep the ego returns to 'an earlier state of things . . . by . . . breaking off its relations with the external world and withdrawing its cathexes from the sense organs.'[2]

One or several such mechanisms are involved in ego-phenomena like attention, thinking, consciousness etc.

Attention-cathexes fulfil an important regultive function. 'The course of our conscious reflections show us that we follow a particular path in our application of attention. If, as we follow this patch, we come upon an idea which will not bear criticism, we break off: we drop the cathexis of attention.'[3] Freud points to an important aspect of this function when he states that 'if a cathexis which releases unpleasure were able to escape attention, the ego's intervention would come too late.'[4] In 'The Project' Freud even spoke of a 'biological rule of attention' regulating 'the displacement of ego-cathexes'. It runs as follows: '*If an indication of reality appears, the perceptual cathexis which is simultaneously present must be hypercathected.*'[5] In his discussion of jokes Freud maintains that 'precisely the cathexis of attention has a great share in the supervision and fresh employment of liberated cathectic energy'.[6]

Thoughts are closely linked with the problem of attention, as it is '*a sine qua non* of the arousing of indications of thought that they shall receive a cathexis of attention'.[7] Secondary process thinking is a mental process which takes place exclusively by means of bound energies. It is mainly for this reason that increased tension can be tolerated while the process of discharge is postponed. 'It is essentially an experimental kind of acting, accompanied by displacement of relatively small quantities of cathexis together with less expenditure (discharge) of them. For this purpose the conversion of freely displaceable cathexes into "bound" cathexes was necessary, and this was brought about by means of raising the level

---

[1] (1900a) *The Interpretation of Dreams*, S.E., Vol. 5, p. 555; cf. also ibid., pp. 543 f., 554, 570, 573.

[2] (1940a [1938]) *An Outline of Psycho-Analysis*, S.E., Vol. 23, p. 166.

[3] (1900a) *The Interpretation of Dreams*, S.E., Vol. 5, p. 593.

[4] (1950a [1887–1902]) *The Origins of Psycho-Analysis*, Imago, London, 1954, p. 415.

[5] ibid., p. 428 f.; cf. also ibid., pp. 386, 387, 417–19, 420, 431 f.

[6] (1905c) *Jokes and their Relation to the Unconscious*, S.E., Vol. 8, p. 151 f.

[7] (1950a [1887–1902]) *The Origins of Psycho-Analysis*, Imago, London, 1954, p. 431.

of the whole cathectic process.'[1] Whereas here Freud seems to imply that thinking entails a certain amount of discharge, he had maintained in 1905 that 'in our thought processes we are constantly in the habit of displacing such cathexes . . . (that have become superfluous) . . . from one path to another without losing any of their energy by discharge'.[2] Another passage seems to support this second point of view: 'A train of thought that has been set going . . . in the preconscious may either cease spontaneously or persist. We picture the first of these outcomes as implying that the energy attaching to the train of thought is diffused along all the associative paths that radiate from it; this energy sets the whole network of thoughts in a state of excitation which lasts for a certain time and then dies away as the excitation in search of discharge becomes transformed into a quiescent cathexis.'[3] Thus the main characteristics of secondary thought processes from a cathectic point of view are that they always employ bound energy and that only small amounts of cathexes are displaced.

Consciousness is dependent on 'cathectic innervations' which 'are sent out and withdrawn in rapid periodic impulses from within into the completely pervious system *Pcpt-Cs*. So long as that system is cathected in this manner, it receives perceptions (which are accompanied by consciousness) . . . but as soon as the cathexis is withdrawn, consciousness is extinguished and the functioning of the system comes to a standstill'.[4] Freud had expressed a similar notion in 'The Project' when he stated that 'consciousness emerges *during the passage* of a quantity . . . that is to say that it is not aroused by a *constant* cathexis'.[5] One of the major functions of consciousness is the perception of 'new qualities' which enables it to contribute to 'directing the mobile quantities of cathexis and distributing them in an expedient fashion'.[6]

6. *Cathectic processes in the id*

The id only contains cathexes of a freely mobile kind which are

[1] (1911b) 'Formulations on the Two Principles of Mental Functioning', S.E., Vol. 12, p. 221; cf. also (1950a [1887–1902]) *The Origins of Psycho-Analysis*, Imago, London, 1954, p. 425 f.

[2] (1905c) *Jokes and their Relation to the Unconscious*, S.E., Vol. 8, p. 151 f.

[3] (1900a) *The Interpretation of Dreams*, S.E., Vol. 5, p. 594.

[4] (1925a) 'A Note upon the "Mystic Writing-Pad"', S.E., Vol. 19, p. 231.

[5] (1950a [1887–1902]) *The Origins of Psycho-Analysis*, Imago, London, 1954, p. 404.

[6] (1900a) *The Interpretation of Dreams*, S.E., Vol. 5, p. 616.

characterized by the ease of their displaceability and by their principal aim of finding discharge. The cathexes in the id are, in the first place, 'the mental representatives of the instincts',[1] i.e. 'an idea or group of ideas which is cathected with a definite quota of psychical energy (libido or interest) coming from an instinct'.[2] The processes are solely governed by the pleasure principle, and Freud's statement that '*releases of pleasure and unpleasure automatically regulate the course of cathectic processes*'[3] seems to have particular application to such id-processes. We infer this from his statement elsewhere that the secondary process can tolerate, 'cathect and work over even what is associated with the release of unpleasure'.[4]

In libidinal regression 'the libido has withdrawn from the ego and its laws. . . . The ideas to which it now transfers its energy as a cathexis belong to the system of the unconscious and are subject to the processes which are possible there, particularly to condensation and displacement'. This regression is made possible by the existence of fixations and consists in a 'regressive cathexis (with libido) of these fixations'.[5]

With regard to repression, Freud emphasizes the fact that the 'repressed idea remains capable of action in the Ucs, and it must therefore have retained its cathexis'. That such ideas, in spite of their cathexis, cannot penetrate into the system Pcs is due to the existence of anticathexes.[6] However, if a 'repressed unconscious wish receives an organic reinforcement' it may make an attempt at forcing its way through, in spite of having lost the 'cathexis from the Pcs. There then follows a defensive struggle—for the Pcs in turn reinforces its opposition to the repressed thoughts (i.e. produces an "anticathexis")—and thereafter the transference thoughts, which are the vehicles of the unconscious wish, force their way through in some form of compromise which is reached by the production of a symptom'.[7]

In the paper on 'Repression' (1915) we find a very important passage with regard to repression and its dependence upon the quantitative aspect of cathexis: 'With unrepressed derivatives of

[1] (1926f) 'Psycho-Analysis', S.E., Vol. 20, p. 265 f.
[2] (1915d) 'Repression', S.E., Vol. 14, p. 152.
[3] (1900a) *The Interpretation of Dreams*, S.E., Vol. 5, p. 574.
[4] ibid., p. 616.
[5] (1916–17) *Introductory Lectures on Psycho-Analysis*, S.E., Vol. 16, p. 359.
[6] (1915e) 'The Unconscious', S.E., Vol. 14, p. 180 f.
[7] (1900a) *The Interpretation of Dreams*, S.E., Vol. 5, p. 604 f.

the unconscious the fate of a particular idea is often decided by the degree of its activity or cathexis . . . such a derivative remains unrepressed so long as it represents only a small amount of energy, although its content would be calculated to give rise to a conflict with what is dominant in consciousness. The quantitative factor proves decisive for this conflict . . . where repression is concerned, an increase of energic cathexis operates in the same sense as an approach to the unconscious, while a decrease of that cathexis operates in the same sense as remoteness from the unconscious or distortion.'[1]

7. Cathectic processes in memories, perceptions, and hallucinations

These three phenomena are considered together because the cathectic processes involved in them are closely linked. Perceptions lead to memories, and the latter may in turn lead to hallucinations under certain conditions. A memory, unlike a perception, 'does not possess enough quality to excite consciousness and thus to attract fresh cathexis to itself'. This fact facilitates the avoidance 'of the memory of anything that had once been distressing', i.e. the ego 'cathects memories in such a way that there is an inhibition of their discharge . . . in the direction of the development of unpleasure'.[2] Most memories are composed of cathexes from several sense modalities (auditory, visual, tactile etc.), but for an understanding of dream-processes in particular it is important to realize that 'some of these memories themselves exist only in the form of visual cathexes and not as translations into the terminology of the later systems', i.e. without any word-cathexes attached to them.[3]

Genetically, memories serve, in the first place, the function of connecting the representations of needs with the experiences following upon them. A link is established between the two, so that—in an experience of satisfaction, for instance 'the mnemic image' of a particular perception 'remains associated thenceforward with the memory trace of the excitation produced by the need'. This facilitates the re-cathexis of the mnemic image of the perception when the need arises again and directs the efforts towards 'a complete cathexis of the perception'.[4]

The capacity to distinguish between a memory and a perception

[1] (1915d) 'Repression', S.E., Vol. 14, p. 152; cf. also (1916–17) *Introductory Lectures on Psycho-Analysis*, S.E., Vol. 16, p. 373.
[2] (1900a) *The Interpretation of Dreams*, S.E., Vol. 5, p. 600 f.
[3] ibid., p. 573 f.   [4] ibid., p. 565 f.

is an essential one from the point of view of mental economics: *'it is the inhibition brought about by the ego that makes possible a criterion for distinguishing between a perception and a memory'*.[1] As Freud points out elsewhere, an 'internal cathexis [i.e. the cathexis of a memory] could only have the same value as an external one [i.e. a perceptual cathexis] if it were maintained unceasingly. . . . In order to arrive at a more efficient expenditure of psychical force, it is necessary to bring the regression to a halt before it becomes complete, so that it does not proceed beyond the mnemic image.'[2] If the topographical regression is not stopped at the mnemic image 'a complete hallucinatory cathexis of the perceptual systems' is the consequence.[3] As Freud expressed it in *The Ego and the Id* (1923): 'when a memory is revived the cathexis remains in the mnemic system, whereas a hallucination, which is not distinguishable from a perception, can arise when the cathexis does not merely spread over from the memory trace on to the *Pcpt* element, but passes over to it *entirely*'.[4] According to Freud, 'the first wishing seems to have been a hallucinatory cathecting of the memory of satisfaction'. In other words, it is the primary process which strives towards a hallucinatory revival of the perception of satisfaction, whereas it is one of the functions of the secondary process not to 'allow the mnemic cathexis to proceed as far as perception and from there to bind the psychical forces'.[5]

Perception in itself is an ego-function for which only small quantities of energy are employed. 'The ego periodically sends out small amounts of cathexis into the perceptual system, by means of which it samples the external stimuli, and then after every such tentative advance it draws back again.'[6]

8. *Object cathexes*

'The first and true object-cathexes' are the 'thing-cathexes of the objects' contained in the system unconscious.[7] This statement seems

---

[1] (1950a [1887–1902]) *The Origins of Psycho-Analysis,* Imago, London, 1954, p. 387 f.

[2] (1900a) *The Interpretation of Dreams,* S.E., Vol. 5, p. 566.

[3] ibid., p. 548.

[4] (1923b) *The Ego and the Id,* S.E., Vol. 19, p. 20.

[5] (1900a) *The Interpretation of Dreams,* S.E., Vol. 5, p. 598 f.; cf. also (1950a [1887–1902]) *The Origins of Psycho-Analysis,* Imago, London, 1954, p. 401 f.

[6] (1925h) 'Negation', S.E., Vol. 14, p. 201; cf. also (1950a [1887–1902]) *The Origins of Psycho-Analysis,* Imago, London, 1954, p. 142.

[7] (1915e) 'The Unconscious', S.E., Vol. 14, p. 201.

to imply a distinction between early, hallucinatory revivals of the perception of objects by a full cathexis of their memory image and the later cathexis of object-representations with their clear distinction between memory and perception. We may see a confirmation of this distinction in Freud's statement that 'primary *narcissism* . . . lasts until the ego begins to cathect the ideas of objects with libido —to transform narcissistic libido into object libido'.[1] This hypothesis that the first object-cathexes emanate from the id is an important factor for the understanding of narcissism in general, and of secondary narcissism in particular. 'The ego deals with the first object-cathexes of the id . . . by taking over the libido from them into itself and binding it to the alteration of the ego produced by means of identification. . . . The narcissism of the ego is thus a secondary one, which has been withdrawn from objects.'[2] Freud seems to allude to an important determining factor for this tendency to withdraw cathexes from objects when he states, in *An Outline of Psycho-Analysis*, that 'to begin with, the child does not distinguish between the breast and its own body; when the breast has to be separated from the body and shifted to the "*outside*" because the child so often finds it absent, it carries with it, as an "*object*", a part of the original narcissistic libidinal cathexis'[3] (see concept on narcissism). The fact of secondary narcissism has the important consequence for later object-choices that if they have 'been effected on a narcissistic basis . . . the object-cathexis, when obstacles come in its way, can regress to narcissism. The narcissistic identification with the object then becomes a substitute for the erotic cathexis'.[4]

The nature of object-relationships is determined both by qualitative (libidinal or aggressive) and quantitative factors. With regard to the latter, Freud says, for instance, that 'the difference between an ordinary erotic object-cathexis and the state of being in love is that in the latter incomparably more cathexis passes over to the object and that the ego empties itself as it were in favour of the object'.[5] It is obvious that Freud refers to the object-representation in the above and many other, similar passages.

The ease with which object-cathexes are transferred from one

[1] (1940a [1938]) *An Outline of Psycho-Analysis*, S.E., Vol. 23, p. 150.
[2] (1923b) *The Ego and the Id*, S.E., Vol. 19, p. 45 f.
[3] (1940a [1938]) *An Outline of Psycho-Analysis*, S.E., Vol. 23, p. 188.
[4] (1917e [1915]) 'Mourning and Melancholia', S.E., Vol. 14, p. 249.
[5] (1927d) 'Humour', S.E., Vol. 21, p. 164 f.

person to another is an important determining factor for the stability of object-relationships, but also for the treatability in analysis. The analytic process is slow in people who 'cannot make up their minds to detach libidinal cathexes from one object and displace them on to another, although we can discover no special reason for this cathectic loyalty'. The treatability of the opposite type whose 'libido seems particularly mobile' and who 'enters readily upon the new cathexes suggested by analysis, abandoning its former ones in exchange for them' is much more doubtful, and 'the results of analysis often turn out to be very impermanent'.[1]

[1] (1937c) 'Analysis Terminable and Interminable', S.E., Vol. 23, p. 241.

[Editor's Note] We have at times used the text of *The Origins of Psycho-Analysis*, Imago's edition instead of that of *The Standard Edition*. The reason for this is that *The Standard Edition* only contains a selection of the material contained in the Imago's edition. Further the translation of certain passages seems to us clearer, at least occasionally, in the latter than in the former.

FREUD'S THEORY OF CONFLICT

One important contribution of psychoanalysis to the understanding of mental life in general and to the theory of the neuroses in particular had been the recognition of the existence of mental forces that could engage themselves in conflicts.

These views, so familiar to us today, were put forward by Freud in the early nineties. At that time accepted scientific opinion considered the neuroses the result of 'heredity and degeneration'.

In his *Introductory Lectures on Psycho-Analysis* (1916–17) he pointed out what the aim of his endeavours were:

'We seek not merely to describe and to classify phenomena, but to understand them as signs of an interplay of forces in the mind, as a manifestation of purposeful intentions working concurrently or in mutual opposition. We are concerned with a *dynamic view* of mental phenomena. On our view the phenomena that are perceived must yield in importance to trends which are only hypothetical.'[1]

Furthermore his theory of the neurosis is based on the existence of these mental forces in a situation of conflict. He wrote:

'The validity of the hypothesis of psychical conflict and of the formation of symptoms by means of compromises between the two mental currents struggling against each other has been demonstrated by me in case of patients observed and medically treated in real life. . . .[2] Without such a conflict there is no neurosis'.[3]

In his *Studies in Hysteria* and while explaining how the concept of defence arose, he wrote: 'The patient's ego had been approached by an idea which proved to be incompatible, which provoked on the part of the ego a repelling force of which the purpose was defence against this incompatible idea. This defence was in fact successful.

[1] (1916–17) *Introductory Lectures on Psycho-Analysis*, S.E., Vol. 15, p. 67.
[2] (1907a) *Delusions and Dreams in Jensen's 'Gradiva'*, S.E., Vol. 9, p. 54.
[3] (1916–17) *Introductory Lectures on Psycho-Analysis*, S.E., Vol. 16, p. 349.

The idea in question was forced out of consciousness and out of memory.' A few lines later he continued: 'Thus a psychical force, aversion on the part of the ego, had originally driven the pathogenic idea out of association and was now opposing its return to memory.'[1] Further he pointed out: *'Conflict coincides with my concept of defence (or fending off). It comprises the cases of acquired neurosis in people who are not hereditarily abnormal.'[2] Similarly:

'Patients . . . enjoyed good mental health up to the moment at which *an occurrence of incompatibility took place in their ideational life*—that is to say, until their ego was faced with an experience, an idea or a feeling which aroused such a distressing affect that the subject decided to forget about it, because he had no confidence in his power to resolve the contradiction between that incompatible idea and his ego by means of thought-activity. . . .'[3] 'At that time, and even before sexuality had been given its rightful place as an aetiological factor, I had maintained that no experience could have a pathogenic effect unless it appeared intolerable to the subject's ego and gave rise to efforts at defence.'[4]

In connection with the conflict in neurotics and the mechanisms of symptom formation that may result from it he pointed out: 'In such people we regularly find indications of a contention between wishful impulses or, as we are in the habit of saying, a psychical conflict. One part of the personality champions certain wishes while another part opposes them and fends them off.' A few lines later he continued: 'The conflict is conjured up by frustration, as a result of which the libido, deprived of satisfaction, is driven to look for other objects and paths. The necessary pre-condition of the conflict is that these other paths and objects arouse displeasure in one part of the personality, so that a veto is imposed which makes the new method of satisfaction impossible as it stands.'[5]

Having explained how the drives may be forced into a regressive

[1] (1895d) With Breuer, *Studies on Hysteria*, S.E., Vol. 2, p. 269.
[2] (1950a [1887–1902]), *The Origins of Psycho-Analysis*, Imago, London 1954, p. 85. (Letter of 21.5.1894.)
[3] (1894a) 'The Neuro-Psychoses of Defence', S.E., Vol. 3, p. 47.
[4] (1906a) 'My Views on the Part Played by Sexuality in the Aetiology of the Neuroses', S.E., Vol. 7, p. 276.
[5] (1916–17) *Introductory Lectures on Psycho-Analysis*, S.E., Vol. 16, p. 349.

path to earlier forms of satisfaction and objects he further characterized the events that follow this regression according to the ego
objecting or accepting these older forms of satisfaction. Libidinal
strivings follow paths of regression and:

'If these strivings, which are incompatible with the subject's
present-day individuality, acquire enough intensity, a conflict must
result between them and the other portion of his personality, which
has maintained its relation to reality. This conflict is resolved by
formation of symptoms. . . .'[1]

'The path to perversion branches off sharply from that to
neurosis. If these regressions rouse no objection from the ego, no
neurosis will come about either; and the libido will arrive at some
real, even though no longer normal satisfaction. But if the ego,
which has under its control not only consciousness but also the
approaches to motor innervation and accordingly to the realization
of mental desires, does not agree with these regressions, conflict
will follow.'[2]

'. . . in all neuroses the pathological symptoms are really the
end-products of such conflicts, which have led to "repression" and
"splitting" in the mind. The symptoms are generated by different
mechanisms: (a) either as formations in substitution for the repressed forces, or (b) as compromises between the repressing and
repressed forces, or (c) as reaction-formations and safeguards
against the repressed forces. . . .'[3]

'Hysterical symptoms arise as a compromise between two
opposite affective and instinctual impulses, of which one is attempting to bring to expression a component instinct or a constituent of
the sexual constitution, and the other is attempting to supress it.'[4]

In the case of Dora the symptoms appeared after the conflict
emerged between her 'temptation to yield to the man's proposal
and a composite force rebelling against that feeling'. It finally led
to the repudiation by the ego forces of her sexual wishes.[5] She was

[1] (1912e) 'Types of Onset of Neurosis', S.E., Vol. 12, p. 232.
[2] (1916–17) *Introductory Lectures on Psycho-Analysis*, S.E., Vol. 16, p. 359.
[3] (1913m [1911]) 'On Psycho-Analysis', S.E., Vol. 12, p. 208.
[4] (1908a) 'Hysterical Phantasies and their Relation to Bisexuality', S.E., Vol.
9, p. 164; cf. also: (1900a) *The Interpretation of Dreams*, S.E., Vol. 5, p. 596, and
The Origins of Psycho-Analysis, Imago, London 1954. (Letters 46 to Fliess.)
[5] (1905e [1901]) 'Fragment of an Analysis of a Case of Hysteria', S.E., Vol.
7, p. 88 f.

full of regret at having rejected his proposal and longed for his company and his affection but these wishes were in conflict with other forces such as her pride and led to repression. To maintain the repression she had to summon up her love for her father, and to exaggerate it.[1]

In repression and obsessional neurosis, there is an unending conflict:

'. . . fresh psychical efforts are continually required to counter-balance the forward pressure of the instinct.'[2]

'Compulsive acts . . . in two successive stages of which the second neutralizes the first . . . their true significance lies in their being a representation of a conflict between two opposing impulses of approximately equal strength: and hitherto I have invariably found that this opposition has been one between love and hate . . . in hysteria a compromise is arrived at which enables both the opposing tendencies to find expression simultaneously—which kills two birds with one stone; whereas here each of the two opposing tendencies finds satisfaction singly, first one then the other. . . .'[3]

In the case of the Rat Man he pointed out:

'It was a complete obsessional neurosis, . . . The child . . . was under the domination of a component of the sexual instinct, the desire to look [scopophilia], as a result of which there was a constant recurrence in him of a very intense wish connected with persons of the female sex who pleased him—the wish, that is, to see them naked. This wish corresponds to the later obsessional or compulsive idea; and if the quality of compulsion was not yet present in the wish, this was because the ego had not yet placed itself in complete opposition to it and did not yet regard it as something foreign to itself. Nevertheless, opposition to this wish from some source or other was already in activity, for its occurrence was regularly accompanied by a distressing affect. A conflict was evidently in progress in the mind of this young libertine. Side by

---

[1] (1905e [1901]) 'Fragment of an Analysis of a Case of Hysteria', S.E., Vol. 7, p. 58 f.

[2] (1907b) 'Obsessive Actions and Religious Practices', S.E., Vol. 9, p. 124.

[3] (1909d) 'Notes upon a Case of Obsessional Neurosis', S.E., Vol. 10, p. 192.

side with the obsessive wish . . . was an obsessive fear: every time he had a wish of this kind he could not help fearing that something dreadful would happen.'

'We find, accordingly: an erotic instinct and a revolt against it; a wish which has not yet become compulsive and, struggling against it, a fear which is already compulsive; a distressing affect and an impulsion toward the performance of defensive acts.'[1]

Delusions too were considered the result of an unending struggle or conflict:

'The symptoms of a delusion—fantasies and actions alike—are in fact the products of compromise between the two mental currents, and in a compromise account is taken of the demands of each of the two parties to it; but each side must also renounce a part of what it wanted to achieve. Where a compromise comes about it must have been preceded by a struggle—in this case it was the conflict we have assumed between suppressed erotism and the forces that were keeping it in repression. In the formation of a delusion this struggle is in fact unending.'[2]

Freud described how the conflict can be to start with, early in life, one with external authority. 'At that time it is the immediate expression of fear of the external authority, a recognition of the tension between the ego and that authority.'[3] At some point in development these conflicts with the external authority become internalized. 'It is in keeping with the course of human development that external coercion gradually becomes internalized; for a special mental agency, man's super-ego, takes it over and includes it among its commandments.'[4]

There are very many different types of conflict observable in mental life. Some of them are found at the basis of certain neurotic, or other types of disturbances. In other cases they are part of normal mental processes or relate to developmental stages. Nevertheless the nature of the forces and structures involved is of great value for the correct identification of the process or disturbance in

[1] ibid., p. 162 f.

[2] (1907a) *Delusions and Dreams in Jensen's 'Gradiva'*, S.E., Vol. 9, p. 52.

[3] (1930a) *Civilization and its Discontents*, S.E., Vol. 21, p. 136 f.

[4] (1927e) *The Future of an Illusion*, S.E., Vol. 21, p. 11; cf. also (1930a) *Civilization and its Discontents*, S.E., Vol. 21, p. 136 f.

question. In 'Libidinal Types' he pointed out for example to the precipitating causes of the neuroses: 'The precipitating causes of it are frustrations and internal conflicts: conflicts between the three major psychical agencies, conflicts arising within the libidinal economy in consequence of our bisexual disposition and conflicts between the erotic and the aggressive instinctual components.'[1]

In the case of the war neurosis he thought the conflict to be between two different ego ideals:

'It is a question of a conflict between two ego ideals, the customary one and the one the war has compelled the person to build. . . . Thus a conflict can come about just as in the ordinary psychoneurosis. The theory of it would be that a *new* ego has been developed on the basis of a libidinal cathexis of an object, and the former ego strives to displace it. There is thus a struggle within the ego instead of between ego and libido, but fundamentally that comes to the same thing. There is a certain parallelism with melancholia, where also a new ego has been instituted, but no ideal—merely a new ego on the basis of an object-cathexis that has been abandoned. . . .'[2]

He extended the above mentioned considerations to the traumatic neuroses in another letter to Ernest Jones, on February 18, 1919. Freud wrote:

'Let me propose to you the following formula: First consider the traumatic neurosis of peace . . .' and a few lines later: 'Now in the case of war there is the conflict between the habitual and the fresh warlike ideal. The first is subjugated, but when the "shell" arrives this older ego understands that it may be killed by the ways of the alter ego. Its opposition leaves this new master of the ego weak and powerless, and thus it, the Ego as a whole, comes under the aetiology of the traumatic neurosis. The difference between peace and war is that with the former the ego is strong but surprised, with the latter it is prepared but weakened. In this way the war neurosis is a case of internal narcissistic conflict within the ego . . .'[3]

[1] (1931a) 'Libidinal Types', S.E., Vol. 21, p. 220.
[2] Letter to E. Jones in: Jones, E., *Sigmund Freud, Life and Work*, Vol. 2, The Hogarth Press, London, 1958, p. 283 f.
[3] Letter to E. Jones in: Jones, E., *Sigmund Freud, Life and Work*, Vol. 2, The Hogarth Press, London, 1958, p. 285.

'. . . there remains the question of conflicts between the various identifications into which the ego comes apart, conflicts which cannot after all be described as entirely pathological.'[1]

On the other hand, Freud pointed out as well how it is not in every instance that illness will be the result of a situation of conflict. He pointed out: 'It is the endeavour of the psychology of the neuroses to discover what makes these processes, which belong to the normal course of mental life, become pathogenic.'[2] Or: '. . . a psychical conflict, *per se*, may also have a normal outcome'.[3] Similarly on his paper 'On Neurosis and Psychosis' he remarked: 'One would like to know in what circumstances and by what means the ego can succeed in emerging from such conflicts . . . without falling ill.'[4]

On other occasions he assumed the conflict to promote development, for example ego development, as in the following context:

'. . . the child also experiences . . . a "psychical conflict" [about conception and birth], in that views for which he feels an instinctual kind of preference, but which are not "right" in the eyes of grown-ups, come into opposition with other views, which are supported by the authority of the grown-ups without being acceptable to him himself.'[5]

'A child's desire for knowledge on this point does not in fact awaken spontaneously, prompted perhaps by some inborn need for established causes; it is aroused under the goad of the self-seeking instincts that dominate him, when—perhaps after the end of his second year—he is confronted by the arrival of a new baby [this stimulates his thought and prompts him to wonder where baby has come from].'[6]

One very important point in relation to the psychoanalytic theory of conflict was referred to by Freud in the following terms:

'In this connection people usually overlook the one essential

---

[1] (1923b) *The Ego and the Id*, S.E., Vol. 19, p. 31.
[2] (1931a) 'Libidinal Types', S.E., Vol. 21, p. 220.
[3] (1913m [1911]) 'On Psycho-Analysis', S.E., Vol. 12, p. 208.
[4] (1924b) 'Neurosis and Psychosis', S.E., Vol. 19, p. 152.
[5] (1908c) 'On the Sexual Theories of Children', S.E., Vol. 9, p. 214.
[6] ibid., p. 212.

point—that the pathogenic conflict in neurotics is not to be confused with a normal struggle between mental impulses both of which are on the same psychological footing. In the former case the dissension is between two powers, one of which has made its way to the stage of what is preconscious or conscious while the other has been held back at the stage of the unconscious. For that reason the conflict cannot be brought to an issue; the disputants can no more come to grips than, in the familiar simile, a polar bear and a whale. A true decision can only be reached when they both meet on the same ground. To make this possible is, I think, the sole task of our therapy.'[1]

He introduced what he called:

'. . . a fresh factor into the structure of the aetiological chain—namely the quantity, the magnitude, of the energies concerned. We have still to take this factor into account everywhere. . . . A purely qualitative analysis of the aetiological determinants is not enough. Or, to put it another way, a merely *dynamic* view of these mental processes is insufficient; an *economic* line of approach is also needed. We must tell ourselves that the conflict between two trends does not break out till certain intensities of cathexis have been reached, even though the determinants for it have long been present so far as their subject-matter is concerned.'[2]

'The quantitative factor proves decisive for this conflict: as soon as the basically obnoxious idea exceeds a certain degree of strength, the conflict becomes a real one, and it is precisely this activation that leads to repression. So that, . . . an increase of energic cathexis operates in the same sense as an approach to the unconscious, while a decrease of that cathexis operates in the same sense as remoteness from the unconscious or distortion.'[3]

He made it clear that either an increase of libido or a decrease and enfeeblement of the ego may cause the emergence of (latent) neurosis.[4]

---

[1] (1916–17) *Introductory Lectures on Psycho-Analysis*, S.E., Vol. 16, p. 433.
[2] ibid., p. 374.
[3] (1915d) 'Repression', S.E., Vol. 14, p. 152.
[4] (1912c) 'Types of Onset of Neurosis', S.E., Vol. 12, p. 236.

We have been referring so far mostly to conflicts between the different structures or its representatives but there is another group of conflicts that Freud frequently referred to as playing an important role in the final shape of the structure of the personality in normal and pathological cases. We refer to the intrasystemic conflicts. Here he had in mind the existence of some contradictory tendencies and instinctual pair of opposites. In the 'id' they can co-exist together but as soon as they look for expression through the agency of the ego structure the inherent contradiction and resultant conflict will become prominent, especially so when of the two impulses the one is ego syntonic and the other is not.

In the *Introductory Lectures*, he said: 'In a whole number of cases, it looks as though there might also be a conflict between different purely sexual trends. But in essence that is the same thing; for of the two sexual trends that are in conflict, one is always, as we might say, "ego-syntonic", while the other provokes the ego's defence.'[1]

Similarly: 'Of the two conflicting sexual impulses one was ego-syntonic, while the other offended the boy's narcissistic interest; it was on *that* account that the latter underwent repression.'[2]

In *The Ego and the Id* he pointed out to the role that innate bisexuality conflicts plays in the oedipus complex as a twofold one, containing positive and negative aspects and even being determinant in the final outcome; '. . . that is to say, a boy has not merely an ambivalent attitude towards his father and an affectionate object-choice towards his mother, but at the same time he also behaves like a girl and displays an affectionate feminine attitude towards his father and a corresponding jealousy and hostility towards his mother'.[3]

In 'Dostoevsky and Parricide' Freud pointed to the importance of innate bisexual conflicts: 'Thus a strong innate bisexual disposition becomes one of the preconditions or reinforcements of neurosis.'[4]

Much earlier and in referring to paranoid cases Freud remarked: 'Yet we were astonished to find that in all of these cases a defence

[1] (1916–17) *Introductory Lectures on Psycho-Analysis*, S.E., Vol. 16, p. 350.
[2] (1918b [1914]) 'From the History of an Infantile Neurosis', S.E., Vol. 17 p. 110.
[3] (1923b) *The Ego and the Id*, S.E., Vol. 19, p. 33.
[4] (1928b) 'Dostoevsky and Parricide', S.E., Vol. 21, p. 184.

against a homosexual wish was clearly recognizable at the very centre of the conflict which underlay the disease, and that it was in an attempt to master an unconsciously reinforced current of homosexuality that they had all of them come to grief.'[1]

Freud frequently pointed out the role of ambivalence, that is, '. . . the simultaneous existence of love and hate towards the same object—lies at the root of many important cultural institutions'.[2]

He observed that ambivalence was always present in the early developmental stages and he believed that normal adults can succeed in finally separating those two attitudes, though 'many people retain this archaic trait all through their lives'[3] (see concept on ambivalence).

At the root of ambivalent feelings he came to see the conflict between the two primal instincts, '. . . the eternal struggle between Eros and the instinct of destruction or death'.[4]

Reference is made by Freud not infrequently to other types of opposite tendencies observable and inherent to human beings. He frequently, for example, pointed to the conflict between active and passive trends: 'No doubt was left in the analysis that these passive trends had made their appearance at the same time as the active-sadistic ones, or very soon after them.'[5]

Similarly in relation to bisexuality:

'It is well known that at all times there have been, as there still are, human beings who can take as their sexual objects persons of either sex without the one trend interfering with the other.

'We call these people bisexual and accept the fact of their existence without wondering much at it. But we have come to know that all human beings are bisexual in this sense and that their libido is distributed between objects of both sexes, either in a manifest or a latent form. But the following point strikes us. While in the individuals I first mentioned the libidinal impulses can take

---

[1] (1911c) 'Psycho-Analytic Notes on an Autobiographical Account of a Case of Paranoia (Dementia Paranoides)', S.E., Vol. 12, p. 59.

[2] (1912–13) *Totem and Taboo*, S.E., Vol. 13, p. 157.

[3] (1931b) 'Female Sexuality' S.E., Vol. 21, p. 235; cf. also (1930a) *Civilization and its Discontents*, S.E., Vol. 21, p. 133.

[4] (1930a) ibid., p. 132; cf. also p. 137.

[5] (1918b [1914]), 'From the History of an Infantile Neurosis', S.E., Vol. 17, p. 26.

both directions without producing a slash, in the other and more frequent cases the result is an irreconcilable conflict. A man's heterosexuality will not tolerate homosexuality, and vice versa. If the former tendency is the stronger, it succeeds in keeping the latter in a state of latency and preventing its attaining satisfaction in actuality. On the other hand there is no greater danger for a man's heterosexual function than disturbance by latent homosexuality.'

He continued:

'We might attempt to explain this by saying that each individual only has a certain quota of libido at his disposal, for which the two rival trends have to struggle. But it is not clear why the rivals do not always divide up the available quota of libido between them according to their relative strength, since they are able to do so in a number of cases. We are forced to the conclusion that the tendency to a conflict is something special, something which is newly added to the situation, irrespective of the quantity of libido. An independently-emerging tendency to conflict of this sort can scarcely be attributed to anything but the intervention on an element of free aggressiveness.

'If we recognize the case we are discussing as an expression of the destructive or aggressive instinct, the question at once arises whether this view should not be extended to other instances of conflict, and, indeed, whether all that we know about psychical conflict should not be revised from this new angle.'[1]

He thought that the same explanation applied when considering the masochism inherent in so many people, the negative therapeutic reaction and the neurotic sense of guilt. All of these phenomena are unmistakable indications of the aggressive or destructive instinct. He stated that: 'Only by the concurrent or mutually opposing action of the two primal instincts—Eros and the death-instinct—never by one or the other alone, can we explain the rich multiplicity of the phenomena of life.'[2]

In 'Analysis Terminable and Interminable' Freud discussed the possibility of influencing the situation of conflict:

[1] (1937c) 'Analysis Terminable and Interminable', S.E., Vol. 23, p. 244.
[2] ibid., p. 243.

'The optimists' expectations [the optimistic analyst] clearly presuppose a number of thing swhich are not precisely self-evident. They assume, firstly, that there really is a possibility of disposing of an instinctual conflict (or, more correctly, a conflict between the ego and an instinct) definitively and for all time; secondly, that while we are treating someone for one instinctual conflict we can, as it were, inoculate him against the possibility of any other such conflicts; and thirdly, that we have the power, for purposes of prophylaxis, to stir up a pathogenic conflict of this sort which is not betraying itself at the time by any indications, and that it is wise to do so.'[1]

He argued that at the present time an answer may not be possible. Still he felt that in relation to the first question economic considerations were essential. If the strength of the instincts is too much we may not be successful. For the second and third questions he had a concrete answer: 'However much our therapeutic ambition may be tempted to undertake such tasks, experience flatly rejects the notion. If an instinctual conflict is not a currently active one, is not manifesting itself, we cannot influence it even by analysis.'[2]

Finally the relationship between the instinct theory, the models of the mind and the conflict theory is to be noted.

The theory of instincts and Freud's models of the mind were the subject of a long theoretical development. This development can be followed historically up to his final formulations for the former in *Beyond the Pleasure Principle* (1920) and for the latter in *The Ego and the Id* (1923).

It was against this constantly changing background that the theory of conflict was formulated. Thus the conflicts are described at different times in terms relating to this changing background.

It will be further noted that many conflicts can be formulated either on the basis of the instinctual forces involved on it or in terms of the different systems or structures taking part. These two different approaches are frequently in the last analysis not very different from each other, since at different times different instincts and different tendencies had been ascribed to the different systems or structures.

[1] (1937c) 'Analysis Terminable and Interminable', S.E., Vol. 23, p. 223.
[2] ibid., p. 231.

We have referred above to several possibilities of instinctual conflicts. It is well to remember here that these instinctual conflicts may have been described differently at different times and according to the stage of development of the theory of instincts reached.

To start with Freud postulated the sexual and the ego instincts. At the time the sexual instincts were more fully described and understood than the 'ego instincts'. The conflict was then represented as being between the two sets of instincts.[1]

'For the final formula which psychoanalysis has arrived at on the nature of neurosis runs thus: The primal conflict which leads to neuroses is one between the sexual instincts and those which maintain the ego [that is, the self]. The neuroses represents a more or less partial overpowering of the ego by sexuality after the ego's attempts at suppressing sexuality have failed.'[2]

'For a neurosis to be generated there must be a conflict between a person's libidinal wishes and the part of his personality we call his ego, which is the expression of his instinct of self-preservation and which also includes his *ideals* of his personality.'[3]

In the next stage in Freud's theory of instincts he 'recognized that a portion of the "ego instincts" is also of a libidinal character and has taken the subject's own ego as its object. . . . The opposition between the ego instincts and the sexual instincts was transformed into one between the ego instincts and the object instincts both of libidinal nature.'[4] Nevertheless he insisted on a difference between ego libido (interest emanating from erotic sources) and 'interest in general' or 'ego interest' or simply 'interest'.[5]

In the next development in the theory of instincts, the aggressive trends were ascribed to the ego instincts.

[1] (1910i) 'The Psychoanalytic View of Psychogenic Disturbances of Vision', S.E., Vol. 11, p. 214.

[2] (1913j) 'The Claims of Psycho-Analysis to Scientific Interest', S.E., Vol. 13, p. 181.

[3] (1916d) 'Some Character-Types Met with in Psychoanalytic Work', S.E., Vol. 14, p. 316.

[4] (1920g) *Beyond the Pleasure Principle*, S.E., Vol. 18, p. 60 f.n.

[5] (1914c) 'On Narcissism: An Introduction', S.E., Vol. 14, p. 80 f.

'Hate . . . derives from the narcissistic ego's primordial repudiation of the external world with its outpouring of stimuli. As an expression of the reaction of unpleasure evoked by objects, it always remains in an intimate relation with the self-preservative instincts; so that sexual and ego-instincts can readily develop an antithesis which repeats that of love and hate. . . . The hate . . . is also in part based on reactions of repudiation by the ego-instincts, which, in view of the frequent conflicts between the interests of the ego and those of love, can find grounds in real and contemporary motives.'[1]

In the final formulation of the theory of instincts, the place of the opposition between the libidinal (ego and object) instincts and others was replaced by an opposition of a different character. 'Our speculations have transformed this opposition into one between the life instincts (Eros) and the death instincts.'[2]

Finally though the 'topographical theory' was formulated specifically in 1915 in his paper 'The Unconscious', the previous model of the mind as described in Chapter VII of 'The Interpretation of Dreams' was similarly based on spatial and topographical propositions.

'By accepting the existence of the two (or three) psychical systems, [*Ucs, Pcs, Cs*] psychoanalysis has departed a step further from the descriptive psychology of consciousness and has raised new problems and acquired a new content. Up till now, it has differed from that psychology mainly by reason of its *dynamic* view of mental processes; now in addition it seems to take account of psychical *topography* as well, and to indicate in respect of any given mental act within what system or between what systems it takes place. On account of this attempt too, it has been given the name of "depth-psychology".'[3]

Even before the structural theory in 1923 he was well aware of the difficulties of describing the 'conflict' in terms of the topographical theory and he thought that the interplay of forces and situations of conflict between the systems is better described in terms of the ego and the repressed:

[1] (1915c) 'Instincts and their Vicissitudes', S.E., Vol. 14, p. 139.
[2] (1920g) *Beyond the Pleasure Principle*, S.E., Vol. 18, p. 60 f.n.
[3] (1925e) 'The Unconscious', S.E., Vol. 14, p. 173.

'We shall avoid a lack of clarity if we make our contrast not between the conscious and the unconscious but between the coherent *ego* and the *repressed*. It is certain that much of the ego is itself unconscious, and notably what we may describe as its nucleus; only a small part of it is covered by the term "pre-conscious".'[1]

' "Repressed" is a dynamic expression, which takes account of the interplay of mental forces; it implies that there is a force present which is seeking to bring about all kinds of psychical effects, including that of becoming conscious, but that there is also an opposing force which is able to obstruct some of these psychical effects, once more including that of becoming conscious.'[2]

'If what was repressed is brought back again into conscious mental activity . . . the resulting psychical conflict, which the patient had tried to avoid, can, under the physician's guidance, reach a better outcome than was offered by repression . . . conscious control of the wish is attained.'[3]

When the topographical theory was superseded by the structural one a much better characterization and description of the situation of conflict was possible as will be noted in what follows. He further insisted that:

'From the point of view of analytic practice, . . . we land in endless obscurities and difficulties if we keep to our habitual forms of expression and try, for instance, to derive neuroses from a conflict between the conscious and the unconscious. We shall have to substitute for this antithesis another, taken from our insight into the structural conditions of the mind—the antithesis between the coherent ego and the repressed which is split off from it.'[4]

In the paper on 'Neurosis and Psychosis' Freud characterizes the nature of the conflict thus:

'. . . a simple formula has now occurred to me which deals

---

[1] (1920g) *Beyond the Pleasure Principle*, S.E., Vol. 18, p. 19.
[2] (1907a) *Delusions and Dreams in Jensen's 'Gradiva'*, S.E., Vol. 9, p. 48.
[3] (1910a [1909]) 'Five Lectures on Psycho-Analysis', S.E., Vol. 11, p. 27 f.
[4] (1923b) *The Ego and the Id*, S.E., Vol. 19, p. 17.

with what is perhaps the most important genetic difference between a neurosis and a psychosis: *neurosis is the result of a conflict
between the ego and its id, whereas psychosis is the analogous outcome
of a similar disturbance in the relations between the ego and the
external world.*[1]

In the same paper Freud refers to the aetiology common to a
neurosis and a psychosis as consisting in a frustration of one of
those childhood wishes and how this frustration is in the last
resort an external one: '. . . but in the individual case it may proceed from the internal agency (in the super-ego) which has taken
over the representation of the demands of reality.'[2] He continues:
'The pathogenic effect depends on whether, in a conflictual tension
of this kind, the ego remains true to its dependence on the external
world and attempts to silence the id, or whether it lets itself be
overcome by the id and thus torn away from reality.'[3] Later: 'The
attitude of the super-ego should be taken into account—which has
not hitherto been done—in every form of psychical illness.' Still
later on: 'Transference neuroses corresponds to a conflict between
the ego and the id; narcissistic neuroses, to a conflict between the
ego and the super-ego; and psychoses, to one between the ego and
the external world.'[4]

Freud described the difficult situation of the ego in *The Ego and
the Id* and in the *New Introductory Lectures* because: the ego is in
the difficult position of serving three masters at the same time (id,
super-ego, external reality). This makes it liable to possible conflicts from three directions.[5]

In his paper 'Neurosis and Psychosis' he commented: 'The
thesis that the neuroses and psychoses originate in the ego's conflicts with its various ruling agencies—that is, therefore, that they
reflect a failure in the functioning of the ego, which is at pains to
reconcile the various demands made on it—this thesis needs to be
supplemented in one further point.' He refers to the circumstances
and means by which the ego manages to emerge from such conflicts—that are always present—without being ill.[6]

---

[1] (1924b) 'Neurosis and Psychosis', S.E., Vol. 19, p. 149.
[2] ibid., p. 151.   [3] ibid., p. 151.   [4] ibid., p. 152.
[5] (1933a) *New Introductory Lectures on Psycho-Analysis*, S.E., Vol. 22, p.
77; cf. also (1923b) *The Ego and the Id*, S.E., Vol. 19, p. 56.
[6] (1924b) 'Neurosis and Psychosis', S.E., Vol. 19, p. 152.

FIXATION

I. DEFINITION

'Fixation' refers to the attachment of a portion of libido or aggression to particular zones, conditions or modes of gratification, objects, so that the fixated portion of the drive is no longer mobile.

Freud gave a general description of fixation in the following passage (he is referring to a term of Jung's 'psychic inertia'): '. . . a peculiar "psychical inertia", which opposes change and progress, is the fundamental precondition of neurosis. . . . If we search for the starting point of this special inertia, we discover that it is the manifestation of very early linkages—linkages which it is hard to resolve—between instincts and impressions and the objects involved in these impressions. These linkages have the effect of bringing the development of the instincts concerned to a standstill. Or in other words, this specialized "psychical inertia" is only a different term, though hardly a better one, for . . . a "fixation" .'[1]

We should note that the concept of fixation emerged in the context of the libido theory, before the introduction of aggression as an instinct. The clinical implications of fixation were thus worked out in terms of libido alone, without reference to aggression, except in so far as 'sadism' is a constituent of the oral and anal phases. Even at present we have no parallel theory of stages of aggressive development, and therefore do not attempt to characterise the fixation points of the aggressive drive with the same precision as we do the libidinal ones.

Freud explained the libido's capacity for fixation in terms of the axiom of general pathology that all biological processes are liable to arrests or inhibitions of development.[2] In the course of normal libidinal development some degree of fixation seems to be inevitable.

II. EARLY USAGES OF THE TERM

Up to 1905, and occasionally afterwards, 'fixated' is usually used simply as an equivalent of the adjective 'fixated'. Something is

[1] (1915f) 'A Case of Paranoia Running Counter to the Psycho-Analytic Theory of the Disease', S.E., Vol. 14, p. 272.
[2] (1916–17) *Introductory Lectures on Psycho-Analysis*, S.E., Vol. 16, p. 339.

'fixated' or undergoes 'fixation' when it is established permanently in a definitive form. Thus Freud may speak of the 'fixation' of a symptom[1] or the 'fixation' of a compulsive act.[2]

The first use of the term is noted by Kris in the letters to Fliess. Kris understands this usage as referring to 'an experience that becomes unconsciously fixed in the subject's memory'.[3] From 1905 fixation is used in the special sense defined above.

III. VARIETIES OF FIXATION

The concept of fixation has been applied to a wide range of different clinical phenomena. Freud described various types of fixation:

(1) Fixation of a component instinct.
(2) Fixation of libido at a stage of the pre-genital organization.
(3) Fixation to an object or to a type of object choice.
(4) Fixation to a traumatic experience (as in the traumatic neuroses).[4]

(1) Fixation *of a component instinct* means that a component instinct of infantile sexuality has been arrested in its development and separated off from the mainstream of libidinal development. Consequently it does not become subordinated to genital sexuality (where, normally, it might contribute to sexual forepleasure), but continues to seek independent gratification.[5] Examples of this can be seen in the perversions, where the gratification of a component instinct is sought rather than coitus.[6]

(2) Fixation *at a stage of pregenital sexuality* means that a portion of libido has failed to move on to the next stage of development, but persists independently in seeking the gratifications (aims) characteristic of that stage (oral, anal, or phallic oedipal). Thus, an

---

[1] (1893h) 'On the Psychical Mechanism of Hysterical Phenomena', S.E., Vol. 3, p. 32.
[2] (1896b) 'Further Remarks on the Neuro-Psychoses of Defence', S.E., Vol. 3, p. 174.
[3] (1950a [1887–1902]) *The Origins of Psycho-Analysis*, Imago, London, 1954, p. 198.
[4] (1916–17) *Introductory Lectures on Psycho-Analysis*, S.E., Vol. 16, p. 274.
[5] ibid., p. 340.
[6] (1905d) *Three Essays on the Theory of Sexuality*, S.E., Vol. 7, p. 191.

anal-sadistic fixation would mean that a certain amount of the anal-sadistic impulses retained their strength while the rest of the libido moved on into the phallic stage. This might be seen for example in those older children who compulsively torture small animals.[1]

(3) 'A particularly close attachment of the instinct to its object is distinguished by the term "fixation".'[2] While Freud could thus speak of 'fixation' to a love object in adult life, as he did in discussing mourning, for the most part the concept of object fixation is applied to the objects of childhood. Freud was chiefly concerned with fixation to the 'incestuous objects' of the oedipus complex. However he assumed that fixations to objects could take place at every stage of the child's pre-oedipal and oedipal relationships. Such fixations would mean that less libido was available to move on to the next developmentally appropriate object relationship. For example, a little girl might be so fixated upon her mother as a pre-oedipal and negative oedipal object, that she establishes only a very weak positive oedipal relationship to her father.[3]

The most general clinical result of pre-genital object fixations is that they affect the type of love object chosen and the type of object relationship which is sought in adult life. In the *Three Essays*, Freud described the task of puberty as the detachment of libido from the oedipal objects. He implied that a degree of fixation to the 'incestuous object' is present even in normal object choice.[4]

IV. HISTORY OF CONCEPT

Fixation emerged as a concept in the context of the theory of libidinal development as set forth in the *Three Essays* in 1905. 'Every step on this long path of development can become a point of fixation, every juncture in this involved combination can be an occasion for a dissociation of the sexual instinct.'[5]

The role of fixation to the oedipal object in hysteria was first shown in the case of Dora.[6]

The formulation of the role of fixation in the aetiology of

[1] ibid., p. 193.
[2] (1915c) 'Instincts and their Vicissitudes', S.E., Vol. 14, p. 123.
[3] (1931b) 'Female Sexuality', S.E., Vol. 21, p. 226.
[4] (1905d) *Three Essays on the Theory of Sexuality*, S.E., Vol. 7, p. 228.
[5] ibid., p. 235.
[6] (1905e [1901]) 'Fragment of an Analysis of a Case of Hysteria', S.E., Vol. 7.

neurosis was established, by implication, in 'Types of Onset of Neurosis',[1] and the formulation that the choice of neurosis depends on the localization of the fixation points was first made in 'The Disposition to Obsessional Neurosis'.[2]

This formulation about the problem of choice of neurosis had a long pre-history in Freud's thought.

V. CAUSES OF FIXATION

Fixation occurs when the component instinct, zone, libidinal stage or object relationship involved has been a source of intense libidinal experiences either of a gratifying or a painful nature. Such intense experiences are the product of the infantile sexual constitution on the one hand and of environmental influences (seductions, over-gratifications, or deprivations) on the other, in a reciprocal relationship. Freud postulated constitutional variations in the strength of the various instinctual components. Where the constitutional strength of an instinct is great, a lesser degree of environmental stimulation will effect fixations in a normal constitution.[3] For this reason the effect of events on a child depends upon the phase of its development in which they occur and whether they meet an impulse which is at its peak of strength, nascent or on the wane.

VI. CLINICAL APPLICATIONS

a. *Fixation in the Aetiology of Neurosis*
Fixation is an important factor in the complementary series of causes which bring about a neurosis. '. . . libidinal fixation represents the predisposing, internal factor in the aetiology of the neuroses, while frustration represents the accidental, external one.'[4] Neurosis arises when the libido regresses to the fixation points, thus reinforcing the fixated impulses of infantile sexuality, which then come into conflict with the ego. The more libido is fixated at pre-genital levels, the weaker will the genital libido be.

---

[1] (1912c) 'Types of Onset of Neurosis', S.E., Vol. 12.
[2] (1913i) 'The Disposition to Obsessional Neurosis', S.E., Vol. 12.
[3] (1905d) *Three Essays on the Theory of Sexuality*, S.E., Vol. 7, p. 211 and p. 242; cf. also (1916–17) *Introductory Lectures on Psycho-Analysis*, S.E., Vol. 16, p. 362 f.
[4] (1916–17) *Introductory Lectures on Psycho-Analysis*, S.E., Vol. 16, p. 346.

'The stronger the fixation on its path of development, the more readily will the function evade external difficulties by regressing to the fixations.'[1]

b. *Fixation Points and Choice of Neurosis*

The choice of neurosis is determined by the nature of the fixation points to which the libido regresses, and not by the nature of the precipitating conflict or frustration. This is because, as seen above, it is the re-cathected infantile sexuality of the respective fixation point which impels the neurotic symptom formation. Thus the impulses and fantasies defended against in a neurosis will differ in content according to which stage in development is regressed to. Furthermore, the type of defence mechanism which is mobilized may be related to the type of impulse which has to be defended against. Thus the form of the symptomatology is also partly determined by the fixation points.[2]

Freud also characterized the fixation points of the neuroses as follows:

(1) *Hysteria.* The fixation point lies in the phallic oedipal phase. At first Freud characterized hysteria in terms of object fixation alone (to the 'incestuous object') and thought that no phase-fixation was involved,[3] but as he came to recognize the phallic phase as distinctive and pre-genital, this view changed. He clearly related hysteria to the final phase of libidinal development characterized by the primacy of the genitals. There is no regression to a pre-genital stage but in women there is regression to phallic, that is, clitoral sexuality.[4]

Obsessional Neurosis. The fixation point lies in the anal-sadistic stage. This accounts for the special conflicts over ambivalence present in obsessional neuroses.[5] In 1913 Freud already suggested 'the possibility that a chronological outstripping of libidinal development by ego development should be included in the disposition to obsessional neurosis', as this would tend to bring about a fixation of the anal sadistic impulses.[6]

[1] ibid., p. 341.
[2] (1913i) 'The Disposition to Obsessional Neurosis', S.E., Vol. 12.
[3] (1916–17) *Introductory Lectures on Psycho-Analysis*, S.E., Vol. 16, p. 343.
[4] (1913i) 'The Disposition to Obsessional Neurosis', S.E., Vol. 12, p. 325 f.
[5] ibid., p. 321. [6] ibid., p. 325.

In the course of an illness, the libido may regress from its later fixation points to earlier ones, with a consequent change in symptomatology. Such a case which regressed from hysteria to an obsessional neurosis is described in 'The Disposition to Obsessional Neurosis'.[1] Multiple fixation points may yield a mixed symptomatology.

The Psychoses. Freud characterized the psychoses in terms of libidinal regression to fixation points before the stage of object-choice has been established—that is in the phase of autoeroticism and narcissism.[2] However, he explained that ego regression might be involved too.[3]

Paranoia. The fixation point lies in the stage of narcissism which is regressed to.[4] *Schizophrenia* (or Dementia Praecox)—The fixation point is 'situated further back than in paranoia, and must lie somewhere at the beginning of the course of development from autoerotism to object love'. More specifically he referred to the stage of auto-erotism.[5]

Melancholia. In melancholia, in contrast to normal mourning, the ego's identification with the lost object is complete; object cathexes are entirely given up.

Among the preconditions for such a process Freud finds: 'On the one hand, a strong fixation to the loved object must have been present; on the other hand, in contradiction to this, the object-cathexis must have had little power of resistance. As Otto Rank has aptly remarked, this contradiction seems to imply that the object-choice has been effected on a narcissistic basis, so that the object-cathexis, when obstacles come in its way, can regress to narcissism.'[6] Where there is a disposition to obsessional neurosis the conflict due to ambivalence gives a pathological cast to mourning and forces it to express itself in the form of self-reproaches.

'. . . This conflict due to ambivalence, which sometimes arises more from real experiences, sometimes more from constitutional

---

[1] (1913i) 'The Disposition to Obsessional Neurosis', S.E., Vol. 12, p. 319 f.
[2] ibid., p. 318.
[3] (1911c) 'Psycho-Analytic Notes on an Autobiographical Account of a Case of Paranoia' S.E., Vol. 12, p. 75.
[4] (1917e [1915]) 'Mourning and Melancholia', S.E., Vol. 14, p. 249.
[5] ibid., p. 251.   [6] ibid., p. 249.

factors, must not be overlooked among the preconditions of melancholia.'[1]

After Abraham's work on the oral phase in 1929, Freud cited his description of the oral sadistic phase as the fixation point for melancholia.[2]

c. The Relation Between Fixation and Perversions, Neuroses, and Character Formation

The mode in which pre-genital fixations manifest themselves in the adult personality depends on the attitude the ego adopts towards the fixation. The same pregenital fixation can function as the source of a perversion, a neurotic symptom, or a character trait.

A *perversion* arises when a pre-genital impulse is permitted direct gratification by the ego. This may occur because genital primacy was never reached[3] or when the fixations are reinforced by regression. 'The path to perversion branches off sharply from that to neurosis. If these regressions rouse no objection from the ego, no neurosis will come about either; and the libido will arrive at some real even though no longer normal, satisfaction.'[4] In some perversions, namely in fetishism, where some other object replaces the female genital, Freud found that the ego condones the perversion because the fetish serves as a defence against castration anxieties, i.e. it represents a denial of the reality of the 'castration' of women.[5]

Neurosis eventuates where the ego is in conflict with the pregenital fixation. Originally, this fixation was repressed. With regression to the fixation point there is a 'return of the repressed', i.e. the reinforced impulses of the fixation attempt to find conscious expression. If this meets with resistance from the ego, symptom formation results.[6]

Character Traits. In character traits, a stable defence against, or sublimated use of, pre-genital fixations has been achieved by the ego. This may be carried out in childhood, or one may see a 'change of character' following regression, as in the menopause.[7]

[1] ibid., p. 251.

[2] (1933a) *New Introductory Lectures on Psycho-Analysis*, S.E., Vol. 23, p. 99.

[3] (1905d) *Three Essays on the Theory of Sexuality*, S.E., Vol. 7, p. 237.

[4] (1916–17) *Introductory Lectures on Psycho-Analysis*, S.E., Vol. 16, p. 359.

[5] (1940e [1938]) 'Splitting of the Ego in the Process of Defence', S.E., Vol. 23, p. 277; cf. (1927e) 'Fetishism' S.E., Vol. 21.

[6] (1911c) Psycho-Analytic Notes on an Autobiographical Account of a Case of Paranoia', S.E., Vol. 12, p. 67 f.

[7] (1913i) 'The Disposition to Obsessional Neurosis', S.E., Vol. 12, p. 323.

'What we describe as a person's "character" is built up to a considerable extent from the material of sexual excitations and is composed of instincts that have been fixed since childhood, of constructions achieved by means of sublimation, and of other constructions, employed for effectively holding in check perverse impulses which have been recognized as being unutilizable.'[1]

'. . . the permanent character traits are either unchanged prolongations of the original instincts, or sublimations of those instincts, or reaction-formations against them.'[2]

We may take as an example a single component instinct, scopophilia. Freud describes how scopophilia may contribute to normal sexuality, become the source of sublimations (interest in art), or become the source of either a perversion (voyeurism)[3] or a neurotic symptom: 'When repression of these inclinations sets in, the desire to see other people's genitals . . . persists as a tormenting compulsion, which in some cases of neurosis later affords the strongest motive force for the formation of symptoms.'[4]

d. *Object Fixation and Types of Object Choice*
In the *Three Essays on the Theory of Sexuality* Freud described how fixation to the oedipal object becomes pathogenic in cases of hysteria where adult sexual life is excessively repudiated because the unconscious incestuous meaning of all possible objects brings them in conflict with the 'incest taboo'.[5]

Freud returned to this theme in his Three Contributions to the Psychology of Love[6] where he described types of object choice based on recreation of aspects of the oedipal situation. A further example is found in 'Those Wrecked by Success'.[7]

[1] (1905d) *Three Essays on the Theory of Sexuality*, S.E., Vol. 7., p. 238 f.
[2] (1908b) 'Character and Anal Erotism', S.E., Vol. 9, p. 175.
[3] (1905d) *Three Essays on the Theory of Sexuality*, S.E., Vol. 7, p. 156 f.
[4] ibid., p. 192.
[5] ibid., p. 225 f.
[6] (1910h) 'A Special Type of Choice of Object Made by Men', S.E., Vol. 11; (1912d) 'On the Universal Tendency to Debasement in the Sphere of Love, S.E., Vol. 11; (1918a) 'The Taboo of Virginity', S.E., Vol. 11.
[7] (1916d) 'Some Character-Types Met with in Psycho-Analytic Work', S.E., Vol. 14, pp. 316–31.

REGRESSION

'Regression' is the term used to describe the flowing back of the drives (Freud developed this concept mainly in relation to the libido theory but it is similarly applicable to the aggressive drives) —because of the intervention of powerful external obstacles—to fixed focal points in its own past. The term as Freud emphasized is used in a descriptive sense: 'Nor can we call regression of the libido a purely psychical process and we cannot tell where we should localize it in the mental apparatus. And though it is true that it exercises the most powerful influence on mental life, yet the most prominent factor in it is the organic one.'[1] In a vivid illustration he compared the process with an advance through hostile territory of a migrating people who have 'left strong detachments behind at the stopping places on its migration'.[2] The more occupiers that are left behind, the weaker would be the vanguard and the sooner would it face the danger of defeat. And in a situation of actual or threatened defeat the foremost naturally would retreat to the strong points they had left behind. Similarly the stronger the fixation, the easier are the chances of a regression taking place if obstacles are encountered.

DIFFERENT USES OF THE TERM

Regression can refer to a regression to certain objects or types of object-relationships or it may refer to topical, temporal or formal regression as formulated in regression in dreams. The term has also been used to describe not only libidinal regressions (in neuroses and psychoses) but regressions on the ego side as well (in the psychoses).

HISTORICAL DEVELOPMENT

Freud compared his studies on fixation and regression to a research project he undertook as a twenty-year-old student working

---

[1] (1916–17) *Introductory Lectures on Psycho-Analysis*, S.E., Vol. 16, p. 342 f.
[2] ibid., p. 341.

for Professor von Brucke in 1876. The subject of his research related to the origin of the dorsal nerve roots in the spinal cord of a
small fish, archaic in form, and it formed the basis of his first
published works (1877–8). His finding was that the cells of the
ganglion had moved out of the spinal cord along the nerve-roots
only for some of them to be arrested on the way. This helped him
recognize the possibility that single portions of every separate
sexual impulse may remain in an early stage of development although other portions of it may have reached their final goal.
Arrests in component impulses at an early stage were called
fixations. And those portions of the component impulses which
revert along the path of phased development—usually when external obstacles hold up their further progress—were said to constitute *regression*.[1]

As the field of Freud's interest broadened in the years that followed, his references to the regressive process were fleeting. It was
in 1897 that he first placed regression at the centre of his dynamic
explanation of neuroses. He did so in a letter to Wilhelm Fliess
introducing his 'discovery' of the development of the libido.[2]
Three years later Freud distinguished between *topical* (or topographical), *temporal* and *formal* regression. But he added that the
three forms are 'one at bottom and occur together as a rule.'[3]

(a) a topographical one, in the sense of the schema of the psychical systems expounded;
(b) a temporal one, in so far as it is a regression to older psychic
structures;
(c) a formal one, where primitive methods of expression and
representation take the place of the usual ones.

Freud showed the importance of regression in dreams '. . .
Dreaming is on the whole an example of regression to the dreamer's
earliest condition, a revival of his childhood, of the instinctual
impulses which dominated it and the methods of expression which
were then available to him. Behind this childhood of the individual
we are promised a picture of a phylogenetic childhood—a picture
of the development of the human race, of which the individual's

[1] (1916–17) *Introductory Lectures on Psycho-Analysis*, S.E., Vol. 16, p. 340.
[2] (1950a[1887–1902]) *The Origins of Psycho-Analysis*, Imago, London, 1954,
p. 230 n.
[3] (1900a) *The Interpretation of Dreams*, S.E., Vol. 5, p. 548.

development is in fact an abbreviated recapitulation influenced by the chance circumstances of life. We can guess how much to the point in Nietszche's assertion that in dreams "some primordial relic of humanity is at work which we can now scarcely reach any longer by a direct path"; and we may expect that the analysis of dreams will lead us to a knowledge of man's archaic heritage, of what is psychically innate in him. Dreams and neuroses seem to have preserved more mental antiquities than we could have imagined possible; so that psychoanalysis may claim a high place among the sciences which are concerned with the reconstruction of the earliest and most obscure periods of the beginning of the human race.'[1]

A further development came in 1909 when he drew attention to the importance of the regressive process in symptom formation: 'The flight from unsatisfactory reality into what, on account of the biological damage involved, we call illness (though it is never without an immediate yield of pleasure to the patient) takes place along the path of involution, of regression, of a return to earlier phases of sexual life, phases from which at one time satisfaction was not withheld.'[2]

In 1916 Freud described 'a return to the objects first cathected by the libido, which as we know, are of an incestuous nature, and a return of the sexual organization as a whole to earlier stages. Both sorts are found in the transference neuroses and play a great part in their mechanism. In particular, a return to the first incestuous objects of the libido is a feature that is found in neurotics with positively fatiguing regularity. There is much more to be said about regressions of the libido itself when we take into account as well another group of neuroses, the narcissistic ones. . . . These disorders give us access to other developmental processes of the libidinal function which we have not yet mentioned, and show us correspondingly new sorts of regression as well.'[3]

Freud has related how the 'discovery' of the mental process he later was to name regression transformed the development of the psychoanalytic technique. Towards the end of the nineteenth century he and Breuer were using the cathartic method in certain treatments in which the patient's attention was led directly to the traumatic scene in which the symptom had arisen. Their aim was,

[1] ibid., p. 548 f.
[2] (1910a [1909]) 'Five Lectures on Psycho-Analysis', S.E., Vol. 11, p. 49.
[3] (1916–17) *Introductory Lectures on Psycho-Analysis*, S.E., Vol. 16, p. 341.

in that way, to pin-point the mental conflict in that scene so as to be able to release the suppressed affect in it:

'In the course of this we discovered the mental process, characteristic of the neuroses, which I later named "regression". The patient's associations moved back from the scene which we were trying to elucidate to earlier experiences, and compelled the analysis, which was supposed to correct the present, to occupy itself with the past. This regression led constantly further backwards: at first it seemed regularly to bring us to puberty; later on, failures and points which still eluded explanation drew the analytic work still further back into years of childhood which had hitherto been inaccessible to any kind of exploration. This regressive direction became an important characteristic of analysis.'[1]

Freud in 1912 also drew attention to the specific part played by regression in meeting difficulties in the analytic situation, and the interaction and relationship of regression with processes like introversion and repression. In the first place he said 'all the forces which have caused the libido to regress will rise up as "resistances" against the work of analysis'. And in the second case, he noted, the libido originally 'entered a regressive course because the attraction of reality had been diminished'. He went on: 'In order to liberate it [from where it is fixated and to where it has regressed] this attraction of the unconscious has to be overcome; that is, the repression of the unconscious instincts and of their productions, which has meanwhile been set up in the subject, must be removed. This is responsible for by far the largest part of the resistance, which so often causes the illness to persist even after the turning away from reality has lost its temporary justification. The analysis has to struggle against the resistances from both these sources.'[2]

(a) *Theoretical Considerations*

'It is plausible to suppose that fixation and regression are not independent of each other. The stronger the fixations on its path of development, the more readily will the function evade external difficulties by regressing to the fixations—the more incapable, there-

---

[1] (1914d) 'On the History of the Psycho-Analytic Movement', S.E., Vol. 14, p. 10.
[2] (1912b) 'The Dynamics of Transference', S.E., Vol. 12, p. 102 f.

fore, does the developed function turn out to be of resisting external obstacles in its course.'[1]

(b) *Clinical Examples*

Hysteria
The libido regresses in hysteria to the primary incestuous sexual objects—but not to an earlier stage of sexual development.[2] 'In place of a change in the external world these substitute a change in the subject's own body . . . something that corresponds, phylogenetically, to a highly significant regression.'[3]

Obsessional Neuroses
In obsessional neurosis the libido is fixated at, or regresses to, a special stage in its development. This is the anal-sadistic phase, characteristically pre-genital. Freud observed: '. . . the regression of libido to the preliminary stage of the sadistic-anal organization is the most striking fact and the one which is decisive for what is manifested in symptoms'. The impulse to love must then mask itself under the sadistic impulse. Regression to primary objects takes place at the same time and these obsessive ideas fill the patient with horror and remain unaccountable to his conscious perception.[4]

Perversion
Freud laid down this general precondition for the emergence of perversion: 'A regression of the libido without repression would never produce a neurosis but would lead to a perversion.'[5]

The Psychoses
In the neuroses libidinal regression can take place without ego regression but in the psychoses there is a detachment of the libido together with its withdrawal on to the ego. Disturbance of the libidinal processes may result from abnormal changes in the ego—in cases where the ego is weak. In his discussion on 'Dementia Praecox and Paranoia' Freud drew attention to the fact that 'their dispositional fixation is to be looked for in a stage of libidinal development *before* object-choice has been established—that is, in

[1] (1916–17) *Introductory Lectures on Psycho-Analysis*, S.E., Vol. 16, p. 341.
[2] ibid., p. 343.   [3] ibid., p. 366.   [4] ibid., p. 343.   [5] ibid., p. 344.

the phase of auto-eroticism and narcissism'. Regression can thus be traced back to the very earliest libidinal fixation.[1]

Freud suggested that the paranoiac withdrawal of love from its former object was always accompanied by a regression and he defined this as a regression from the previously substituted homosexuality to narcissism: 'in paranoia the liberated libido becomes attached to the ego, and is used for the aggrandizement of the ego. A return is thus made to the stage of narcissism (known to us from the development of the libido), in which a person's only sexual object is his own ego . . .'.[2]

In dementia praecox 'the regression extends not merely to narcissism (manifesting itself in the shape of megalomania) but to a complete abandonment of object-love and a return to infantile auto-erotism.'[3]

Melancholia

Freud observed three preconditions of melancholia—'loss of the object, ambivalence, and regression of libido into the ego'.[4] The regressive factor appeared to him responsible for the result. Melancholia, he noted, borrows some features from mourning and others from the 'process of regression from narcissistic object-choice to narcissism'.[5]

It may be as well to point out that regression also occurs in normal functioning, as for instance in states of reduced consciousness such as dreams and jokes.[6]

[1] (1913i) 'The Disposition to Obsessional Neurosis', S.E., Vol. 12, p. 318.
[2] (1911c) 'Psycho-Analytic Notes on an Autobiographical Account of a Case of Paranoia', S.E., Vol. 12, p. 72.
[3] ibid., p. 77.
[4] (1917e [1915]) 'Mourning and Melancholia', S.E., Vol. 14, p. 258.
[5] ibid., p. 250.
[6] (1905c) *Jokes and their Relation to the Unconscious*, S.E., Vol. 8, pp. 171-9.

ANXIETY

'Anxiety is an affective condition—that is, a combination of certain feelings in the pleasure – unpleasure series with corresponding innervations of discharge and a perception of them, but probably also the precipitate of a particular important event, incorporated by inheritance . . .'.[1]

Historically there are three main phases in the development of Freud's views on anxiety. In the first, he postulated a transformation of undischarged libido into anxiety. During this phase there was, however, present in 'The Project', *The Interpretation of Dreams* and the paper on 'The Unconscious', the notion of slight release of unpleasure (anxiety) to act as a signal to prevent further unpleasure. This idea was developed more fully in the second phase in *Inhibitions, Symptoms and Anxiety*, after the publication in 1923 of the structural theory. At this stage he still retained the previous (transformation) theory in connection with anxiety neurosis. In the third phase this, too, was rejected and full acceptance given to his signal anxiety theory.

In the early days of psychoanalysis Freud considered anxiety as the result of a purely biological process. He believed that it occurred in neurosis because of some interference with the discharge of sexual tension leading to an accumulation of undischarged libido which was directly transformed into anxiety. He said that such regression of an affect from the unwelcome sexual idea 'cannot be proved by any clinico-psychological analysis. Perhaps it would be more correct to say that these processes are not of a psychical nature at all . . . they are physical processes . . .' with 'psychical consequences'.[2]

Following Fechner, who postulated the 'principle of constancy', i.e. the inherent tendency in the nervous system to keep the quantity of excitation in it as low as possible, or at least to keep it constant, Freud was led to believe that any interference with the discharge of sexual tension would cause accumulated excitation that would find an outlet in the form of anxiety. This explained the

[1] (1933a) *New Introductory Lectures on Psycho-Analysis*, S.E., Vol. 22, p. 81.
[2] (1894a) 'The Neuro-Psychoses of Defence', S.E., Vol. 3, p. 53.

presence of anxiety in 'anxiety neuroses' or the 'actual neuroses', but it did not so clearly do so in the 'psychoneuroses' (phobias, obsessional neuroses etc.) where the possibility of psychological events could not be excluded. He solved this problem by assuming that whereas in the 'actual neuroses' the cause of accumulated tension was physical, e.g. coitus interruptus, in the 'psychoneuroses' it was due to repression.

In the telescopic model of the mind anxiety was conceptualized as '. . . a libidinal impulse which has its origin in the unconscious and is inhibited by the preconscious'.[1] Anxiety in dreams was originally explained on the same basis as anxiety anywhere else. In *Jensen's 'Gradiva'* Freud stated: 'The anxiety in anxiety-dreams, like neurotic anxiety in general . . . arises out of libido by the process of repression.'[2] In the paper on 'Repression' Freud referred to the quantitative factor of the instinctual representative as following three possible vicissitudes: (1) it can be suppressed, and no trace is found of it, (2) it may appear as an effect which is somehow qualitatively coloured, or (3) it is changed into anxiety.[3]

At the time of the topographical theory the same view in relation to anxiety prevailed in Freud's work (transformation theory) though in places there are short references to what he was to develop later in *Inhibitions, Symptoms and Anxiety*. For example in 'The Unconscious' Freud says: 'Excitation . . . must . . . give rise to a slight development of anxiety; and this is now used . . . to inhibit, by means of a fresh flight on the part of the [*Pcs*] cathexis, the further progress of the development of anxiety.'[4]

In the structural model of mental functions Freud mostly discarded the previous hypothesis and adopted the model of anxiety as a signal. But in *Inhibitions, Symptoms and Anxiety* he was still saying that though the matter was unimportant it was very possible that in anxiety neurosis 'what finds discharge in the generating of anxiety is precisely the surplus of unutilized libido'. It was not until a passage in the *New Introductory Lectures on Psychoanalysis* that he settled this question by saying that even in anxiety neurosis the appearance of anxiety was a reaction to a traumatic situation. He no longer maintained that it was libido that turned into anxiety.

[1] (1900a) *The Interpretation of Dreams*, S.E., Vol. 4, p. 337 f.
[2] (1907a) *Delusions and Dreams in Jensen's 'Gradiva'*, S.E., Vol. 9. p. 60 f.
[3] (1915d) 'Repression', S.E., Vol. 14, p. 153.
[4] (1915e) 'The Unconscious', S.E., Vol. 14, p. 183.

Anxiety was now an ego-function; affects were no longer safety valves but were used as signals by the ego. The 'ego is the actual seat of anxiety. . . . Anxiety is an affective state and as such can . . . only be felt by the ego. The id cannot have anxiety as the ego can for it is an organization and cannot make a judgement about situations of danger'. However 'processes . . . begin to take place in the id which cause the ego to produce anxiety'.[1]

In the *New Introductory Lectures* Freud restated his views of 1926 that only the ego can produce and feel anxiety and that objective anxiety is felt by the ego in relation to the external world, neurotic anxiety in relation to the id and moral anxiety in relation to the super-ego. He added that 'the question of what the material is out of which anxiety is made loses interest . . .'.[2] He also referred to his discovery of two new facts—that anxiety causes repression and not repression anxiety as was previously thought, and that frightening instinctual situations can be traced back to external situations of danger.

He stated that certain specific developmental occurrences are liable to precipitate traumatic situations: birth, separation anxiety, castration anxiety, loss of the objects love, loss of super-ego love.[3] These situations arouse automatic anxiety, the essence of which is an experience of helplessness on the part of the ego in the face of an accumulation of excitation, whether external or internal.[4] Anxiety as a signal is the response of the ego to the threat of an impending traumatic situation.[5]

[1] (1926d) *Inhibitions, Symptoms and Anxiety*, S.E., Vol. 20, p. 140.
[2] (1933a) *New Introductory Lectures on Psycho-Analysis*, S.E., Vol. 22, p. 81.
[3] (1926d) *Inhibitions, Symptoms and Anxiety*, S.E., Vol. 20, p. 82 (Editor's Introduction) and pp. 136, 138, 143.
[4] ibid., pp. 137 and 166.
[5] ibid., pp. 145-7.

AMBIVALENCE

I. DEFINITION

'Emotional ambivalence in the proper sense of the term' is the 'simultaneous existence of love and hate towards the same object'[1] and 'is present to a greater or lesser amount in the innate disposition of everyone';[2] 'affectionate and hostile impulses . . . persist side by side, often to the end of one's life, without either of them being able to do away with the other'.[3] Freud confirmed that alongside the child's intense love there is always a strong aggressive tendency[4] but that 'we cannot go so far as to assert that the ambivalence of emotional cathexes is a universally valid law, and that it is absolutely impossible to feel great love for a person without its being accompanied by a hatred that is perhaps equally great, or vice versa. Normal adults do undoubtedly succeed in separating those two attitudes from each other, and do not find themselves obliged to hate their love-objects and to love their enemy as well as hate him. But this seems to be the result of later developments. In the first phases of erotic life, ambivalence is evidently the rule. Many people retain this archaic trait all through their lives'.[5] He defined the conflict due to ambivalence as 'a well-grounded love and a no less justifiable hatred',[6] expanding this definition finally in his last theory of instincts into the conflict between the two primal instincts, 'the eternal struggle between Eros and the instinct of destruction or death'.[7]

II. DIFFERENT USES OF THE TERM

Although Freud's general use of the term 'ambivalence' is as defined above, he occasionally used it to describe the simultaneous presence of active and passive impulses. 'The fact that, at this later

[1] (1912–13) *Totem and Taboo*, S.E., Vol. 13, p. 157.
[2] ibid., p. 60.
[3] (1914f) 'Some Reflections on Schoolboy Psychology', S.E., Vol. 13, p. 243.
[4] (1933a) *New Introductory Lectures on Psycho-Analysis*, S.E., Vol. 22, p. 124.
[5] (1931b) 'Female Sexuality', S.E., Vol. 21, p. 235.
[6] (1926d) *Inhibitions, Symptoms and Anxiety*, S.E., Vol. 20, p. 102.
[7] (1930a) *Civilization and its Discontents*, S.E., Vol. 21, p. 132.

period of development of an instinctual impulse, its (passive) opposite may be observed alongside it, deserves to be marked by the very apt term introduced by Bleuler—"ambivalence".[1] 'The third antithesis of loving, the transformation of loving into being loved, corresponds to the operation of the polarity of activity and passivity, and is to be judged in the same way as the cases of scopophilia and sadism.'[2]

This use of the term occurs in Freud's description of the analysis of the Wolf Man: 'No doubt was left in the analysis that these passive trends had made their appearance at the same time as the active-sadistic ones, or very soon after them. This is in accordance with the usually clear, intense, and constant *ambivalence* of the patient, which was shown here for the first time in the even development of both members of the pairs of contrary component instincts.'[3]

III. HISTORICAL SURVEY

(a) *General*

Freud first hinted at the concept of ambivalence in his manuscript to Fliess in May 1897 when as he approached the idea of the oedipus complex, he noted the existence of hostile impulses against parents.[4] He was recognizing its significance in his clinical work in 1907 when he was preparing the 'Notes Upon a Case of Obsessional Neurosis' (published in 1909); and he indicated love and hate are bound together in contrary pairs which in the adult do not as a rule become simultaneously conscious, but in children can exist peaceably side by side for a considerable time. 'The feelings which are aroused in these relations between parents and children and in the resulting ones between brothers and sisters are not only of a positive or affectionate kind but also of a negative or hostile one.'[5] The cause of 'the *chronic* co-existence of love and hatred, both directed towards the same person and both of the highest degree of intensity . . . appears to be that at a very early age, somewhere in the prehistoric period of his infancy, the two opposites should

---

[1] (1915c) 'Instincts and their Vicissitudes', S.E., Vol. 14, p. 131.

[2] ibid., pp. 139–40.

[3] (1918b [1914]) 'From the History of an Infantile Neurosis', S.E., Vol. 17, p. 26.

[4] (1950a [1887–1902]) *The Origins of Psycho-Analysis*, Imago, London, 1954, Draft N, pp. 207–10.

[5] (1910a [1909]) 'Five Lectures on Psycho-Analysis', S.E., Vol. 11, p. 47.

have been split apart and one of them, usually the hatred, have been repressed'.[1]

In 1912 Freud adopted for the concept the term ambivalence coined by Bleuler in 1910 in a lecture delivered by him in Berne. In his paper 'The Dynamics of Transference' (1912) acknowledging Bleuler's valuable contribution, he stressed that a high degree of ambivalence is certainly a peculiarity of neurotic people but some amount is present in everyone. He established its historical significance in noting the connection between taboo and neurosis in *Totem and Taboo* (1913) showing how primitive man dealt with the conflict between his love and hate by projecting the hostility, displacing it usually on to the loved person, and then establishing taboos to protect himself from the oppression from without, in a similar way to that which is used in obsessional neurosis, melancholia ('Mourning and Melancholia', (1917)), hysteria (*Inhibitions, Symptoms and Anxiety*, 1926), paranoia (Dostoevsky and Parricide', 1929), and homosexuality ('The Psychogenesis of a Case of Female Homosexuality', 1920).

(b) *The Metapsychological Aspects*

It would seem that until 1915 Freud was considering ambivalence only in terms of a pair of opposite effects of 'antithetical emotions':[2] However, in 'Instincts and their Vicissitudes' he began his metapsychological formulation of the concept in relation to his developing theories of instinct culminating with the assertion that the conflict of love and hate is the conflict of the two primal instincts. (See concepts on theory of instincts and death instinct.) In 1915 he considered 'the case of love and hate acquires a special interest from the circumstance that it refuses to be fitted into our scheme of the instincts'.[3] Love could be transformed into hate but it was common to find them co-existing and directed towards the same object, furnishing a most important example of ambivalence of feeling; however, 'the attitudes of love and hate cannot be made use of for the relations of *instincts* to their objects, but are reserved for the relations of the *total ego*, [Freud here means self, the total person] to objects'.[4] He used the polarity of love and hate

---

[1] (1909d) 'Notes Upon a Case of Obsessional Neurosis', S.E., Vol. 10, p. 239.
[2] (1912–13) *Totem and Taboo*, S.E., Vol. 13, p. 145.
[3] (1915c) 'Instincts and their Vicissitudes', S.E., Vol. 14, p. 133.
[4] ibid., p. 137.

to illustrate his thesis of the relationship between the sexual and the ego instincts; hate is older than love and 'as an expression of the reaction of unpleasure evoked by objects, it always remains in an intimate relation with the self-preservative instincts; so that sexual and ego-instincts can readily develop an antithesis which repeats that of love and hate'.[1] He appreciated that love and hate sprang from different sources and saw ambivalence as 'characterized by the fact that in it the opposing pairs of instincts are developed to an approximately equal extent'.[2]

It was not until 1920 in *Beyond the Pleasure Principle* that he directly connected 'the polarity of love [affection] and hatred [aggressiveness in object-love] with a hypothetical opposition between instincts of life and death',[3] noting that 'wherever the original sadism has undergone no mitigation or intermixture, we find the familiar ambivalence of love and hate in erotic life'.[4] He queried whether 'ordinary ambivalence, which is so often un-usually strong in the constitutional disposition to neurosis, should not be regarded as the product of a defusion; ambivalence, how-ever, is such a fundamental phenomenon that it more probably represents an instinctual fusion that has not been completed'.[5] Aware of the opposition to his theory of the death instinct he in-sisted in 1930 that there was an 'inborn conflict arising from ambivalence, of the eternal struggle between the trends of love and death'[6] and that whatever is hostile and dangerous in love cannot be ascribed to an original bipolarity in its own nature but to a conflict between the life and death instincts (see concept: fusion-defusion).

(c) *Origin of Ambivalence*

Freud's fluctuating views of the origin of ambivalence unfold side by side with the development of his instinct theories. He always considered it a fundamental phenomenon of emotional life[7] present to a greater or less amount in the innate disposition of everyone; a law which 'governs our emotional relations'.[8] But in

---

[1] ibid., p. 139.
[2] (1905d) *Three Essays on the Theory of Sexuality*, S.E., Vol. 7, p. 199.
[3] (1921c) *Group Psychology and the Analysis of the Ego*, S.E., Vol. 18, p. 102, n1.
[4] (1920g) *Beyond the Pleasure Principle*, S.E., Vol. 18, p. 54.
[5] (1923b) *The Ego and the Id*, S.E., Vol. 19, p. 42.
[6] (1930a) *Civilization and its Discontents*, S.E., Vol. 21, p. 133.
[7] (1912–13) *Totem and Taboo*, S.E., Vol. 13, p. 60.
[8] (1915b) 'Thoughts for the Times on War and Death', S.E., Vol. 14, p. 293.

133

1913 he speculated whether originally ambivalence had formed no part of emotional life but was acquired by the human race in connection with their father complex—precisely where the psychoanalytic examination of modern individuals still finds it revealed at its strongest in the contradictory feelings towards the powerful father. Following his formulation of the theory of the death instinct he considered in 1923 whether, as quoted above, ambivalence represented an incomplete instinctual fusion, but in the same book he put forward 'that the ambivalence displayed in the relation to the parents should be attributed entirely to bisexuality and that it is not, as I have represented . . . developed out of identification in consequence of rivalry'.[1] In 1933 he showed his uncertainty of its origin when he queried whether one might reject 'the idea that there is an original ambivalence such as this in erotic cathexes', i.e. in the child's first love relation to its object and pointed to the fact 'that it is the special nature of the mother-child relationship'.[2] However, in 'Analysis Terminable and Interminable' in 1937 he still equated love and life instinct, hate and the death instinct.

Parallel with the development of the place of ambivalence in the instinct theories was its place in the phases of development of the sexual organization. Freud noted in 1915 that the preliminary stage of love which has as its sexual aim the devouring of the object is an ambivalent one; identification, a preliminary stage of object choice, is so from the first and behaves like a derivative of the first oral phase of the organization of the libido, i.e. the oral cannibalistic phase, where there is the wish to destroy and to keep the object. In the sadistic anal stage the aim to master the object continues the ambivalent relationship to such a degree that it is difficult to distinguish love from hate. 'The predominance in it of sadism and the cloacal part played by the anal zone give it a quite peculiarly archaic colouring.'[3] The ambivalent identification with the parent of the opposite sex becomes manifest in the oedipal conflict; the hostile impulses and the affectionate feelings which had existed side by side in the preceding stages break into conflict perhaps as a result of an increase in the affective fantasy, the content of which naturally runs directly counter to some pre-

[1] (1923b) *The Ego and the Id*, S.E., Vol. 19, p. 33.
[2] (1933a) *New Introductory Lectures on Psycho-Analysis*, S.E., Vol. 22, p. 124.
[3] (1905d) *Three Essays on the Theory of Sexuality*, S.E., Vol. 7, p. 199.

dominant tendency,[1] the intensity of the struggle varying with the strength of the predisposition and of real experiences. 'Not until the genital organization is established does love become the opposite of hate.'[2] Boys and girls may then deal differently with their ambivalence. 'The explanation I have attempted to give is at once met by a question: "How is it, then, that boys are able to keep intact their attachment to their mother, which is certainly no less strong than that of girls?" The answer comes equally promptly: "Because boys are able to deal with their ambivalent feelings towards their mother by directing all their hostility on to their father." But, in the first place, we ought not to make this reply until we have made a close study of the pre-oedipus phase in boys, and, in the second place, it is probably more prudent in general to admit that we have as yet no clear understanding of these processes, with which we have only just become acquainted'[3] (see concept: oedipus complex). Freud pointed out that although ambivalence decreases in normal development, it does not disappear completely. Contrary feelings exist side by side in relationships other than in the immediate family such as with school teachers.[4]

(d) *Cultural Aspects*

As well as the relationship of ambivalence to normal and neurotic development, Freud considered the concept was of importance in the origins of religion and conscience and that it had great significance in the evolution of civilizations. He thought that the ambivalence of the oedipus complex governed the relations of mankind to its deity. He stated that; 'the ideational image belonging to his childhood is preserved and becomes merged with the inherited memory traces of the primal father to form the individual's idea of God'.[5] In 1913 he considered 'it seems probable that conscience too arose, on a basis of emotional ambivalence';[6] and although Freud's view of the origin and nature of conscience changed as he further developed his theory the ambivalent element consistently formed part of his formulations. The institution of an internal

---

[1] (1921c) *Group Psychology and the Analysis of the Ego*, S.E., Vol. 18, p. 79, n1.
[2] (1915c) 'Instincts and their Vicissitudes', S.E., Vol. 14, p. 139.
[3] (1931b) 'Female Sexuality', S.E., Vol. 21, p. 235.
[4] (1914f) 'Some Reflections on Schoolboy Psychology', S.E., Vol. 13, p. 243.
[5] (1923d) 'A Seventeenth-Century Demonological Neurosis' S.E., Vol. 19, p. 85.
[6] (1912–13) *Totem and Taboo*, S.E., Vol. 13, p. 68.

authority, the super-ego, by which a sense of guilt could be produced not only by an act of violence but also by the intention, in no way altered the fact that 'the conflict arising from ambivalence left the same result'.[1]

In *Totem and Taboo* Freud suggested that owing 'to the indestructibility and insusceptibility to correction which are attributes of unconscious processes, it [ambivalence] may have survived from very early times to which it was appropriate into later times and circumstances in which its manifestations are bound to seem strange. These are no more than hints, but if they were attentively developed their importance for our understanding of the growth of civilization would become apparent'.[2] 'If civilization is a necessary course of development from the family to humanity as a whole, than—as a result of the inborn conflict arising from ambivalence—there is inextricably bound up with it an increase of the sense of guilt, which will perhaps reach heights that the individual finds hard to tolerate.'[3]

IV. CLINICAL APPLICATIONS

Freud appreciated that the emotional life of a man is made up of pairs of contraries. 'Indeed, if it were not so, repressions and neuroses would perhaps never come about.'[4] The conflict due to ambivalence plays a vital part in the formation of neurosis; as he equated the struggle between love and hate to that between the life and death instincts, he wondered in 'Analysis Terminable and Interminable' 'whether we ought not to review all our knowledge of psychical conflict from this new angle'.[5] 'Ambivalence in the emotional trends of neurotics is the best explanation of their ability to enlist their transference in the service of resistance in their analysis'[6] and is of importance to the outcome.

Obsessional Neurosis
Freud originally formulated the concept of ambivalence in relation to this illness; an ambivalent 'relation between love and hatred . . . is among the most frequent, the most marked, and,

---

[1] (1930a) *Civilization and Its Discontents*, S.E., Vol. 21, p. 133.
[2] (1912–13) *Totem and Taboo*, S.E., Vol. 13, p. 70 f.
[3] (1930a) *Civilization and its Discontents*, S.E., Vol. 21, p. 133.
[4] (1909b) 'Analysis of a Phobia in a Five-Year-Old Boy', S.E., Vol. 10, p. 113.
[5] (1937c) 'Analysis Terminable and Interminable', S.E., Vol. 23, p. 244.
[6] (1912b) 'The Dynamics of Transference', S.E., Vol. 10, p. 107.

probably, therefore, the most important characteristics of obses-sional neurosis'.[1] In 1913 he assumed that 'the presence of a particularly large amount of this original emotional ambivalence is characteristic of the disposition of obsessional neurotics'.[2] It is, however, very probable that the whole defensive process of reaction formation 'is made possible by the ambivalent relationship into which the sadistic impulsion that has to be repressed has been introduced'.[3] The power of the conflict of ambivalence is clearly demonstrated in the obsessional states of depression following upon the death of a loved one; and also in its ability to make most of the symptoms of the neurosis acquired 'in addition to their original meaning, a directly contrary one'.[4] Freud did not, however, con-sider he knew the reason why ambivalence plays such a large part in the neurosis.

Hysteria

In 1909 Freud queried whether the suppressed hostile and jealous feeling to his father may have gone to form the predisposition for his subsequent illness and in 1913 he pointed out how Hans dealt with the conflict by displacing his hostile and fearful feelings on to a substitute. 'The conflict due to ambivalence is not dealt with in relation to one and the same person; it is circumvented . . . by one of the pair of conflicting impulses being directed to another person as a substitutive object,'[5] thus avoiding the conflict. Freud pointed out how, 'There are clearly different ways of egress from a conflict due to ambivalence.'[6] Little Hans' phobia must have been one attempt to solve it; obsessional neurotics make use of reaction formations which have the universality of character traits, and in hysteria reaction formation is limited to the particular object of the ambivalence.

Melancholia

Freud saw the conflict due to ambivalence as a precondition of melancholia and one which complicates the relationship to the object. 'The ambivalence is either constitutional, i.e. is an element of every love-relation formed by this particular ego, or else it

[1] (1909d) 'Notes on a Case of Obsessional Neurosis', S.E., Vol. 10, p. 239.
[2] (1912–13) *Totem and Taboo*, S.E., Vol. 13, p. 60.
[3] (1915d) 'Repression' S.E., Vol. 14, p. 157.
[4] (1926d) *Inhibitions, Symptoms and Anxiety*, S.E., Vol. 20, p. 113.
[5] ibid., p. 103.   [6] ibid., p. 120.

proceeds precisely from those experiences that involved the threat of losing the object.'[1] 'Constitutional ambivalence belongs by its nature to the repressed; traumatic experiences in connection with the object may have activated other repressed material. Thus everything to do with these struggles due to ambivalence remains withdrawn from consciousness,'[2] while it is the influence of the conflict due to ambivalence that enables the erotic cathexis to regress to the sadistic and to the oral cannibalistic stages.

Paranoia and Homosexuality
In this discussion of the Schreber case in 1911 Freud specifically stated that the main purpose of the projection of the hatred on to the once loved object was to justify the change in the emotional attitudes, i.e. the conflict due to ambivalence. 'The typical case of such a conflict [paranoia] is one between two members of a pair of opposites—the case of an ambivalent attitude.'[3] 'The persecuted paranoiac sees in . . . others the reflection of his own hostile impulses against them. Since we know that with the paranoiac it is precisely the most loved person of his own sex that becomes his persecutor, the question arises where this reversal of affect takes its origin; the answer is not far to seek—the ever-present ambivalence of feeling provides its source . . . and serves the same purpose for the persecuted paranoiac . . . of a defence against homosexuality.'[4] 'An ambivalent attitude is present from the outset and the transformation is effected by means of a reactive displacement of cathexis.'[5]

The ambivalence in the relation of the girl to the mother and the boy to the father helps to bring about a pathogenic solution of homosexuality to the oedipal and pre-oedipal conflicts.

Normal Functioning
Freud considered that ambivalence is present in everyone as is demonstrated in dreams[6] and that it is the quantitative factor which is of importance in psychopathology.[7]

[1] 1917e [1915]) 'Mourning and Melancholia', S.E., Vol. 14, p. 256.
[2] ibid., p. 257.
[3] (1912–13) *Totem and Taboo*, S.E., Vol. 13, p. 92.
[4] (1922b) 'Some Neurotic Mechanisms in Jealousy, Paranoia and Homosexuality', S.E., Vol. 18, pp. 226–7.
[5] (1923b) *The Ego and the Id*, S.E., Vol. 19, pp. 42–3.
[6] (1900a) *The Interpretation of Dreams*, S.E., Vol. 5, p. 431.
[7] (1922b) 'Some Neurotic Mechanisms in Jealousy, Paranoia and Homosexuality', S.E., Vol. 18, p. 229.

DIFFERENT USES
OF THE TERM 'OBJECT'

The term 'object' has been used in several different ways and with various implications all through Freud's work.

In spite of the various uses Freud is very consistent always as to what he means in the one case or the other.

There are two sets of contrasts which are of extreme importance when assessing in which sense 'object' as a concept is being used.

The first contrast is between something (object) outside the child's body or something (object) which is in fact a part of the child's body. The second set of contrasts refers to the uses of 'object' as the object of the component instincts as contrasted with object of the ego.

In relation to the first set of contrasts we can see that Freud used the term to describe something outside the child, that is, the mother, the breast etc. Here Freud was using the term 'object' descriptively, as an external observer would: 'At a time at which the first beginnings of sexual satisfaction are still linked with the taking of nourishment, the *sexual instinct* has a *sexual object* outside the infant's own body in the shape of his mother's breast. It is only later that the instinct loses that object, just at the time, perhaps, when the child is able to form a total idea of the person to whom the organ that is giving him satisfaction belongs. As a rule the sexual instinct *then becomes auto-erotic*, and not until the period of latency has been passed through is the original relation restored. There are thus good reasons why a child sucking at his mother's breast has become the prototype of every relation of love. The finding of an object is in fact a refinding of it.'[1]

Later in a 1920 addition to the *Three Essays on the Theory of Sexuality*, it becomes clear what he means by object when used in a psychological sense (object of the ego) and not with a biological connotation (as object of the component instinct when very early in life). We quote: 'We were then obliged to recognize, as one of our most surprising findings, that this early efflorescence of infantile sexual life (between the ages of two and five) already gives rise

[1] (1905d) *Three Essays on The Theory of Sexuality*, S.E., Vol. 7, p. 222.

Sets of contrasts in the use of the term 'object'

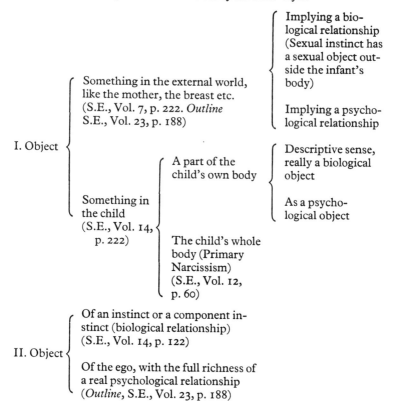

to the choice of an object, with all the wealth of mental activities which such a process involves.'[1]

In the same paper, under the heading 'Diphasic Choice of Objects', Freud says: 'It may be regarded as typical of the choice of an object that the process is diphasic, that is, that it occurs in two waves. The first of these begins between the age of two [there is an editor's note here saying that in 1915 this figure was three; it was altered to two in 1920] and five, and is brought to a halt or to a retreat by the latency period; it is characterized by the infantile nature of the sexual aims. The second wave sets in with puberty and determines the final outcome of sexual life.'[2]

[1] (1905d) *Three Essays on The Theory of Sexuality.* S.E., Vol. 7, p. 234.
[2] ibid., p. 200.

It must be borne in mind that the two above mentioned quotations describes the choice of an object for the phallic oedipal strivings of the child once this degree of organization has developmentally taken place. It is clear that a psychological relationship to an object exists long before such development as the one described here.

Furthermore, in 'Instincts and their Vicissitudes' he says: 'Thus we become aware that the attitudes of love and hate cannot be made use of for the relations of *instincts* to their objects, but are reserved for the relations of the *total ego* to objects.'[1]

In the quotation that follows, taken from *An Outline of Psycho-Analysis,* Freud makes quite clear at which point the sexual biological object in the form of the mother's breast is transformed into a psychological meaningful object for the ego of the child. He clearly points here to the necessary precondition being a differentiation between the child's self and that of the mother. 'A child's first erotic object is the mother's breast that nourishes it; love has its origin in attachment to the satisfied need for nourishment. There is no doubt that, to begin with, the child does not distinguish between the breast and its own body; when the breast has to be separated from the body and shifted to the "*outside*" because the child so often finds it absent, it carries with it as an "*object*" a part of the original narcissistic libidinal cathexis.'[2]

It is thus clear that if we take the term 'object' loosely and out of the context in which it may appear in Freud, we make a serious mistake by mixing concepts of different orders, belonging to totally different developmental stages, and using them as if they were equivalents. Clearly something completely different is implied in each case.

In this first set of contrasts we are dealing with object as used to designate a part of the child's own body. This part of his body acts as the object of one of his component instincts. For example, in 'Instincts and their Vicissitudes': 'The object is not necessarily something extraneous: it may equally well be a part of the subject's own body. It may be changed any number of times in the course of the vicissitudes which the instinct undergoes during its existence.'[3] Furthermore, earlier in the same paper he has stated while

[1] (1915c) 'Instincts and their Vicissitudes', S.E., Vol. 14, p. 137.
[2] (1940a [1938]) *An Outline of Psycho-Analysis*, S.E., Vol. 23, p. 122.
[3] (1915c) 'Instincts and their Vicissitudes', S.E., Vol. 14, p. 122.

discussing how all the component instincts had not been as yet equally accessible to analysis: 'In general we can assert of them that their activities are *auto-erotic*; that is to say, their object is negligible in comparison with the organ which is their source, and as a rule *coincides with that organ*' (our italics).[1]

He described in the same paper the object of an instinct as follows: 'The object of an instinct is the thing in regard to which or through which the instinct is able to achieve its aim. It is what is most variable about an instinct and is not originally connected with it, but becomes assigned to it only in consequence of being peculiarly fitted to make satisfaction possible.'[2] This makes even clearer what was meant by Freud when he referred to the breast or the mother at the very early stage. One can compare the relatively unimportant link and attachment of the given component instinct to its object (either in the external world or in the body of the child) as described here by Freud with the close link in later stages of development when the mother has become the object of the ego.

In this set of contrasts, a third use of the term 'object' can be noted. Freud refers now not to a part of the child's body, but also to the child's body as a whole. Such references can be found in several of Freud's works like *Leonardo, Schreber's Case, Totem and Taboo,* etc. In his paper on the *Schreber Case* he wrote: 'This stage has been given the name of narcissism. What happens is this. There comes a time in the development of the individual at which he unifies his sexual instincts (which have hitherto been engaged in auto-erotic activities) in order to obtain a love-object; and he begins by taking himself, his own body, as his love-object; and only subsequently proceeds from this to the choice of some person other than himself as his object.'[3]

Our second set of contrasts consists of 'object' as the object of a component instinct, or as the 'object' of the ego. The relevant quotations for the second set of contrasts have already been given in connection with the first set of contrasts discussed. The question of the relation of the ego to the object is further complicated by the fact that this relation varies in complexity and richness, according

[1] (1915c) 'Instincts and their Vicissitudes', S.E., Vol. 14 p. 132.
[2] ibid., p. 122.
[3] (1911c) 'Psycho-Analytic Notes on an Autobiographical Account of a Case of Paranoia (Dementia Paranoides)', S.E., Vol. 12, p. 60; cf. (1905d) *Three Essays on the Theory of Sexuality*, S.E., Vol. 7, p. 144 n; and (1910c) *Leonardo da Vinci and a Memory of His Childhood*, S.E., Vol. 11, p. 100.

to the developmental stage of the particular ego and child considered, as well as with his age. This type of relationship will consequently vary from the relatively simple to the most complex.

The relationship of a component instinct to an object is in the nature of a biological relationship while that of the ego to the object is a much more complex one belonging to the psychological realm.

One can say that the need satisfying type of relationship to an object is in the nature of the relationship of a component instinct to its object. That is why the so-called objects of need satisfaction suffer the same fate as the objects of the component instincts. They exist for as long as they yield satisfaction and disappear or are readily changed for others as soon as they do not comply with this function, as indeed happens to the object of the component instincts.

A HISTORICAL REVISION OF THE THREE ESSAYS ON THE THEORY OF SEXUALITY

The *Three Essays* first published in 1905 has suffered in its various editions a greater number of corrections and additions than any other of Freud's published works. To help the reader place historically the most significant corrections and additions this summary has been prepared.*

i. *The Sexual Aberrations* (p. 135)

* All references to pages are to the S.E., Vol. 7.

'Thus the sexual object is a kind of reflection of the subject's own bisexual nature' a footnote added in 1915.

A footnote (pp. 144–5)   1910
That analysis shows that the invert development is characterized by phase (early) of intense, short attachment to a woman, they identify with woman and take selves as sexual object (p. 144).

Second footnote (pp. 145–6)   1915
Examines further factors which influence the way in which the individual will develop. Choice of hetero- versus homosexual object made after puberty, on basis of many factors; essential characteristics: the coming into operation of narcissistic object-choice and a retention of the erotic significance of the anal zone. Some determining accidental factors are frustration and presence of both parents.

Third footnote (pp. 146–7)   1920
Cites recent biological work (and Ferenzi's distinction between 'subject homo-erotics' who merely exchanged a female for a male object) on organic determinants of homosexual-characters (p. 147).

CONCLUSION (p. 146)   1905

B. SEXUALLY IMMATURE PERSONS AND ANIMALS
AS SEXUAL OBJECTS points out that this question   1905
of the sexual object, is one of degree, not question of insanity, etc. (p. 145).
Footnote: distinction between us and ancients . . . they stressed instinct itself, we the object (p. 149).   1910

II. DEVIATIONS IN RESPECT OF THE SEXUAL AIM

A. ANATOMICAL EXTENSIONS   1905
OVERVALUATION OF THE SEXUAL OBJECT (p. 150)   1905
Footnote quotes Ferenzi as having brought suggestibility (to authority of object) in relation with 'parental complex'.   1910
Second footnote deals with relation between overvaluation of object and sexual activities concerned with other parts of the body than genital, the 'craving for stimulation'.   1915

Third footnote recast text—Freud does not see
'craving for stimulation' as an important factor
(p. 151).   1920
Fourth footnote—that women exhibit sexual over-
valuation toward their children, but not their men.   1920
SEXUAL USE OF THE MUCUS MEMBRANE OF
LIPS AND MOUTH (p. 151)   1905
SEXUAL USE OF THE ANAL ORIFICE (p. 152)   1905
SIGNIFICANCE OF OTHER REGIONS OF THE
        BODY (p. 152)   1905
UNSUITABLE SUBSTITUTES FOR THE SEXUAL
        OBJECT-FETISHISM (p. 153)   1905
In discussion of the precondition of 'weakness in the
sexual apparatus' required there is a footnote—that
this represents the 'conditional' precondition, also
that it can be 'accidentally' determined (by the
early occurence of deterrence for fear—from sexual
object).   1915
Another footnote points to origin of fetish as being a
mask for a forgotten phase in sexual development . . .
that this phase turns to fetishism and choice of
fetish, are 'constitutionally determined factors'.   1920
Footnote pointing to shoe or slipper as symbol for
female genital.   1910
Importance of repression of pleasure in smell (re
feet and hair) discussed in several footnotes. In
addition in childhood, the foot represents woman's
penis.   1910
Link between foot fetishism and scoptophilic
instinct, repression.   1915
B. FIXATIONS OF PRELIMINARY SEXUAL AIMS   1905
APPEARANCE OF NEW AIMS (p. 155)   1905
TOUCHING AND LOOKING (p. 156)   1905
Footnote first published use of term 'sublimate'.   1905
Footnote: link between exhibitionism and castration
fear (p. 157).   1920
SADISM AND MASOCHISM (p. 157)
'the most common and most significant of all the
perversions—the desire to inflict pain upon the sexual
object, and its reverse . . . active and passive forms

sadism in normal male aggressiveness . . . desire to
subjugate . . . sadism an aggressive component'.   1905
Masochism . . . sexual overvaluation . . . sentences
omitted in 1915 and addition of two paragraphs
precisely defining both terms (p. 168).
A footnote further distinguishes masochism—a
primary or erotogenic masochism out of which two
later forms, feminine and moral masochism. Sadism
without expression turns on self and produces
secondary masochism.   1924
Short paragraph on pain in original edition.   1905
'Sadism and masochism occupy a special position
among perversions, since contrast between activity
and passivity which lies behind them is among
universal characteristics of sexual life.'   1915
Paragraph on pre-genital (oral) aspect.   1905
Footnote placing these outside class of other
perversions.   1924
Active and passive forms of this perversion occur
in same individual. 'A sadist is always at same time
a masochist.'   1905
'Certain perversions occur as pairs of opposites'
(p. 160).   1905
Presence of these opposites are connected with
opposing activity and passivity. . . .   1915
and with masculinity and feminity . . .
bisexuality. . . .   1924

III. THE PERVERSIONS IN GENERAL (p. 160)
      VARIATION AND DISEASE
      Perversion is a pathological symptom when it is a
      replacement for, not addition to, normal sexuality.   1905
      MENTAL FACTOR IN THE PERVERSIONS (p. 161)
      Horrifying perversions represent 'idealization of the
      instinct'.   1905
      TWO CONCLUSIONS (p. 162)
      1. Forces (resistances, shame and disgust) restrain
      sexual instinct, if these develop before sexual instinct,
      they influence it.   1905
          Footnote: link between individual development and
          psychogenesis of human race.   1915

147

2. Composite nature of sexual instinct, many con-
verging, component instincts show up in study of
abnormalities.   1905

    Note: 'Perversions are a residue of development
    toward the oedipus complex and after the repression
    of that complex the components of the sexual
    instinct which are strongest in the disposition of the
    individual concerned emerge once more' (p. 162–3).   1920

IV. THE SEXUAL INSTINCT IN NEUROTICS (p. 163)
PSYCHOANALYSIS
Analysis demonstrates that 'the symptoms constitute
activity of the patient'.   1905

    Added later 'symptoms based on one hand on
    demands of libido and on other, the ego reaction'.   1920

FINDINGS OF PSYCHOANALYSIS (p. 164)
. . . illness offers a way of escape between pressure of
instinct and antagonism to sexuality.   1905

NEUROSES AND PERVERSION (p. 155)
'Neuroses are . . . the negative of perversions'
(a) all neurotics show inverted (unconscious)
impulses.   1905

    Note: emphasizes importance of this on any theory of
    homosexuality.   1920

(b) every kind of anatomical extension of sexual
activity found, especially membrane of mouth and anus
which are given role of genital.   1905

(c) very important role of component instincts most
part emerge as pair of opposites, one shows presence of
other.   1905

V. COMPONENT INSTINCTS AND EROTOGENIC
    ZONES (p. 167)
First sentence tracing perversions to 'component
instincts'.   1905
Remainder of this paragraph defines instinct,
stimulus, source and aim.   1915

    A footnote states that the instinct theory is 'the most
    important, least complete' portion of the theory.   1924

Paragraph 2 (p. 168), somatic organs cause excitations
of a chemical nature to arise. One of these excitations
is described as specifically sexual—the organ concerned

Footnote, further example, adult girl's description
of her feelings of bliss in thumb sucking (p. 181).   1920

AUTO-EROTISM (p. 181)

First paragraph introduces concept, quotes H. Ellis.   1905
Footnote distinguishes difference between Ellis
and psychoanalytic definitions.   1920
Sentence refers to hysterical disturbance of many
women patients, constriction of throat, vomiting,
they have indulged in much childhood sucking.   1915
Early edition refers to two essential characteristics
of infantile sexual manifestations, made three in   1915
Sentence added 'At its origin it (Manifestation)
attaches itself to one of the vital somatic
functions; it has as yet no sexual object, and is thus
auto-erotic; and its sexual aim is dominated by an
erotogenic zone.'   1915

(3) THE SEXUAL AIM OF INFANTILE SEXUALITY
CHARACTERISTICS OF EROTOGENIC ZONES (p. 183)
Early edition states 'Erotogenic and hysterogenic
zones show the same characteristics.'   1905
Later 'after further reflection . . . I ascribe
quality of erotogenicity to all parts of body and all
internal organs'.   1915
THE INFANTILE SEXUAL AIM (p. 184)   1905
A footnote points to dangers of teleological
expressions as 'nature will have made provisions so
that this experience of satisfaction shall not be left
to chance' (the satisfaction of stimulation of an
erotogenic zone).   1920

(4) MASTURBATORY SEXUAL MANIFESTATIONS (p. 185)
ACTIVITY OF THE ANAL ZONE (p. 185)
How sexuality attaches itself to somatic functions,
how shown in bowel disturbances, etc.   1905
Paragraph discusses way faeces are felt by child as
'gift' i.e. object related (p. 186) aspect, also child
fantasies faeces as baby.   1915
Footnote, cites Salome paper, on meaning of 1st
prohibition (of pleasures of anality), the child
views environment as hostile to his impulses, from
then on what is 'anal' is excluded from life.   1920

ACTIVITY OF THE GENITAL ZONES (p. 187)
Early editions (1905, 1910) contain a teleological-
sounding phrase as to how nature makes sure
genital area is subject to stimulation and excitation
(masturbation) by urination, etc. and washing.
This sentence removed in 1915.
   Paragraph distinguishes more sharply between
   2nd and 1st phase of infantile sexual activity,
   assigns precise date—about fourth year—to 2nd
   phase, 3rd corresponds to pubertal masturbation.   1915
SECOND PHASE OF INFANTILE MASTURBATION
   (p. 189)
This phase leaves deepest unconscious impressions
in subject's memory, etc. and basis of neurosis.   1905
   Footnote: Footnote raises question as to why sense
   of guilt is attached to this masturbatory phase.   1915
   Second footnote: masturbation takes over all guilt
   over sexuality.   1920
RETURN OF EARLY INFANTILE MASTURBATION
   (p. 190)   1905
POLYMORPHOUSLY PERVERSE DISPOSITION (p. 191)
Children easily seduced into it.   1905
COMPONENT INSTINCTS (p. 191)   1905
   Footnotes added to this section deal primarily
   with the question of the link between cruelty and the
   later insight into the early development of object
   choice (age 3–5).   1910
(5) THE SEXUAL RESEARCHES OF CHILDREN
   Whole section appeared in 1915.   1915
THE INSTINCT FOR KNOWLEDGE (p. 194)   1915
THE RIDDLE OF THE SPHINX (p. 194)   1915
CASTRATION COMPLEX AND PENIS ENVY (p. 195)   1915
   A footnote indicates that women as well as men,
   suffer from this complex, believing that the woman
   have lost it by castration. This belief causes many
   men to have low opinion of women.   1920
THEORIES OF BIRTH (p. 196)   1915
SADISTIC VIEW OF SEXUAL INTERCOURSE (p. 196)   1915
TYPICAL FAILURE OF INFANTILE SEXUAL
   RESEARCHES (p. 196)   1915

(2) THE PROBLEM OF SEXUAL EXCITATION   1905
   PART PLAYED BY THE SEXUAL SUBSTANCES
     (p. 213)   1905
   IMPORTANCE OF THE INTERNAL SEXUAL
     ORGANS (p. 214)
   Discussions and footnotes show Freud's increased
   conviction that the chemical aspects are not very
   important (see pp. 213–14).   1905
   CHEMICAL THEORY (p. 215)
   This paragraph was modified from the original
   edition, in accordance with more research and
   information available.   1920
(3) THE LIBIDO THEORY (p. 217)
   Section is largely based on the narcissism paper.
   Three footnotes further elaborate this but do not
   essentially change this.   1915
     Last paragraph of this section in 1920. This para-
     graph emphasizes the concept of libido as restricted
     to 'sexual instinctual forces' distinct from Jung's
     equating it to psychical instinctual force in general.
(4) THE DIFFERENTIATION BETWEEN MEN AND
    WOMEN (p. 219)
   Discussion of essentially 'masculine' (phallic)
   character of childhood sexuality so far as
   masturbatory activity is concerned.   1905
     Footnote deals rather extensively with the concept
     of masculinity and feminity in the sense of
     activity-passivity, biologically and sociologically.   1915
   LEADING ZONES IN MEN AND WOMEN (p. 220)
   Discussion deals mainly with zone development in
   women from clitoris to vagina.   1905
(5) THE FINDING OF AN OBJECT (p. 222)
   First paragraph describes infant sucking as
   prototype of later object finding, lost at a later period,
   then returning in puberty.   1905
   The editor notes that the text of this paragraph
   written in 1905 (p. 222) states that the oral phase is
   object related but that after this sexuality is
   auto-erotic until puberty. This does not coincide with
   the remarks written in 1915 (on p. 200) on the

diphasic choice of object. There are accordingly two
waves, the first beginning between age of 2 and 5,
being stopped by latency period and the second,
final wave appearing in puberty. In 1920 another
comment emphasizes that between ages of 2 and 5
the first choice of object takes place (p. 234).
  Footnote elaborates on two methods of finding the
  object, based on narcissism paper, anaclitic, then
  narcissistic (p. 222).   1915
THE SEXUAL OBJECT DURING EARLY INFANCY
  (p. 222).   1905
INFANTILE ANXIETY (p. 224).   1905
  A footnote states that 'neurotic anxiety arises out
  of libido', 'related to it as vinegar is to wine' (a view
  modified later).   1920
THE BARRIER AGAINST INCEST (p. 225)   1905
  Footnote added refers to anthropological data in
  Totem and Taboo, referring to oedipus complex, etc.   1915
  Footnote discusses pubertal fantasies, link to early
  fantasies, dreams, and oedipus complex.   1920
  Another footnote to same reference . . . refers to
  Rank's theories of intra-uterine period.   1924
AFTER-EFFECTS OF INFANTILE OBJECT-CHOICE
  (p. 228)   1905
  A later footnote points out that the process of falling
  in love is so full of peculiarities and compulsions,
  it can only be understood in terms of being residual
  effect of childhood.   1915
PREVENTION OF INVERSION (p. 229)   1905
  A footnote describes changes in the text relating to
  the oedipus complex and the role it has to this
  subject.   1915
                      SUMMARY
An introductory paragraph about perversions   1905
  Footnote points out that perversions as well as neuroses
  result from regressions, therefore analysis can also help
  perversions.   1915
  There is a sentence relating to the age at which
  childhood sexuality, including object choice, begins in one
  year (1915). Age given was 3–5.   1915

A HISTORICAL REVISION ON THE THEORY OF SEXUALITY

Age given as 2 to 5 later in 1920.
A parenthesis to the effect that *any* organ can function as
an erotogenic zone was added.   1915
That the sexual instinct is 'not unified and is at first'
without an object were added in following the extensive
work on narcissism.   1920
Three paragraphs dealing with two pregenital
organizations, choice of object, precursor of final sexual
organization. One paragraph deals with latency period,
being peculiar to human civilization.   1920
One sentence in above three paragraphs elucidates on
the phallic phase, emphasizing that only phallus exists
in childhood genital sexuality.   1924
FACTORS INTERFERING WITH DEVELOPMENT (p. 235)   1905
CONSTITUTION AND HEREDITY (p. 235)   1905
FURTHER MODIFICATION (p. 237)   1905
Footnote points out that under certain neurotic
circumstances at puberty a normal sexual current might
begin to operate, but then break down, regression to
perversion.   1915
REPRESSION (p. 237)   1905
SUBLIMATION (p. 238)   1905
Comment on character traits such as thrift, etc. link to
anal erotism.   1920
ACCIDENTAL EXPERIENCES (p. 239)   1905
Part of paragraph and following one deals with relative
efficacy of the accidental and constitutional factors on
course of sexual development—'aetiological series' the
dispositional and the definitive.   1915
Term 'aetiological series' altered to 'complemental
series'.   1920
PRECOCITY (p. 240)   1905
TEMPORAL FACTORS (p. 241)   1905
PERTINACITY OF EARLY IMPRESSIONS (p. 242)   1905
FIXATION (p. 242)   1905

REALITY TESTING

A. DEFINITION

Reality testing is an ego function which distinguishes between the perceptions or stimuli of the external world and the impulses or wishes of the unconscious and which compares reality and fantasy.*

The term 'reality testing' was first used in 'Two Principles of Mental Functioning' (1911b) in a discussion on fantasy, though the function was fully implied from the beginning of Freud's writings.[1]

In 'The Project' (1895) were Freud's first attempts to distinguish between inner and outer reality (wish fulfilment, idea, fantasy, memory from reality perception), his idea that the finding of an object in reality was indeed a re-finding of it and his central thesis that it was an inhibition brought about by the ego that makes possible the distinguishing between a perception and a memory (or idea).[2]

B. DEVELOPMENT OF REALITY TESTING: PERCEPTION AND WISH FULFILMENT

In 'The Project', Freud tried to understand the thinking and reality testing necessary to distinguish between perception and wish-fulfilment as growing out of the tension associated with striving for wish satisfaction. 'The craving involves a state of tension in the ego; and as a result of it the idea of the loved object (the "wishful idea") is cathected. Biological experience has taught us that this idea must not be cathected so intensely that it might be

---

* *Footnote* to the definition: Reality testing is often confused with the concepts of reality orientation, reality awareness and reality adaptation. Reality orientation is a descriptive psychiatric concept involving evidence of an individual's awareness of a situation in relation to time, space, people, etc. Reality awareness comes as a result of reality testing, a greater or lesser cognizance of the separateness of the external and internal worlds. Reality adaptation, then, encompasses both the individual's awareness of the differences between the perceptions or stimuli of the external world and the impulses, wishes and fantasies of the internal world and his action in regard to this awareness.

[1] (1911b) 'Formulations on Two Principles of Mental Functioning', S.E., Vol. 12, p. 222.

[2] (1950a [1887–1902]) *The Origins of Psycho-Analysis*, Imago, London, 1954.

confused with a perception, and that its discharge must be post-poned till indications of quality arise from it which prove that it is real—that the cathexis is a perceptual one. If a perception arises which is identical with or similar to the wishful idea, the perception finds its neurones precathected by the wish—that is to say, some or all of them are cathected, according to the degree to which the idea and the perception tally. The difference between the idea and the perception then gives rise to the process of thought; and this reaches its conclusion when a path has been found by which the discordant perceptual cathexes can be merged into ideational cathexes. *Identity* is then attained.'[1]

In *The Interpretation of Dreams* (1900) Freud wrote of the link in the infant between 'the memory trace of the excitation produced by the need' and the mnemic image of the perception which is 'an essential component of this experience of satisfaction'.[2] The next time this need appears, 'a psychical impulse will at once emerge which will seek to re-cathect the mnemic image of the perception and to re-evoke the perception itself . . .'. In order to obtain satisfaction, the perceptual identity will need to be established as coming from the direction of the external world since the path of regression does not bring about the discontinuance of the need and can only lead to frustration. In a footnote added in 1919 he wrote, 'In other words, it becomes evident that there must be a means of "reality testing" (i.e. of testing things to see whether they are real or not.).'[3] Later in this book he wrote that a second system (*Pcs*) must alter the world 'in such a way that it became possible to arrive at a real perception of the object of satisfaction'.[4]

C. REALITY TESTING AND THE RE-FINDING OF OBJECTS

Reality testing as a re-finding of objects which have formerly afforded real satisfaction was clearly formulated in Freud's paper on 'Negation' (1925h)[5] but was first discussed in 'The Project' (1895)[6] in the infant's attempts to establish an identity between the memory-image of the mother's breast and the real perception of it.

[1] ibid., p. 418.
[2] (1900a) *The Interpretation of Dreams*, S.E., Vol. 5, p. 565 f.
[3] ibid., p. 566, n2.   [4] ibid., p. 598 f.
[5] (1925h) 'Negation', S.E., Vol. 19, p. 237 f.
[6] (1950a [1887–1902]) *The Origins of Psycho-Analysis*, Imago, London, 1954 pp. 389–92.

In 1900a Freud followed on this discussion in terms of the aim of the earliest psychical activity as being to 'produce a "perceptual identity" ', to repeat the perception that had been linked with the satisfaction of the need. This desired perceptual identity is then established as coming from the direction of the external world.[1] In 'Negation' this was further developed: 'The first and immediate aim, therefore, of reality testing, is not to *find* an object in real perception which corresponds to the one presented, but to *re-find* such an object, to convince oneself that it is still there. Another capacity of the power of thinking offers a further contribution to the differentiation between what is subjective and what is objective. The reproduction of a perception as a presentation is not always a faithful one; it may be modified by omissions, or changed by the merging of various elements. In that case, reality testing has to acertain how far such distortions go. But it is evident that a precondition for the setting up of reality testing is that objects shall have been lost which once brought real satisfaction.'[2]

D. REALITY-TESTING AND NORMAL AND HALLUCINATORY REGRESSION

In *The Interpretation of Dreams* Freud wrote that 'Nothing prevents us from assuming that there was a primitive state of the psychical apparatus in which this path was actually traversed, that is, in which wishing ended in hallucinating.' This path of regression did not bring about a cessation of the need. 'In order to arrive at a more efficient expenditure of psychical force, it is necessary to bring the regression to a halt before it becomes complete, so that it does not proceed beyond the mnemic image, and is able to seek out other paths which lead eventually to the desired perceptual identity being established from the direction of the external world. This inhibition of the regression and the subsequent diversion of the excitation become the business of a second system, which is in control of voluntary movement—which for the first time, that is, makes use of movement for purposes remembered in advance. But all the complicated thought activity which is spun out from the mnemic image to the moment at which the perceptual identity is established by the external world—all this activity of thought merely

[1] (1900a) *The Interpretation of Dreams*, S.E., Vol. 5, pp. 565–7.
[2] (1925h) 'Negation', S.E., Vol. 19, p. 237 f.

constitutes a roundabout path to wish fulfilment which has been made necessary by experience.'[1]

In discussing hallucinatory regression, Freud stated in the same book, 'In the waking state, however, . . . it does not succeed in producing a hallucinatory revival of the *perceptual* images.'[2] He further stated in 'A Metapsychological Supplement to the Theory of Dreams' (1917d [1915]) '. . . we may be allowed to assume that hallucination consists in a cathexis of the system Cs (*Pcpt*), which, however, is not effected—as normally—from without, but from within, and that a necessary condition for the occurrence of halluci- nation is that regression shall be carried far enough to reach this system itself and in so doing be able to pass over reality testing.'[3]

E. REALITY TESTING AND EGO INHIBITION

This distinguishing between fantasy and reality interested Freud from the beginning of his writings and much on this subject can be found in 'The Project' (Part I, Sections 15 and 16, and in Part III, Section 1).[4] The discussion in 'The Project', according to Strachey is similar to the one in 'A Metapsychological Supplement to the Theory of Dreams', 'It included two main lines of thought. Freud argued that the "primary psychical processes" do not by themselves make any distinction between an idea and a perception; they re- quire, in the first place, to be inhibited by the "secondary psychical processes", and these can only come into operation where there is an "ego" with a large enough store of cathexis to provide the energy necessary to put the inhibition into effect. The aim of the inhibi- tion is to give time for "indications of reality" to arrive from the perceptual apparatus. But, in the second place, besides this inhibiting and delaying function, the ego is also responsible for directing cathexes of "attention" on to the external world, without which the indications of reality could not be observed.'[5]

In 'The Project's' own language Freud wrote, 'Where inhibition is operated by a cathected ego, the indications of w-discharge [perceptual neurones] serve in general as indications of reality

[1] (1900a) *The Interpretation of Dreams*, S.E., Vol. 5, p. 566 f.

[2] ibid., p. 543.

[3] (1917d [1915]) 'A Metapsychological Supplement to the Theory of Dreams', S.E., Vol. 14, p. 232.

[4] (1950a [1887–1902]) *The Origins of Psycho-Analysis*, Imago, London, 1954.

[5] (1917d [1915]) 'A Metapsychological Supplement to the Theory of Dreams', S.E., Vol. 14, p. 220.

which Ψ [nervous system as a whole] learns, by biological experience, to make use of. If the ego is in a state of wishful tension at the moment when an indication of reality emerges, it will allow discharge to follow along the lines of the specific action. If an increase of unpleasure coincides with the indication of reality, Ψ will institute a defence of normal magnitude by an appropriately large lateral cathexis at the point indicated. If neither of these is the case (i.e., if there is neither a wishful state nor an increase of unpleasure at the moment when an indication of reality is received), the cathexis will be allowed to proceed unhindered, according to the nature of the facilitations prevailing. Wishful cathexis carried to the point of hallucination and a complete generation of unpleasure, involving a complete expenditure of defence, may be described as "psychical primary processes". On the other hand, those processes which are only made possible by a good cathexis of the ego and which represent a moderation of the primary processes may be described as "psychical secondary processes". . . . It will be seen that the *sine qua non* of the latter is a correct exploitation of the indications of reality and that this is only possible when there is inhibition on the part of the ego.'[1]

In *The Interpretation of Dreams*, Freud brought in the ego activity and inhibition necessary for reality testing in many different ways (see quotation in previous 'Normal and Hallucinatory Regression'). Another quotation relevant here in the same book is, 'The first wishing seems to have been a hallucinatory cathecting of the memory of satisfaction. Such hallucinations, however, if they were not to be maintained to the point of exhaustion, proved to be inadequate to bring about the cessation of the need or, accordingly, the pleasure attaching to satisfaction. A second activity—or, as we put it, the activity of a second system—became necessary, which would not allow the mnemic cathexis to proceed as far as perception and from there to bind the psychical forces; instead, it diverted the excitation arising from the need along a roundabout path which ultimately, by means of voluntary movement, altered the external world in such a way that it became possible to arrive at a real perception of the object of satisfaction.'[2]

Just as reality testing grows out of and is dependent upon the

[1] (1950a [1887–1902]) *The Origins of Psycho-Analysis*, Imago, London, 1954, p. 388 f.
[2] (1900a) *The Interpretations of Dreams*, S.E., Vol. 5, p. 598 f.

inhibiting function of the ego, so is the ego dependent upon reality testing for its preservation and safety. In *An Outline of Psycho-Analysis* (1938) Freud wrote, 'Conscious processes on the periphery of the ego and everything else in the ego unconscious—such would be the simplest state of affairs that we might picture. And such may in fact be the conditions prevailing in animals. But in men there is an added complication owing to which internal processes in the ego may also acquire the quality of consciousness. This complication is produced by the function of speech, which brings the material in the ego into a firm connection with the memory traces of visual and more particularly of auditory perceptions. Thenceforward the perceptual periphery of the cortex of the ego can be stimulated to a much greater extent from inside as well; internal events such as sequences of ideas and intellective processes can become conscious; and a special apparatus becomes necessary in order to distinguish between the two possibilities—that is, what is known as *reality testing*. The equation "perception = reality (external world)" no longer holds. Errors, which can now easily arise and do in fact habitually arise in dreams are called *hallucinations*.'[1]

Later in the same book he wrote, 'Just as the id is directed exclusively to obtaining pleasure, so the ego is governed by considerations of safety. The ego has set itself the task of self-preservation, which the id appears to neglect. It makes use of sensations of anxiety as a signal to give a warning of dangers threatening its integrity. Since memory traces can become conscious just as much as perceptions, especially through their association with verbal residues, the possibility arises of a confusion which would lead to a mistaking of reality. The ego guards itself by establishing a function for *reality testing*, which can be allowed to fall into abeyance in dreams on account of the conditions governing the state of sleep.'[2]

F. SYSTEMS CONTAINING REALITY TESTING

In 'The Project', Freud wrote that 'The biological rule of attention, in so far as it concerns the ego, runs as follows: If an indication of reality appears, the perceptual cathexis which is simultaneously present must be hypercathected.'[3] There is the

[1] (1940a [1938]) *An Outline of Psycho-Analysis*, London, 1949, p. 22.
[2] ibid., p. 110 f.
[3] (1950a [1887–1902]) *The Origins of Psycho-Analysis*, Imago, London, 1954, p. 429 f.

beginning thought here which over the years finally places reality testing as an ego function. In *The Interpretation of Dreams*, as written previously, reality testing is placed in the 'second system'. In 'The Unconscious' (1915) Freud attributed reality testing to the system *Pcs*. 'Further, it devolves upon the system *Pcs* to make communication possible between the different ideational contents so that they can influence one another, to give them an order in time, and to set up a censorship or several censorships; "reality testing" too, and the reality principle, are in its province.'[1]

In 'Mourning and Melancholia' (1917e [1915]), again he placed reality testing in the still undefined ego, '. . . we shall count it, [conscience] along with the censorship of consciousness and reality testing, among the major institutions of the ego . . .'.[2]

However, in 'A Metapsychological Supplement to the Theory of Dreams' (1917d [1915]) in which he was attempting to differentiate *Cs* from *Pcs* and in which he wrote of *Cs* as he had previously written of *Pcs*, he attributed reality testing to *Cs*, though in the same paragraph he also places it in the ego. 'This function of orientating the individual in the world by discrimination between what is internal and what is external must now, after detailed dissection of the mental apparatus, be ascribed to the system *Cs* (*Pcpt*) alone. The *Cs* must have at its disposal a motor innervation which determines whether the perception can be made to disappear or whether it proves resistant. Reality testing need be nothing more than this contrivance. We can say nothing more precise on this point, for we know too little as yet of the nature and mode of operation of the system *Cs*. We shall place reality testing among the major *institutions of the ego*, alongside the *censorships* which we have come to recognize between the psychical systems . . .'.[3]

Freud ascribed the reality testing function to the ego ideal in *Group Psychology and The Analysis of The Ego* (1921c): 'The fact that the ego experiences in a dream-like way whatever he may request or assert reminds us that we omitted to mention among the functions of the ego ideal the business of testing the reality of things. No wonder that the ego takes a perception for real if its reality is vouched for by the mental agency which ordinarily dis-

---

[1] (1915e) 'The Unconscious', S.E., Vol. 14, p. 188.
[2] (1917e [1915]) 'Mourning and Melancholia', S.E., Vol. 14, p. 247.
[3] (1917d [1915]) 'A Metapsychological Supplement to the Theory of Dreams', S.E., Vol. 14, p. 233.

charges the duty of testing the reality of things.' In a footnote added in 1923 he wrote, 'There seems, however, to be some doubt whether the attribution of this function to the ego ideal is justified.'[1]

In *The Ego and the Id* (1923b) Freud definitely ascribed reality testing to the ego: '. . . I seem to have been mistaken in ascribing the function of "reality testing" to this super-ego—a point which needs correction. It would fit in perfectly with the relations of the ego to the world of perception if reality testing remained a task of the ego itself.'[2] In this same book he further wrote, 'Our ideas about the ego are beginning to clear, and its various relationships are gaining distinctness. We now see the ego in its strength and in its weaknesses. It is entrusted with important functions. By virtue of its relation to the perceptual system it gives mental processes an order in time and submits them to "reality testing".'[3]

G. GENESIS OF REALITY DIFFERENTIATION

In thinking through the genesis of reality differentiation, Freud wrote that the ego learns to differentiate between inner and outer stimuli by the persistence of the stimuli and whether or not escape from it is possible.

In 'Instincts and Their Vicissitudes' (1915c) he wrote, 'Let us imagine ourselves in the situation of an almost entirely helpless living organism, as yet unorientated in the world, which is receiving stimuli in its nervous substance. This organism will very soon be in a position to make a first distinction and a first orientation. On the one hand, it will be aware of stimuli which can be avoided by muscular action (flight); these it ascribes to an external world. On the other hand, it will also be aware of stimuli against which such action is of no avail and whose character of constant pressure persists in spite of it; these stimuli are the signs of an internal world, the evidence of instinctual needs. The perceptual substance of the living organism will thus have found in the efficacy of its muscular activity a basis for distinguishing between an "outside" and an "inside".'[4]

He added in 'A Metapsychological Supplement to the Theory

---

[1] (1921c) *Group Psychology and the Analysis of the Ego*, S.E., Vol. 18, p. 114.
[2] (1923b) *The Ego and the Id*, S.E., Vol. 19, p. 28, n2.
[3] ibid., p. 55.
[4] (1915c) 'Instincts and their Vicissitudes', S.E., Vol. 14, p. 119.

of Dreams' (1917d [1915]), 'In an earlier passage we ascribed to the still helpless organism a capacity for making a first orientation in the world by means of its perceptions, distinguishing "external" and "internal" according to their relation to its muscular action. A perception which is made to disappear by an action is recognized as external, as reality; where such an action makes no difference, the perception originates within the subject's own body—it is not real. It is of value to the individual to possess a means such as this of recognizing reality, which at the same time helps him to deal with it . . .'.[1]

Another dimension of the genesis of reality was discussed in 'Negation' (1925h): 'The function of judgement is concerned in the main with two sorts of decisions. It affirms or disaffirms the possession by a thing of a particular attribute; and it asserts or disputes that a presentation has an existence in reality. The attribute to be decided about may originally have been good or bad, useful or harmful. Expressed in the language of the oldest— the oral—instinctual impulses, the judgement is: "I should like to eat this", or "I should like to spit it out"; and put more generally: "I should like to take this into myself and to keep that out". That is to say: "It shall be inside me" or "it shall be outside me". As I have shown elsewhere, the original pleasure-ego wants to introject into itself everything that is good and to eject from itself everything that is bad. What is bad, what is alien to the ego and what is external are, to begin with, identical.'[2]

H. PSYCHICAL REALITY AND MATERIAL REALITY

In 'The Project'[3] Freud commented on the difference between 'thought reality' and 'external reality' and in *The Interpretation of Dreams* in attempting to come to grips with what is inner and outer reality he wrote, 'Whether we are to attribute *reality* to unconscious wishes, I cannot say. It must be denied, of course, to any transitional or intermediate thoughts.'[4] In 1909 he added, ' "If we look at unconscious wishes reduced to their most fundamental and truest shape, we shall have to remember, no doubt, that psychical

[1] (1917d [1915]) 'A Metapsychological Supplement to the Theory of Dreams', S.E., Vol. 14, p. 232.
[2] (1925h) 'Negation', S.E., Vol. 19, p. 236 f.
[3] (1950a [1887–1902]) *The Origins of Psycho-Analysis*, Imago, London, 1954, p. 430.
[4] (1900a) *The Interpretation of Dreams*, S.E., Vol. 5, p. 620.

reality too has more than one form of existence." '[1] In 1919 the sentence read, 'If we look at unconscious wishes reduced to their most fundamental and truest shape, we shall have to conclude, no doubt, that *psychical* reality is a particular form of existence not to be confused with *material* reality.'[2]

In *The Interpretation of Dreams*, Freud identified the unconscious as the true psychical reality and found it essentially as much unknown to the individual as the reality of the external world. The former is *'as incompletely presented by the data of consciousness as is the external world by the communications of our sense organs'*.[3]

I. NORMAL AND CLINICAL IMPLICATIONS OF REALITY TESTING

Freud discussed reality testing in connection with a wide range of normal, neurotic and psychotic conditions. He used the pathological condition of 'Meynert's Amentia' in 'A Metapsychological Supplement to the Theory of Dreams' (1917d [1915]) to show how the break with reality can occur. 'Amentia is the reaction to a loss which reality affirms, but which the ego has to deny, since it finds it unsupportable. Thereupon the ego breaks off its relation to reality; it withdraws the cathexis from the system of perceptions, *cs*—or rather, perhaps, it withdraws a cathexis. . . . With this turning away from reality, reality testing is got rid of, the (unrepressed, completely conscious) wishful fantasies are able to press forward into the system, and they are there regarded as a better reality.'[4]

In *Group Psychology and the Analysis of the Ego* (1921) he wrote of the distortion in reality in the neurotic: 'We have pointed out that this predominance of the life of fantasy and of the illusion born of an unfulfilled wish is the ruling factor in the psychology of neuroses. We have found that what neurotics are guided by is not ordinary objective reality but psychological reality. A hysterical symptom is based upon phantasy instead of upon the repetition of real experience, and the sense of guilt in an obsessional neurosis is based upon the fact of an evil intention which was never carried out. Indeed, just as in dreams and in hypnosis, in the mental

---

[1] ibid., p. 620 n1.   [2] ibid., p. 620.   [3] ibid., p. 613.
[4] (1917d [1915]) 'A Metapsychological Supplement to the Theory of Dreams', S.E., Vol. 14, p. 233.

operations of a group the function for testing the reality of things falls into the background in comparison with the strength of wishful impulses with their affective cathexis.'[1]

Freud differentiated a neurosis from a psychosis in 'Neurosis and Psychosis' (1924 [1923])[2] and in 'The Loss of Reality in Neurosis and Psychosis' (1924)[3] in that in neurosis the ego supresses some of the id because of the ego's dependence on reality but that in psychosis the ego will withdraw from some of the reality because of the predominance of the id.

The process of mourning requires reality testing *par excellence*. In 'Mourning and Melancholia' (1917e [1915]) Freud noted that 'Reality testing has shown that the loved object no longer exists, and it proceeds to demand that all libido shall be withdrawn from its attachments to that object. This demand arouses understandable opposition. . . . This opposition can be so intense that a turning away from reality takes place and a clinging to the object through the medium of a hallucinatory wishful psychosis. Normally, respect for reality gains the day.'[4] In *Inhibitions, Symptoms and Anxiety*, (1926 [1925]) Freud added: 'Mourning occurs under the influence of reality testing; for the latter function demands categorically from the bereaved person that he should separate himself from the object, since it no longer exists.'[5]

Freud in 'The Uncanny' (1919) commented that '. . . anyone who has completely and finally rid himself of animistic beliefs will be insensible to this type of the uncanny. . . . The whole thing is purely an affair of "reality testing", a question of the material reality of the phenomena'.[6]

In the paper, 'Fetishism' (1927)[7] and in *An Outline of Psycho-Analysis* (1940a [1938])[8] Freud wrote of the defensive reality distortion that takes place in the ego defence of splitting its reactions in response to an intolerable external reality.

The various ways of dealing with reality were discussed at length in *Civilization and its Discontents* (1930a [1929]) 'Another

---

[1] (1921c) *Group Psychology and the Analysis of the Ego*, S.E., Vol. 18, p. 80.
[2] (1924b) 'Neurosis and Psychosis', S.E., Vol. 19, pp. 150–151.
[3] (1924e) 'The Loss of Reality in Neurosis and Psychosis', S.E., Vol. 19, p. 183.
[4] (1917e [1915]) 'Mourning and Melancholia', S.E., Vol. 14, p. 244.
[5] (1926d) *Inhibitions, Symptoms and Anxiety*, S.E., Vol. 20, p. 172.
[6] (1919h) 'The "Uncanny"', S.E., Vol. 17, p. 248.
[7] (1927e) 'Fetishism', S.E., Vol. 21, pp. 153–154.
[8] (1940a [1938]) *An Outline of Psycho-Analysis*, S.E., Vol. 23, pp. 202–204.

technique for fending off suffering is the employment of the displacements of libido which our mental apparatus permits of and through which its function gains so much in flexibility. The task here is that of shifting the instinctual aims in such a way that they cannot come up against frustration from the external world. In this, sublimation of the instincts lends its assistance.'[1]

'. . . While this procedure already clearly shows an intention of making oneself independent of the external world by seeking satisfaction in internal, psychical processes, the next procedure brings out those features yet more strongly. In it, the connection with reality is still further loosened; satisfaction is obtained from illusions, which are recognized as such without the discrepancy between them and reality being allowed to interfere with enjoyment. The region from which these illusions arise is the life of the imagination; at the time when the development of the sense of reality took place, this region was expressly exempted from the demands of reality testing and was set apart for the purpose of fulfilling wishes which were difficult to carry out.'[2]

'. . . Another procedure operates more energetically and more thoroughly. It regards reality as the sole enemy and as the source of all suffering, with which it is impossible to live, so that one must break off all relations with it if one is to be in any way happy', i.e. the hermit, the madman, the mass delusions of reality, etc.[3]

[1] (1930a) *Civilization and its Discontents*, S.E., Vol. 21, p. 79.
[2] ibid., p. 80.   [3] ibid., p. 81.

TRANSFERENCE

Definition
'Transference arises spontaneously in all human relationships . . .
psychoanalysis does not create it but merely reveals it to consciousness and gains control of it in order to guide psychical processes towards the desired goal of cure.'[1] This phenomenon,
transference, is itself only a piece of repetition of the forgotten past
but this revival of early attitudes which have become unconscious,
occurs not as belonging to the past but on to the physician in the
present and is based on no real relation between them. 'The
patient sees in him the return, the reincarnation, of some important
figure out of his childhood [his parents] or past, and consequently
transfers on to him feelings and reactions which undoubtedly
applied to this prototype.'[2] These were and are ambivalent, com-
prising of positive (affectionate) as well as negative (hostile)
attitudes towards the analyst.

'This fact of transference soon proves to be a factor of undreamt-
of importance, [in treatment] on the one hand an instrument of
irreplaceable value and on the other hand a source of serious
dangers.'[3] It is used as a weapon by the resistances both when
positive and negative; but it is only in the re-experiencing in the
transference that part of his emotional life which the patient can no
longer recall to memory, that he becomes convinced of the existence
and power of his unconscious impulses and the validity of the
connections which have been constructed during the analysis.

Technically, handling the transference is the 'hardest part of the
whole task. . . . Transference is the one thing the presence of
which has to be detected almost without assistance and with the
slightest clues to go upon, while at the same time the risk of making
arbitrary inferences has to be avoided'.[4]

'All the patient's tendencies including the hostile ones . . . are
turned to account for the purpose of the analysis by being made

[1] (1910a [1909]) 'Five Lectures on Psycho-Analysis', S.E., Vol. 11, p. 51.
[2] (1940a [1938]) *An Outline of Psycho-Analysis*, S.E., Vol. 23, p. 174.
[3] ibid., p. 174.
[4] (1905e [1901]) 'Fragment of an Analysis of a Case of Hysteria', S.E., Vol.
7, p. 116.

conscious. . . . Transference, which seems ordained to be the greatest obstacle to psychoanalysis, becomes its most powerful ally, if its presence can be detected.'[1] It is 'an essential feature to my picture of analysis and which can claim, alike technically and theoretically, to be regarded as of the first importance'.[2]

The phenomenon of transference, 'the special emotional relation regularly formed between the patient and the physician'[3] was seen by Freud as proof of 'the truth that the motive forces behind the formation of neurotic synptoms are of a sexual nature'.[4]

BEGINNING

Historical Survey

The term 'transference' was first used by Freud in his 'Studies on Hysteria'[5] where he began to recognize the surprising phenomenon which neither he nor Breuer was prepared to encounter in their new cathartic, pressure technique which had replaced hypnotic treatment. Unlike Breuer who acquired an aversion to further work on the elucidation of the neuroses when he discovered the sexual motivation of his woman patient Anna O's transference on to him, not understanding the universal nature of this unexpected phenomenon Freud was not overwhelmed but he was able to begin his lifelong study of the process, clinically and theoretically.

Freud had recognized from the beginning of his clinical work the importance of the affective factor, i.e. the personal influence of the physician. With patients,

'I say, it is almost inevitable that their personal relation to him will force itself, for a time at least, unduly into the foreground. It seems, indeed, as though an influence of this kind on the part of the doctor is a *sine qua non* to a solution of the problem. I do not think any essential difference is made in this respect whether hypnosis can be used or whether it has to be by-passed and replaced by something else.'[6]

He thought that the physician could use his influence based on this positive relationship to be the elucidator, the teacher, the

[1] ibid., p. 117.
[2] (1925d [1924]) *An Autobiographical Study*, S.E., Vol. 20, p. 42.
[3] (1923a) 'Two Encyclopedia Articles', S.E., Vol. 18, p. 247.
[4] ibid., p. 247.
[5] (1895d) *Studies on Hysteria*, S.E., Vol. 2, p. 302.
[6] ibid., p. 266.

representative of a freed or superior view of the world, father con-
fessor, etc. to enable patients to overcome resistances and 'start on
the truly curative psychical work [cartharsis] . . . reproducing the
pathogenic impressions that caused it [the hysterical symptom]
and by giving utterance to them with an expression of affect'.[1]
This relationship could, however, be disturbed and it is 'the worst
obstacle we can come across. We can, however, reckon on meeting
it in every comparatively serious analysis.'[2] The obstacle was an
external one, not inherent in the material, arising from three
principal causes.

(1) The patient's personal estrangement from the physician, e.g.
if she feels insulted by him and this can be overcome by explanation and clearly, was not seen at this time as a transference;

(2) The patient's dread of becoming too dependent on the
physician arising out of the special solicitude inherent in the treatment itself. This may create considerable difficulties as the new
motive of the resistance remains as a rule unconscious but also not
recognized as transferred.

(3) 'If the patient is frightened at finding that she is transferring
on to the figure of the physician the distressing ideas which arise
from the content of the analysis. This is a frequent, and indeed in
some analyses a regular, occurrence. Transference on to the
physician takes place through a *false connection*.'[3]

He explained that this meant a past wish appeared in the
patients' consciousness but without any of the memories to place
it at an appropriate time. Therefore,

'The wish which was present was then, owing to the compulsion to associate which was dominant in her consciousness,
linked to my person, with which the patient was legitimately concerned; and as the result of this *mesalliance*—which I described as
a "false connection"—the same affect was provoked which had
forced the patient long before to repudiate this forbidden wish.
Since I have discovered this, I have been able, whenever I have
been similarly involved personally, to presume that a transference
and a false connection have once more taken place.'[4]

[1] (1895d) *Studies on Hysteria*, S.E., Vol. 2, p. 283.
[2] ibid., p. 301.   [3] ibid., p. 302.
[4] (1895d) *Studies on Hysteria*, S.E., Vol. 2, p. 303.

By his brilliant realization that these resistances were based on the old model and 'that the whole process followed a law',[1] Freud was able to apply the same treatment to them as to the old symptoms and so begin to understand the significant meaning of this 'obstacle' and eventually turn it into a major instrument of psychoanalytic technique and theory.

He was already aware in 1893 that the patient has

'. . . to overcome the distressing affect aroused by having been able to entertain such a wish [erotic] even for a moment; and it seemed to make no difference to the success of the treatment whether she made this psychical repudiation the theme of her work in the historical instance or in the recent one connected with me. The patients, too, gradually learnt to realize that in these transferences on to the figure of the physician it was a question of a compulsion and an illusion which melted away with the conclusion of the analysis'.[2]

Its vital importance therapeutically was, however, much more fully recognized in 'A Case of Hysteria' written in 1901. By then he appreciated that transference was an inevitable necessity in all analysis, the latest creation of the patients' ongoing disease. Unless it were recognized and handled skilfully, no treatment could be sustained; he realized that it was his failure to do this with his patient, Dora, that had brought about the premature ending of her analysis. His understanding of the theoretical implications of the phenomenon had clearly increased and developed in the intermediate years. He realized in 1901 that

'It may be safely said that during psychoanalytic treatment the formation of new symptoms is invariably stopped. But the productive powers of the neurosis are by no means extinguished; they are occupied in the creation of a special class of mental structures, for the most part unconscious, to which the name of "*transferences*" may be given.'[3]

He recognized then as a revival of a whole series of psychological experiences applied in the present to the analyst but belonging to

[1] ibid., p. 304.   [2] ibid., p. 304.
[3] (1905e [1901]) 'Fragment of an Analysis of a Case of Hysteria', S.E., Vol. 7, p. 116.

past figures. They obviously occurred in other situations such as mental institutions, but no one there was aware of them. Psychoanalysis aimed at recognizing them, the hostile as well as the affectionate ones, making them conscious and then destroying them. This process was seen as essential because of the use patients 'made of transference to set 'up all the obstacles that make the material inaccessible to treatment, and since it is only after the transference has been resolved that a patient arrives at a sense of conviction of the validity of the connections which have been constructed during the analysis'.[1] Freud then considered, as he does throughout his writing, that working with the transference was the hardest task of the analytic technique since the patient's assistance cannot be expected. But working the transferences into the analysis at an early stage although it retards and obscures the course of the analysis, does guarantee it against sudden and overwhelming resistances and possible premature termination.

In the Dora case, Freud was still approaching the phenomenon from the surface; he indicated that the transference could develop because of some unknown quantity in the physician which reminded the patient of some figure in the past. He thought it made no difference whether the particular impulse of the patient so revived had to be overcome in connection with the doctor or with some one else. When it was made conscious and explained to the patient, it would immediately be destroyed. If, however, it were not recognized, acting out of the fantasies would replace reproducing them verbally in treatment—and bring about premature termination.

'If cruel impulses and revengeful motives, which have already been used in the patient's ordinary life for maintaining her symptoms, become transferred on to the physician during treatment, before he has had time to detach them from himself by tracing them back to their sources, then it is not to be wondered at if the patient's condition is unaffected by his therapeutic efforts. For how could the patient take a more effective revenge than by demonstrating upon her own person the helplessness and incapacity of the physician ?'[2]

However, already in 'A Case of Obsessional Neurosis', 1909,

[1] (1905e [1901]) 'Fragment of an Analysis of a Case of Hysteria', S.E., Vol. 7, pp. 116 and 117.
[2] ibid., p. 120 f.

The Rat Man had to go 'along the painful road of transference'[1] on to the physician to reach a conviction of his unconscious wishes.

'With the help of a transference fantasy, he experienced, as though it were new and belonged to the present, the very episode from the past which he had forgotten, or which had only passed through his mind unconsciously.'[2]

Freud had also come to realize fully that:

'The process of cure is accomplished in a relapse into love, if we combine all the many components of the sexual instinct under the term "love"; and such a relapse is indispensable, for the symptoms on account of which the treatment has been undertaken are nothing other than precipitates of earlier struggles connected with repression or the return of the repressed, and they can only be resolved and washed away by a fresh high tide of the same passions. Every psychoanalytic treatment is an attempt at liberating repressed love which has found a meagre outlet in the compromise of a symptom. Indeed, the agreement between such treatments and the process of cure described by the author of *Gradiva* reaches its climax in the further fact that in analytic psychotherapy too the re-awakened passion, whether it is love or hate, invariably chooses as its object the figure of the doctor.'[3]

It still seemed to him in his interpretation of the Schreber Case, 1911, that the transference had arisen because the figure of the doctor had 'reminded' the patient of his brother or father. But as the theoretical meanings of the phenomenon were explored, this concept was greatly expanded. By 1910, Freud could summarize his attitude in a letter to Oskar Pfister:

'As for the transference it is altogether a curse. The intractable and fierce impulses in the illness, on account of which I renounced both indirect and hypnotic suggestion, cannot be altogether abolished even through psychoanalysis; they can only be restrained, and what remains expresses itself in the transference. That is

---

[1] (1909d) 'Notes upon a Case of Obsessional Neurosis', S.E., Vol. 10, p. 209.
[2] ibid., p. 199.
[3] (1907a) *Delusions and Dreams in Jensen's 'Gradiva'*, S.E., Vol. 9, p. 90.

often a considerable amount. The analytic rules fail us; one has to adapt oneself to the individuality of the patient and keep some personal note of one's own. In general I agree with Stekel that the patient should be kept in a state of abstinence, of unrequited love, and that is not always entirely possible. The more affection you allow him the more readily you reach his complexes, but the less the definite result, since he disposes of the previous gratification in his complexes by exchanging them for what he experiences in the transference. The therapeutic result is very good, but it is quite dependent on the transference. One perhaps achieves a cure, but not the necessary degree of independence or a guarantee against relapse.'[1]

THEORETICAL AND TECHNICAL EVALUATIONS, 1909–15

Strachey has pointed out Freud's reluctance to publish material on the technique of psychoanalytic treatment but sufficient explicit assessments were made throughout his writings to clarify the relevant factors and distinguish their comparative importance. The fullest account was in the period 1908–15 when he was engaged also in his metapsychological formulations.

Freud had planned in his metapsychological formulations to publish a systematic work on psychoanalytic technique in 1908 in which he intended to deal with the 'powerful mechanism'[2] of transference which helped patients to find the repressed unconscious wishes in themselves. He explained to his American audience in 1909:

'In every psychoanalytic treatment of a neurotic patient the strange phenomenon that is known as "transference" makes its appearance. The patient, that is to say, directs towards the physician a degree of affectionate feeling (mingled, often enough, with hostility) which is based on no real relation between them and which—as is shown by every detail of its emergence can only be traced back to old wishful phantasies of the patient's which have become unconscious. Thus the part of the patient's emotional life which he can no longer recall to memory is re-experienced by him in his rela-

---

[1] Letter to Pfister: June 5, 1910, Jones, E., *Life of Sigmund Freud*, Vol. 2, The Hogarth Press, p. 497.

[2] (1910d) 'The Future Prospects of Psycho-Analytic Therapy', S.E., Vol. 11, p. 142.

tion to the physician; and it is only this re-experiencing in the "transference" that convinces him of the existence and of the power of these unconscious sexual impulses. His symptoms, to take an analogy from chemistry, are precipitates of earlier experiences in the sphere of love (in the widest sense of the word), and it is only in the raised temperature of his experience of the transference that they can be resolved and reduced to other psychical products. In this reaction the physician, if I may borrow an apt phrase from Ferenczi (1909), plays the part of a catalytic ferment, which temporarily attracts to itself the affects liberated in the process.'[1]

He was convinced that everywhere this spontaneous transference is the true vehicle of therapeutic influence. As, however, technique had been transformed from the cathartic aim of elucidation of symptoms to one of finding out and overcoming of resistances, he insisted that a patient 'must have formed a sufficient attachment (transference) to the physician for his emotional relationship to him to make a fresh flight impossible'[2] from the intensification of his conflict through the disclosure of the unconscious wishes in the transference.

In his paper, 'The Dynamics of Transference' Freud outlined not only the importance of the positive transference but the theoretical explanation of how one occurred, developed, became resistant and could be used for therapeutic cure.

BASIS OF TRANSFERENCE

'It must be understood that each individual, through the combined operation of his innate disposition and the influences brought to bear on him during his early years, has acquired a specific method of his own in his conduct of his erotic life—that is, in the preconditions to falling in love which he lays down, in the instincts he satisfies and the aims he sets himself in the course of it. This produces what might be described as a stereotype plate (or several such), which is constantly repeated—constantly reprinted afresh—in the course of the person's life, so far as external circumstances and the nature of the love-objects accessible to him permit, and which is certainly not entirely insusceptible to change in the face of

[1] (1910a [1909]), 'Five Lectures on Psycho-Analysis', S.E., Vol. 11, p. 51.
[2] (1910k) '"Wild" Psycho-Analysis', S.E., Vol. 11, p. 226.

recent experiences. Now, our observations have shown that only a portion of these impulses which determine the course of erotic life have passed through the full process of psychical development. That portion is directed towards reality, is at the disposal of the conscious personality, and forms a part of it. Another portion of the libidinal impulses has been held up in the course of development; it has been kept away from the conscious personality and from reality, and has either been prevented from further expansion except in phantasy or has remained wholly in the unconscious so that it is unknown to the personality's consciousness. If someone's need for love is not entirely satisfied by reality, he is bound to approach every new person whom he meets with libidinal anticipatory ideas; and it is highly probable that both portions of his libido, the portion that is capable of becoming conscious as well as the unconscious one, have a share in forming that attitude.'[1]

The anticipatory libidinal cathexis which the patient directs to the analyst cannot be tied to any particular stereotype, any particular infantile figure since transference has been set up not only by conscious anticipatory ideas but also by those which are unconscious, and it is this factor which makes the amount and nature of the transference exceed anything which could be justified on sensible or rational grounds. In every neurosis 'the portion of the libido which is capable of becoming conscious and is directed towards reality is diminished, and the portion which is directed *away* from reality and is unconscious, and which, though it may still feed the subject's phantasies, nevertheless belongs to the unconscious, is proportionately increased'.[2]

SOURCES OF RESISTANCE

Analytic treatment aims at seeking out libido which had regressed to its infantile imagos, make it accessible to consciousness and enter into the service of reality. This must, of course, provoke resistances; the original libidinal regression came about by a frustration of satisfaction between the subject and the external world in reality, but even more, by the attraction exerted in the libido by the portions of the complexes belonging to the unconscious. Therefore, this

---

[1] (1912b) 'The Dynamics of Transference', S.E., Vol. 12, p. 99 f.
[2] ibid., p. 102.

attraction of the unconscious instincts and their impulses must be overcome. 'Every single association, every act of the person under treatment must reckon with the resistance'.[1]

'If now we follow a pathogenic complex from its representation in the conscious (whether this is an obvious one in the form of a symptom or something quite inconspicuous) to its root in the unconscious, we shall soon enter a region in which the resistance makes itself felt so clearly that the next association must take account of it and appear as a compromise between its demands and those of the work of investigation. It is at this point, on the evidence of our experience, that transference enters on the scene. When anything in the complexive material (in the subject-matter of the complex) is suitable for being transferred on to the figure of the doctor, that transference is carried out; it produces the next association, and announces itself by indications of a resistance—by a stoppage, for instance. We infer from this experience that the transference idea has penetrated into consciousness in front of any other possible associations *because* it satisfies the resistance.'[2]

TYPES OF TRANSFERENCE

The patient will make use of the distortion of his material through the transference as the most advantangeous and strongest weapon of the resistence; the latter can be assessed according to the intensity and persistence of the transference. But it is now clearly essential to differentiate transference into its various aspects: positive (affectionate) and negative (hostile) transferences and to assess their contribution to the treatment process; as clearly some are an ally of treatment while others are a resistant.

Positive Transference
The positive transference can be subdivided according to Freud's earlier explanation in this paper of the dispersion of libidinal cathexis. The conscious affectionate feelings are available to the patient and the physician for the establishment of a positive relationship on which to embark upon treatment and to be the vehicle of the success of treatment.

[1] (1912b) 'The Dynamics of Transference', S.E., Vol. 12, p. 103.
[2] ibid., p. 103.

'*So long as the patient's communications and ideas run on without any obstruction, the theme of transference should be left untouched.* One must wait until the transference, which is the most delicate of all procedures, has become a resistance'.[1]

This inevitably occurs because the unconscious positive feelings invariably go back to their erotic sources on the original sexual infantile objects. Therefore, when treatment seeks out the libido in the unconscious, the reactions are those of the unconscious system.

'The unconscious impulses do not want to be remembered in the way the treatment desires them to be, but endeavour to reproduce themselves in accordance with the timelessness of the unconscious and its capacity for hallucination. Just as happens in dreams, the patient regards the products of the awakening of his unconscious impulses as contemporaneous and real; he seeks to put his passions into action without taking any account of the real situation.'[2]

(This basic problem was explored further in 'Remembering, Repeating and Working Through', 1914, and eventually led to the defining of the Repetition Compulsion in *Beyond the Pleasure Principle*, 1920.)

The analyst must endeavour to prevent the impulses being put into action.

'The doctor tries to compel him to fit these emotional impulses into the nexus of the treatment and of his life-history, to submit them to intellectual consideration and to understand them in the light of their psychical value. This struggle between the doctor and the patient, between intellect and instinctual life, between understanding and seeking to act, is played out almost exclusively in the phenomena of transference. It is on that field that the victory must be won—the victory whose expression is the permanent cure of the neurosis. It cannot be disputed that controlling the phenomena of transference presents the psychoanalyst with the greatest difficulties. But it should not be forgotten that it is precisely they that do us the inestimable service of making the patient's hidden and

---

[1] (1913c) 'On Beginning the Treatment (Further Recommendations on the Technique of Psycho-Analysis, I)', S.E., Vol. 12, p. 139.
[2] (1912b) 'The Dynamics of Transference', S.E., Vol. 12, p. 108.

forgotten erotic impulses immediate and manifest. For when all is said and done, it is impossible to destroy anyone *in absentia* or *in effigie*.'[1]

Transference Love

Freud was more explicit about transference love, bringing it into his formulation of conscious and unconscious feelings. He pointed out how the patient who has shown conscious affectionate feelings towards the physician for a long time; becomes 'swallowed up in her love . . . precisely at a point of time when one is having to try to bring her to admit or remember some particularly distressing and heavily repressed piece of her life history'.[2] This state of being in love with the analyst is undoubtedly genuine, it is provoked by the analytic situation, intensified by the resistance and is less concerned about reality than in the case of normal love, but it is based on the old traits and repeats the infantile reactions in the ways characteristic of every state of being in love.

Therefore, accepting it as a transference, the analyst handles it as any other transference manifestation.

'He must take care not to steer away from the transference-love, or to repulse it or to make it distasteful to the patient; but he must just as resolutely withhold any response to it. He must keep firm hold of the transference-love, but treat it as something unreal, as a situation which has to be gone through in the treatment and traced back to its unconscious origins and which must assist in bringing all that is most deeply hidden in the patient's erotic life into her consciousness and therefore under control. The more plainly the analyst lets it be seen that he is proof against every temptation, the more readily will he be able to extract from the situation its analytic content. The patient, whose sexual repression is of course not yet removed but merely pushed into the background, will then feel safe enough to allow all her preconditions for loving, all the phantasies springing from her sexual desires, all the detailed characteristics of her state of being in love, to come to light; and from these she will herself open the way to the infantile roots of her love.'[3]

[1] (1912b) 'The Dynamics of Transference', S.E., Vol. 12, p. 108.
[2] (1915a) 'Observations on Transference Love (Further Recommendations on the Technique of Psycho-Analysis, III)', S.E., Vol. 12, p. 162.
[3] ibid., p. 166.

Negative Transference

With the negative transference, Freud considered that it also had two definite aspects.

'In the curable forms of psychoneurosis it is found side by side with the affectionate transference, often directed simultaneously towards the same person. Bleuler has coined the excellent term 'ambivalence' to describe this phenomenon. . . .

Ambivalence in the emotional trends of neurotics is the best explanation of their ability to enlist their transferences in the service of resistance.'[1]

When the hostile feelings are recognized and made conscious in the transference they too can come into the service of reality and furtherance of the treatment, the ultimate aim of which is for the patient to be free of neurotic anxiety and inhibitions in his real life by working them through and destroying them in transference manifestations.

Freud appreciated that in order to achieve this, the treatment itself must reinforce the patient's primary motive of treatment of relief of suffering, by supplying 'the amounts of energy that are needed for overcoming the resistances by making mobile the energies which lie ready for the transference; and, by giving the patient information at the right time, it shows him the paths along which he should direct those energies'.[2]

The second aspect of the negative transference was only touched upon at this period; Freud considered where it was essentially negative as in paranoics, no treatment was possible as the weapon of cure was the positive transference. He elaborated more fully later what types of illness could be cured or helped by psychoanalytic treatment in discussing the narcissistic disorders.

COMPULSION TO REPEAT

The strength of the unconscious aspects of the transference phenomenon with all the dangerous possibilities arising out of the patients' compulsion to repeat rather than to remember if 'the untamed instincts assert themselves before there is time to put the

[1] (1912b) 'The Dynamics of Transference', S.E., Vol. 12, p. 106 f.
[2] (1913c) 'On Beginning the Treatment (Further Recommendations on the Technique of Psycho-Analysis, I)', S.E., Vol. 12, p. 143.

reins of transference on them'[1] was fully recognized and explored in the penultimate paper 'Remembering, Repeating and Working Through' (1914) of this main series of discussions on technique.

Freud pointed out that the patients' compulsion to repeat is his way of remembering what is repressed and that he cannot escape from it in treatment. The transference which is clearly a repetition of this forgotten past will not be confined on to the treatment but must affect all other aspects of the patients' current situation. Repeating in analysis must imply 'conjuring up a piece of real life; and for that reason it cannot always be harmless and unobjectionable. This consideration opens up the whole problem of what is so often unavoidable—"deterioration during treatment" '.[2] The dangers may also be increased by the probability that new and deeper-lying instinctual impulses which had not been allowed to be felt may be '"repeated"'. Basically, this must happen because the patient's state of being ill is not an event of the past but a present-day force.

'This state of illness is brought, piece by piece, within the field and range of operation of the treatment, and while the patient experiences it as something real and contemporary, we have to do our therapeutic work on it, which consists in a large measure in tracing it back to the past.'[3]

TRANSFERENCE NEUROSIS

The analyst perpetually struggles to keep in the psychical sphere all the impulses which the patient would like to direct into the motor sphere. The means chosen are the conscious positive relationship the patient has established with the physician and the main instrument, the handling of the transference itself.[4]

'We render the compulsion harmless, and indeed useful, by giving it the right to assert itself in a definite field. We admit it into the transference as a playground in which it is allowed to expand in almost complete freedom and in which it is expected to display to us everything in the way of pathogenic instincts that is hidden in the patient's mind. Provided only that the patient shows compliance

[1] (1914g) 'Remembering, Repeating and Working Through (Further Recommendations on the Technique of Psycho-Analysis, II)', S.E., Vol. 12, p. 154.

[2] ibid., p. 152.   [3] ibid., p. 151 f.   [4] ibid., p. 153.

enough to respect the necessary conditions of the analysis, we regularly succeed in giving all the symptoms of the illness a new transference meaning and in replacing his ordinary neurosis by a "transference-neurosis" of which he can be cured by the therapeutic work. The transference thus creates an intermediate region between illness and real life through which the transition from the one to the other is made. The new condition has taken over all the features of the illness; but it represents an artificial illness which is at every point accessible to our intervention. It is a piece of real experience, but one which has been made possible by especially favourable conditions, and it is of a provisional nature. From the repetitive reactions which are exhibited in the transference we are led along the familiar paths to the awakening of the memories, which appear without difficulty, as it were, after the resistance has been overcome.'[1]

Freud later explained in the *Introductory Lectures on Psycho-Analysis* (1916–17) that the 'transference neurosis' develops from the fact that the illness still alive when treatment begins continues to develop. 'When, however, the treatment has obtained mastery over the patient, what happens is that the whole of his illness's new production is concentrated upon a single point—his relation to the doctor. . . . When the transference has risen to this significance, work upon the patient's memories retreats far into the background. Thereafter it is not incorrect to say that we are no longer concerned with the patient's earlier illness but with a newly created and transformed neurosis which has taken the former's place.'[2] All the symptoms now have a new sense in a relation to the transference but as the analyst is situated in the centre of the illness, he is well able to find his way about it.

'The mastering of this new, artificial neurosis coincides with getting rid of the illness which was originally brought to the treatment—with the accomplishment of our therapeutic task. A person who has become normal and free from the operation of repressed instinctual impulses in his relation to the doctor will remain so in his own life after the doctor has once more withdrawn from it.'[3]

---

[1] (1914g) 'Remembering, Repeating and Working Through (Further Recommendations on the Technique of Psycho-Analysis, II)', S.E., Vol. 12, p. 154 f.

[2] (1916–17) *Introductory Lectures on Psycho-Analysis*, S.E., Vol. 15–16, p. 444.

[3] ibid., p. 444 f.

In his penultimate major work, 'Analysis Terminable and Interminable' Freud greatly qualified this claim.

The repetitive reactions, reproductions, seen in the transference and the transference neurosis always have as their subject some portion of infantile sexual life—of the oedipus complex and its derivatives; Freud insisted they must be repeated as contemporary experience but the analyst tries to ensure that the patient retains some degree of aloofness which will enable him to recognize that what appears to be reality is in fact only a reflection of a forgotten past. This formulation is more clearly understood in terms of the structural theory.

WORKING THROUGH

The importance of working through of the material was emphasized as being the part of treatment which effects the greatest changes and which so sharply differentiates psychoanalytic treatment from any suggestion therapy. This is much changed from the earlier formulations when making material conscious was considered enough. He explained it theoretically as correlating it 'with the "abreacting" of the quotas of affect strangulated by repression'[1] and he attributed its necessity to the resistance of the unconscious. This was explored in relation to the revision of the Instinct Theories in *Beyond the Pleasure Principle*.

Thus in this group of brilliant papers on Technique written between 1908 and 1915, Freud had laid down in some detail his basic understanding of the transference. Few changes and additions were made later as all the major components had been indicated.

FURTHER DEVELOPMENTS 1915–39

The later developments consisted only of different stress placed on some particular aspects; further clarification of the resistances in the light of the structural theory; the application and limitation of the technique to all types of mental illness and, varied estimations of the success of treatment.

---

[1] (1914g) 'Remembering, Repeating and Working Through (Further Recommendations on the Technique of Psycho-Analysis, II); S.E., Vol. 12, p. 156.

CONTENTS OF TRANSFERENCE

Freud commented in his *Introductory Lectures on Psycho-Analysis* on the regressive return not only 'to the objects first cathected by the libido' but to the 'return of the sexual organization as a whole to earlier stages'.[1] Although this had been implied in his case presentations such as the Wolf Man, it did not seem to have been stated so specifically previously. He also drew attention in 'Civilization and its Discontents' to the 'quota of plain inclination to aggression'[2] which appears in the transference over and above the sadistic components of the erotic relationship.

Frustration

It had been stated in the Technique Papers that abstinence and lack of gratification of the unconscious wishes were necessary conditions for the continuation of treatment. Freud was more explicit in his 'Lines of Advance in Psychoanalytic Therapy', 1919. Frustration with his objects had made the patient ill; in order to ensure the necessary continuation of treatment, 'Cruel though it may sound, we must see to it that the patient's suffering, to a degree that is in some way or other effective, does not come to an end prematurely.'[3] One definite way is through the non-gratification of the patient's wishes in the transference. 'As far as his relations with the physician are concerned, the patient must be left with unfulfilled wishes in abundance. It is expedient to deny him precisely those satisfactions which he desires most intensely and expresses most importunately.'[4]

Hostility

The inevitable emergence of hostile feelings in the transference was pin-pointed more precisely. Transference, present in the beginning of treatment, changes into a resistance when firstly an affectionate trend has become so powerful, betrays signs of its origin in a sexual need so clearly, that it inevitably provokes an internal opposition to itself and when, secondly, it consists of hostile instead of affectionate impulses. 'The hostile feelings make their appearance as a

[1] (1916–17) *Introductory Lectures on Psycho-Analysis*, S.E., Vol. 16, p. 341.
[2] (1930a) *Civilization and its Discontents*, S.E., Vol. 21, p. 106.
[3] (1919a [1918]) 'Lines of Advance in Psycho-Analytic Therapy', S.E., Vol. 17, p. 163.
[4] ibid., p. 164.

rule later than the affectionate ones and behind them. . . . The hostile feelings are as much an indication of an emotional tie as the affectionate ones . . . and deserve to be called a "transference" since the situation in the treatment quite certainly offers no adequate grounds for their origin.'[1] It is the analyst's task constantly to show the patient his illusion that his new real life in the transference is but a reflection of the past.[2] To ensure that the patient remains accessible to the evidence, the analyst must take care that neither the love nor the hostility reach an extreme height. He stressed that he thought

'it most undesirable if the patient *acts* outside the transference instead of remembering. The ideal conduct for our purposes would be that he should behave as normally as possible outside the treatment and express his abnormal reactions only in the transference'.[3]

Children's Analysis
Freud commented on the value of children's analysis both as a therapeutic measure and as a teaching vehicle.

'We had no misgivings over applying analytic treatment to children who either exhibited unambiguous neurotic symptoms or who were on the road to an unfavourable development of character. The apprehension expressed by opponents of analysis that the child would be injured by it proved unfounded. What we gained from these undertakings was that we were able to confirm on the living subject what we had inferred (from historical documents, as it were) in the case of adults. But the gain for the children was also very satisfactory. It turned out that a child is a very favourable subject for analytic therapy; the results are thorough and lasting. The technique of treatment worked out for adults must, of course, be largely altered for children. A child is psychologically a different object from an adult. As yet he possesses no super-ego, the method of free association does not carry far with him, transference (since the real parents are still on the spot) plays a different part. The internal resistances against which we struggle in adults are replaced for the most part in children by external difficulties. If

[1] (1916–17) *Introductory Lectures on Psycho-Analysis*, S.E., Vol. 16, p. 443.
[2] (1940a [1938]) *An Outline of Psycho-Analysis*, S.E., Vol. 23, p. 179.
[3] ibid., p. 177.

the parents make themselves vehicles of the resistance, the aim of the analysis—and even the analysis itself—is often imperilled. Hence it is often necessary to combine with a child's analysis a certain amount of analytic influencing of his parents. On the other hand, the inevitable deviations of analyses of children from those of adults are diminished by the circumstance that some of our patients have retained so many infantile character-traits that the analyst (once again adapting himself to his subject) cannot avoid making use with them of certain of the techniques of child-analysis.'[1]

Resistance

Freud has stated in 'The Dynamics of Transference' that resistance seen in the transference came from two sources: (1) the patient's frustration with the real world and his partial withdrawal from it and (2) the attraction of the unconscious complexes which is greater than that of reality. However, in the *Introductory Lectures* (1916–17), chapter 'General Theory of Neuroses' it was noted that the resistances are the outcome of attitudes of the ego striving against alterations of what it had repressed. The intensity of resistance fluctuates in ratio to the intensity of the repression and the unpleasure caused by its lifting. It was clear to him that

'. . . the resistance too is derived from a repression—from the same one that we are endeavouring to resolve, or from one that took place earlier. It was set up by the anticathexis which arose in order to repress the objectionable impulse. Thus we now do the same thing that we tried to do to begin with: interpret, discover and communicate; but now we are doing it at the right place. The anticathexis or the resistance does not form part of the unconscious but of the ego, which is our collaborator, and is so even if it is not conscious'.[2]

By 1920, in *Beyond the Pleasure Principle*, he was insisting that:

'. . . we must above all get rid of the mistaken notion that what we are dealing with in our struggle against resistances is resistance on the part of the *unconscious*. The unconscious—that is to say, the "repressed"—offers no resistance whatever to the efforts of the

[1] (1933a) *New Introductory Lectures on Psycho-Analysis*, S.E., Vol. 22, p. 148.
[2] (1916–17) *Introductory Lectures on Psycho-Analysis*, S.E., Vol. 16, p. 437.

treatment. Indeed, it itself has no other endeavour than to break through the pressure weighing down on it and force its way either to consciousness or to a discharge through some real action. Resistance during treatment arises from the same higher strata and systems of the mind which originally carried out repression. But the fact that, as we know from experience, the motives of the resistances, and indeed the resistances themselves, are unconscious at first during the treatment, is a hint to us that we should correct a shortcoming in our terminology. We shall avoid a lack of clarity if we make our contrast not between the conscious and the unconscious but between the coherent *ego* and the *repressed*'.[1]

The resistance of the conscious and unconscious ego operates under the domination of the pleasure principle, seeking to avoid the unpleasure the liberation of the repressed would cause. Yet in the transference, patients repeat all of the unwanted situations of childhood and all the painful emotions and this compulsion to repeat must be ascribed to the unconscious repressed, the id. Thus, the transference reflects fully both the untamed instinctual and the defensive ego aspects.

'The phenomena of transference are obviously exploited by the resistance which the ego maintains in its pertinacious insistance upon repression; the compulsion to repeat, which the treatment tries to bring into its service is, as it were, drawn over by the ego to *its* side (clinging as the ego does to the pleasure principle).'[2]

The Addendum in *Inhibitions, Symptoms and Anxiety* 1926 does, however, embrace both aspects of resistance discussed in 'The Dynamics of Transference' as well as noting the super-ego aspect recognized by Freud in *The Ego and the Id*.

'This action undertaken to protect repression is observable in analytic treatment as *resistance*. Resistance presupposes the existance of what I have called *anticathexis*.'[3]

It proceeds from the ego which clings to its anti-cathexis to avoid unpleasure. When, however, through the work of the analysis the

[1] (1920g) *Beyond the Pleasure Principle*, S.E., Vol. 18, p. 19.
[2] ibid., p. 23.
[3] (1926d) *Inhibitions, Symptoms and Anxiety*, S.E., Vol. 20, p. 157.

ego relinquishes its resistances, it still has difficulty in undoing the repressions because of the resistance of the unconscious, the id, i.e. of 'the attraction exerted by the unconscious prototypes upon the repressed instinctual process'.[1] A further resistance which opposes every move towards success in the analysis comes from the super-ego and originates from the sense of guilt or need for punishment. In the transference, the analyst can be seen as the super-ego in the form of its original objects.

Freud also subdivides the ego's resistance into three kinds all of which are seen in treatment—(1) against lifting the repression; (2) against the loss of the secondary gain from the illness; and (3) the transference resistance which also aims against the lifting of the repressed but 'which has different and much clearer effects in analysis, since it succeeds in establishing a relation to the analytic situation or the analyst himself and thus re-animating a repression which should only have been recollected'.[2]

Freud pointed out in 'Analysis Terminable and Interminable' that the patient's habitual mode of defences was also transferred; the ego refuses to allow these defences to be tampered with and thus the positive transference is replaced by a negative one which may completely annul the analytic situation. There is the resistance against the uncovering of resistances [defences] and the analysis as a whole. This may prove insuperable as the analysis can only draw upon definite and limited amounts of energy which have to be measured against the hostile forces. However, the overcoming of the resistances 'is worth while . . . for it brings about the advantageous alteration of the ego which will be maintained independently of the outcome of the transference and will hold good in life'.[3] But Freud stressed the many factors working against success and the difficulties inherent in the analytic treatment situation.

Use in Narcissistic Disorder

Freud had clearly understood that 'the capacity for transference, of which we make use for therapeutic purposes in these affections [transference neuroses—anxiety hysteria, conversion hysteria and obsessional neurosis], presupposes an unimpaired object cathexis'.[4]

[1] (1926d) *Inhibitions, Symptoms and Anxiety*, S.E., Vol. 20, p. 159.
[2] ibid., p. 160.
[3] (1940a [1938]) *An Outline of Psycho-Analysis*, S.E., Vol. 23, p. 179.
[4] (1915e) 'The Unconscious', S.E., Vol. 14, p. 196.

The object cathexis in general is retained with great energy even when the libido is withdrawn from the real object on to a phantasied and then repressed object. It has to be assumed that the object cathexis persists in the system *Ucs* which contains the 'thing-cathexes of the objects, the first and true object-cathexes'.[1] The repression denies to this rejected thing-presentation translation into words; hypercathexis is stopped and entry into the *Pcs* system is prevented. This may be linked with the peculiar indifference in regard to the object evident in the transferences arising in analysis, which develop inevitably, irrespective of the persons who are their objects.[2] 'A capacity for directing object-cathexis on to people must of course be attributed to every normal person. The tendency to transference of the neurotics . . . is only an extraordinary increase of this universal characteristic.'[3]

However, in certain disorders object cathexis is not available; no transference is manifest and for that reason the diseases are not accessible to a complete cure by psychoanalytic methods. Freud considered that in schizophrenia

'. . . we have been driven to the assumption that after the process of repression the libido, that has been withdrawn does not seek a new object, but retreats into the ego; that is to say, that here the object-cathexes are given up and a primitive objectless condition of narcissism is re-established. The incapacity of these patients for transference (so far as the pathological process extends), their consequent inaccessibility to therapeutic efforts, their characteristic repudiation of the external world, the appearance of signs of a hypercathexis of their own ego, the final outcome in complete apathy—all these clinical features seem to agree excellently with the assumption that their object-cathexes have been given up.'[4]

Karl Abraham had observed in 1908 how in megalomania and dementia praecox, the libidinal cathexis of objects was lacking and the libido had turned back upon the ego. The libido that is liberated from the real object by frustration does not remain attached to fantasy objects but withdraws on to the ego. Freud classified this

[1] (1915e) 'The Unconscious', S.E., Vol. 14, p. 201.
[2] (1923b) *The Ego and the Id*, S.E., Vol. 19, p. 45.
[3] (1916–17) *Introductory Lectures on Psycho-Analysis*, S.E., Vol. 16, p. 446.
[4] (1915e) 'The Unconscious', S.E., Vol. 14, p. 196 f.

further in his *Introductory Lectures*. On the basis of his clinical impressions, he maintained that in the narcissistic neuroses (dementia praecox, paranoia, melancholia) the patients' object cathexis must have been given up and their object libido transformed into ego libido. Therefore, they have no capacity for transference or only small residues; they reject the doctor, not with hostility but with indifference. For that reason they cannot be influenced by him.[1] Their therapeutic inaccessibility has not prevented analysis from making the most fruitful beginning in the deeper study of these illnesses which are counted among the psychoses, and as a result of these investigations, Freud noted:

'Transference is often not so completely absent but that it can be used to a certain extent; and analysis has achieved undoubted success with cyclical depressions, light paranoia modifications and partial schizophrenia.'[2]

Different Usages
Freud used the word transference to describe a rather different but not unrelated psychological process in *Studies on Hysteria*, and in Chapters IV and VII of *The Interpretation of Dreams*. He noted how 'an unconscious idea as such is quite incapable of entering the preconscious and that it can only exercise any effect there by establishing a connection with an idea which already belongs to the preconscious, by transferring its intensity on to it and by getting itself covered by it. The preconscious idea, which thus acquires an undeserved degree of intensity, may either be left unaltered by the transference, or it may have a modification forced upon it, derived from the content of the idea which effects the transference'.[3]

This same need of transference on the part of the repressed ideas to obtain entry into the preconscious is probably also the explanation for the significant part played by the day's residues in dream formation. These recent, indifferent elements of the day's residues have the least to fear from the censorship and they, therefore, offer the unconscious the indispensable necessary point of attachment for a transference. 'A train of thought comes into being in the preconscious which is without a preconscious cathexis

[1] (1916–17) *Introductory Lectures on Psycho-Analysis*, S.E., Vol. 16, p. 447.
[2] (1925a [1924]) *An Autobiographical Study*, S.E., Vol. 20, p. 60.
[3] (1900a) *The Interpretation of Dreams*, S.E., Vol. 5, p. 562 f.

but has received a cathexis from an unconscious wish,'[1] derived from infancy and in a state of repression.

'The memories on the basis of which the unconscious wish brings about the release of affect were never accessible to the *Pcs*, and consequently the release of the affect attaching to those memories cannot be inhibited either. It is for the very reason of this generation of affect that these ideas are now inaccessible even by way of the preconscious thoughts on to which they have transferred their wishful force. On the contrary, the unpleasure principle takes control and causes the *Pcs* to turn away from the transference thoughts. They are left to themselves—"repressed"—and thus it is that the presence of a store of infantile memories, which has from the first been held back from the *Pcs*, becomes a *sine qua non* of repression.'[2]

It is very possible to see some connection between this process, and transference as Freud was to use it as a re-experiencing on a contemporary person unconscious infantile wishes.

There is also some very slight connection between the usual theoretical understanding of transference and Freud's speculations on thought-transference in 'Dreams and Occultism' 1932. He noted that it was claimed that mental processes in one person, e.g. emotional states and ideas—could be transferred to another person through empty space without the familiar methods of communication. He thought this did exist in the animal kingdom and it could possibly by the original archaic method of communication between individuals; he assumed if it were a real process it might eventually be seen in such instances as cases of simultaneous analysis. Certainly at the present level of knowledge it has little known significance.

Handling the Transference
Freud pointed out the hard task involved in dealing with the transference; the analyst 'becomes convinced that the only really serious [technical] difficulties he has to meet lie in the management of the transference'.[3] He was convinced that the most satisfactory method

---

[1] (1900a) *The Interpretation of Dreams*, S.E., Vol. 5, p. 595 f.
[2] ibid., p. 604.
[3] (1915a) 'Observations on Transference-Love (Further Recommendations on the Technique of Psycho-Analysis, III)', S.E., Vol. 12, p. 159.

of learning it was through the experience of a personal analysis, but he gave some hints on technique.

The first aim of treatment must be to attach the patient to the treatment and to the person of the doctor.

'To ensure this, nothing need be done but to give him time. If one exhibits a serious interest in him, carefully clears away the resistances that crop up at the beginning and avoids making certain mistakes, he will of himself form such an attachment and link the doctor up with one of the imagos of the people by whom he was accustomed to be treated with affection.'[1]

This is essential in that the personal influence of the doctor is the most powerful dynamic weapon in the treatment.

Some kind of relationship to the analyst is established from the beginning, usually one transferred from an infantile one. For a while it is the most powerful motive for the advance of treatment; the analyst need not bother about it so long as it operates for the joint work of the analysis. However,

'Lengthy preliminary discussions before the beginning of the analytic treatment, previous treatment by another method and also previous acquaintance between the doctor and the patient who is to be analysed, have special disadvantageous consequences for which one must be prepared. They result in the patient's meeting the doctor with a transference attitude which is already established and which the doctor must first slowly uncover instead of having the opportunity to observe the growth and development of the transference from the outset.'[2]

The use of the couch was seen by Freud as of great importance 'to prevent the transference from mingling with the patient's associations imperceptibly, to isolate the transference and to allow it to come forward in due course sharply defined as a resistance'.[3] He advised analysts to be aware of the patient's attempts to offset its use by remarks before and after they have got up—these may well be a partition the patient tries to erect—a transference-resis-

---

[1] (1913c) 'On Beginning the Treatment (Further Recommendations on the ↴ Technique of Psycho-Analysis, I)', S.E., Vol. 12, p. 139.
[2] ibid., p. 125.   [3] ibid., p. 134.

tance. He advised that consideration of charging fees must also be seen in the context of the transference.

'The absence of the regulating effect offered by the payment of a fee to the doctor makes itself very painfully felt; the whole relationship is removed from the real world, and the patient is deprived of a strong motive for endeavouring to bring the treatment to an end.'[1]

Until an effective transference, a proper rapport, has been made with the patient, initiation into the postulates and technical procedures of analysis should be postponed. Then it becomes the analyst's

'. . . task to assist the patient in getting to know, and afterwards in overcoming, the resistances which emerged in him during treatment and of which, to begin with, he himself was unaware. And it was found at the same time that the essential part of the process of cure lay in the overcoming of these resistances and that unless this was achieved no permanent mental change could be brought about in the patient'.[2]

The first resistance emerges as the patient insists he has nothing to say:

'. . . he can be driven by our insistence to acknowledge that he has nevertheless overlooked certain thoughts which were occupying his mind. He had thought of the treatment itself, though nothing definite about it, or he had been occupied with the picture of the room in which he was, or he could not help thinking of the objects in the consulting room and of the fact that he was lying here on a sofa—all of which he has replaced by the word "nothing". These indications are intelligible enough: everything connected with the present situation represents a transference to the doctor, which proves suitable to serve as a first resistance. We are thus obliged to begin by uncovering this transference; and a path from it will give rapid access to the patient's pathogenic material.'[3]

[1] ibid., p. 132.
[2] (1923a [1922]) 'Two Encyclopaedia Articles, S.E., Vol. 18, p. 249.
[3] (1913c) 'On Beginning the Treatment (Further Recommendations on the Technique of Psycho-Analysis, I)', S.E., Vol. 12, p. 138.

This first resistance may possess considerable significance and betray the complex which governs the neurosis, e.g. men with over-strong repressed homosexuality probably will withhold their ideas at the outset of treatment because of the special dangers of the situation in exciting their unconscious wishes.

Freud suggested ways of approaching the patient to help him recognize his resistances. He thought it valuable to enlist the

'. . . help of his intelligence, to which we give support by our interpretation. There is no doubt that it is easier for the patient's intelligence to recognize the resistance and to find the translation corresponding to what is repressed if we have previously given him the appropriate anticipatory ideas.'[1]

But he noted this intelligence is always in danger of losing its value as a result of the clouding of judgement that arises from the resistances. The main source of strength which the analyst can give to the patient is in the transference and he only can make use of his acquired knowledge so far as he is induced to do so by trans-ference.

As the analysis proceeds, by searching for the repression through uncovering the resistances, the transference increasingly changes.

The growing intensity of the affectionate or hostile trends transferred on to the analyst must be handled with the greatest skill. The 'transference neurosis' is the point in the treatment when the gravest mistakes can be made or the greatest successes be registered.

'It would be folly to attempt to evade the difficulties by suppressing or neglecting the transference; whatever else had been done in the treatment, it would not deserve the name of an analysis. To send the patient away as soon as the inconveniences of his trans-ference-neurosis make their appearance would be no more sensible, and would moreover be cowardly. It would be as though one had conjured up spirits and run away from them as soon as they appeared.'[2]

It should be the physician's endeavour to keep this transference neurosis within the narrowest limits: to force as much as possible

[1] (1916–17) *Introductory Lectures on Psycho-Analysis*, S.E., Vol. 16, p. 437.
[2] (1926e) *The Question of Lay Analysis*, S.E., Vol. 20, p. 227.

into the channel of memory and to allow as little as possible to emerge as acting, repetition. But it would be clearly senseless and technically wrong to urge the patient to repress what had just been recovered telling her to suppress, renounce or sublimate instincts at the moment when in the transference she acknowledged her erotic wishes.

It would be as senseless to prepare 'patients for the emergence of the erotic transference or even urge them to "go ahead and fall in love with the doctor so that the treatment may make progress"'.[1] This would, if anything at all were achieved, destroy the vital spontaneity of the transference.

The analyst's line of action must be to use the transference which he has helped to promote to cure the neurosis. Plainly he must not derive any personal advantage from it and equally plainly,

'It is out of question for us to yield to the patient's demands deriving from the transference; it would be absurd for us to reject them in an unfriendly, still more in an indignant, manner. We overcome the transference by pointing out to the patient that his feelings do not arise from the present situation and do not apply to the person of the doctor, but that they are repeating something that happened to him earlier. In this way we oblige him to transform his repetition into a memory. But that means the transference, which, whether affectionate or hostile, seemed in every case to constitute the greatest threat to the treatment, becomes its best tool, by whose help the most secret compartments of mental life can be opened.'[2]

The analytic treatment itself must intensify the patients' feelings of frustration which had been a cause of his falling ill. The physician must ensure that this instinctual force behind the frustration continues to impel the patient towards recovery, otherwise relief of symptoms might cause a premature termination of the treatment. But,

'. . . danger threatens from two directions. On the one hand, when the illness has been broken down by the analysis, the patient makes the most assiduous efforts to create for himself in place of his

[1] (1915a) 'Observations on Transference-Love (Further Recommendations on the Technique of Psycho-Analysis, III)', S.E., Vol. 12, p. 161.
[2] (1916–17) *Introductory Lectures on Psycho-Analysis*, S.E., Vol. 16, p. 443 f.

symptoms new substitutive satisfactions, which now lack the feature of suffering.'

'He makes use of the enormous capacity for displacement possessed by the now partly liberated libido, in order to cathect with libido and promote to the position of substitutive satisfactions the most diverse kinds of activities, preferences and habits, not excluding some that have been his already. He continually finds new distractions of this kind, into which the energy necessary to carrying on the treatment escapes, and he knows how to keep them secret for a time. It is the analyst's task to detect these divergent paths and to require him every time to abandon them.'[1]

The physician must energetically oppose any premature substitutive satisfactions proposed in real life. He must get the promise of the patient's not to enter into any major changes such as divorce without working it through in treatment. However, the patient may look for his substitutive satisfactions in the transference:

'. . . and he may even strive to compensate himself by this means for all the other privations laid upon him. Some concessions must of course be made to him, greater or less, according to the nature of the case and the patient's individuality. But it is not good to let them become too great. Any analyst who out of the fullness of his heart, perhaps, and his readiness to help, extends to the patient all that one human being may hope to receive from another, commits the same economic error as that of which our non-analytic institutions for nervous patients are guilty. Their one aim is to make everything as pleasant as possible for the patient, so that he may feel well there and be glad to take refuge there again from the trials of life. In so doing they make no attempt to give him more strength for facing life and more capacity for carrying out his actual tasks in it. In analytic treatment all such spoiling must be avoided'.[2]

The great dangers then to be guarded against is the patients compulsion to repeat instead of remembering, both outside and inside treatment.

[1] (1919a [1918]) 'Lines of Advance in Psycho-Analytic Therapy', S.E., Vol. 17, p. 163.
[2] ibid., p. 164.

'Remembering, as it was induced in hypnosis, could not but give the impression of an experiment carried out in the laboratory. Repeating, as it is induced in analytic treatment according to the newer technique, on the other hand, implies conjuring up a piece of real life; and for that reason it cannot always be harmless and un-objectionable.'[1]

'It is the analyst's task constantly to tear the patient out of his menacing illusion and to show him again that what he takes to be new real life is a reflection of the past. And lest he should fall into a state in which he is inaccessible to all evidence, the analyst takes care that neither the love nor the hostility reach an extreme height. This is effected by preparing him in good time for these possibilities and by not overlooking the first signs of them. Careful handling of the transference on these lines is as a rule richly rewarded. If we succeed, as we usually can, in enlightening the patient on the true nature of the phenomena of transference, we shall have struck a powerful weapon out of the hand of his resistance and shall have converted dangers into gains. For a patient never forgets again what he has experienced in the form of transference; it carries a greater force of conviction than anything he can acquire in other ways.'[2]

Freud stressed the vital need to work through and dissolve the transferences; making resistances and repressions known to the patient was not enough. The arduous but most rewarding part of the analyst's work was the slow convincing of the patient that in his transference-attitude he is re-experiencing emotional relations which had their origin in his earliest object-attachments during the repressed period of his childhood.

The transference is used 'to induce the patient to perform a piece of psychical work—the overcoming of his transference-resistances—which involves a permanent alteration in his mental economy. Any treatment which does not aim at this cannot be called psychoanalysis—nevertheless the handling of the transference remains the most difficult as well as the most important part of the technique of analysis'.[3]

---

[1] (1914g) 'Remembering, Repeating and Working Through (Further Recommendations on the Technique of Psycho-Analysis, II)', S.E., Vol. 12, p. 152.
[2] (1940a) *An Outline of Psycho-Analysis*, S.E., Vol. 23, p. 177.
[3] (1925a [1924]) *An Autobiographical Study*, S.E., Vol. 20, p. 43.

SUMMARY

Its importance therapeutically

Freud recognized that in the hands of the analyst transference becomes the most powerful therapeutic instrument whose value cannot be overestimated. Transference in treatment is a way of uncovering unconscious repressions, of repeating affects belonging to the repressed material of re-living and re-experiencing in the present the forgotten infantile conflicts. He constantly insisted that conviction was obtained through this re-activation in the transference which enabled the patient to become aware of and accept the reality of his unconscious infantile wishes. Unless the conflicts were lived through in relation to the analyst they could not be cured. But the intensity of the transference must have been utilized for the overcoming of the resistances for only then has being ill become impossible, even when the transference has once more been dissolved.[1] The positive transference, too, is the chief way in which the patient acquires strength to fight his way through this conflict with the resistances.

The dangers inherent in this irreplaceable tool arose chiefly from its use for resistance and the greatest skill was needed to handle it.

Its importance theoretically

'The theory of psychoanalysis is an attempt to account for two striking and unexpected facts of observation which emerge whenever an attempt is made to trace the symptoms of a neurotic back to their sources in his past life: the facts of transference and of resistance.'[2] 'The analytic theory of the neuroses is based on three corner stones: the recognition of (1) *"repression"*, of (2) the importance of the sexual instinct and of (3) *"transference"*.'[3]

'The transference possesses this extraordinary, and for the treatment, positively central, importance in hysteria, anxiety hysteria and obsessional neurosis which are for that reason rightly classed together as "transference neuroses". No one who has taken in a full impression of the fact of transference from his analytic

[1] (1914g) 'Remembering, Repeating and Working Through Further Recommendations on the Technique of Psycho-Analysis', S.E., Vol. 12, pl 149f.; cf. also (1940a [1938]) *An Outline of Psycho-Analysis*, S.E., Vol. 23, p. 177.

[2] (1914d) 'On the History of the Psycho-Analytic Movement', S.E., Vol. 14, p. 16.

[3] (1926f) 'Psycho-Analysis', S.E., Vol. 20, p. 267.

work will any longer doubt the nature of the suppressed impulses that obtain expression in the symptoms of these neuroses, and will call for no more powerful evidence of their libidinal character. It may be said that our conviction of the significance of symptoms as substitutive satisfactions of the libido only received its final confirmation after the enlistment of the transference.'[1]

Freud considered that the emergence of the transference in its crudely sexual form whether affectionate or hostile in every treatment of a neurosis remained the decisive one proving that the source of the driving forces of the neurosis lies in sexual life.

Its limitations

'Compared with other psychotherapeutic procedures, psychoanalysis is beyond any doubt the most powerful. . . . But it has its very appreciable limits.

'. . . The radical inaccessibility of the psychoses to analytic treatment should, in view of their close relationship to the neuroses, restrict out pretentions in regard to the latter. The therapeutic effectiveness of psycho-Analysis remains cramped by a number of weighty and scarcely assailable factors.'[2]

Freud considered that the attempts to overcome these difficulties through trying to perfect analysis particularly the transference was not feasible.

He also considered that analysis might not be a prophylactic treatment against instinctual conflicts which were not of the past. Patients cannot themselves bring all their conflicts into the transference; nor is the analyst able to call all their possible instinctual conflicts from the transference situation. Treatment is limited according to what can be made available.

There are cases in which the analyst cannot master the unleashed transference and the analysis has to be broken off; e.g. one class of women with whom one attempts unsuccessfully to preserve the erotic transference without satisfying it. Freud saw the value of recognizing these limitations as the way to avoid wasted efforts to force the treatment into an impossibly all-powerful process.

[1] (1916–17) *Introductory Lectures on Psycho-Analysis*, S.E., Vol. 16, p. 445.
[2] (1933a) *New Introductory Lectures on Psycho–Analysis*, S.E., Vol. 22, p. 153 f.

COUNTER-TRANSFERENCE

Freud did not enter into a full discussion of counter-transference in any of his writings. His comments were mainly confined to his paper on 'Recommendations to Physicians Practising Psycho-Analysis', 1912, and one of his last works, 'Analysis Terminable and Interminable', 1937. Strachey considered that this paucity might be the result of Freud's reluctance to make available to patients detailed knowledge of his technique.

The concept was first formulated in 1910 in 'The Future Prospects of Psychoanalytic Therapy'. Ernest Jones noted that Ferenczi, who had written a paper on technique in 1909, suggested to Freud that he should include in it the theme of the fundamental mental state of the analyst. Freud noted:

'We have become aware of the "counter-transference", which arises in him as a result of the patient's influence on his unconscious feelings, and we are almost inclined to insist that he shall recognize this counter-transference in himself and overcome it. Now that a considerable number of people are practising psychoanalysis and exchanging their observations with one another, we have noticed that no psychoanalyst goes further than his own complexes and internal resistances permit; and we consequently require that he shall begin his activity with a self-analysis and continually carry it deeper while he is making his observations on his patients. Anyone who fails to produce results in a self-analysis of this kind may at once give up any idea of being able to treat patients by analysis.'[1]

However, it became increasingly clear to Freud that self-analysis for would-be analysts was often inadequate and insufficient. In his 'Recommendations to Physicians Practising Psycho-Analysis' he put forward the idea of training analysis, while in 'Analysis Terminable and Interminable', he recommended that analysts should resume their analysis approximately every five years.

Freud indicated in 'Recommendations to Physicians Practising

[1] (1910d) 'The Future Prospects of Psycho-Analytic Therapy', S.E., Vol. 11, p. 144 f.

Psycho-Analysis', what he saw as the analyst's personal share in the treatment process:

'. . . he must turn his own unconscious like a receptive organ towards the transmitting unconscious of the patient. He must adjust himself to the patient as a telephone receiver is adjusted to the transmitting microphone. Just as the receiver converts back into sound-waves the electric oscillations in the telephone line which were set up by sound waves, so the doctor's unconscious is able, from the derivatives of the unconscious which are communicated to him, to reconstruct that unconscious, which has determined the patient's free associations'.[1]

In order to do this, the analyst must fulfil one psychological condition to a high degree:

'. . . if the doctor is to be in a position to use his unconscious in this way as an instrument in the analysis . . . he may not tolerate any resistances in himself which hold back from his consciousness what has been perceived by his unconscious; otherwise he would introduce into the analysis a new species of selection and distortion which would be far more detrimental than that resulting from concentration of conscious attention. It is not enough for this that he himself should be an approximately normal person. It may be insisted, rather, that he should have undergone a psychoanalytic purification and have become aware of those complexes of his own which would be apt to interfere with his grasp of what the patient tells him. There can be no reasonable doubt about the disqualifying effect of such defects in the doctor; every unresolved repression in him constitutes what has been aptly described by Stekel as a "blind spot" in his analytic perception'.[2]

Such dangers as mistakes in the process of remembering which occur only at times when one is disturbed by some personal consideration, i.e. when one had fallen seriously below the standard of the ideal analyst, would then be avoided.

'The correct behaviour for an analyst lies in swinging over according to need from the one mental attitude to the other, in avoiding

---

[1] (1912e) 'Recommendations to Physicians Practising Psycho-Analysis', S.E., Vol. 12, p. 115 f.
[2] ibid., p. 116.

speculation or brooding over cases while they are in analysis, and in submitting the material obtained to a synthetic process of thought only after the analysis is concluded.'[1]

'I cannot advise my colleagues too urgently to model themselves during psychoanalytic treatment on the surgeon, who puts aside all his feelings, even his human sympathy, and concentrates his mental forces on the single aim of performing the operation as skilfully as possible. . . . The justification for requiring this emotional coldness in the analyst is that it creates the most advantageous conditions for both parties: for the doctor a desirable protection for his own emotional life and for the patient the largest amount of help that we can give him today.'[2]

This is particularly essential when the patient has fallen in love with the analyst in the transference.

'For the doctor the phenomenon signifies a valuable piece of enlightenment and a useful warning against any tendency to a counter-transference which may be present in his own mind. He must recognize that the patient's falling in love is induced by the analytic situation and is not to be attributed to the charms of his own person; so that he has no grounds whatever for being proud of such a "conquest", as it would be called outside analysis. And it is always well to be reminded of this.'[3]

'. . . the experiment of letting oneself go a little way in tender feelings for the patient is not altogether without danger. Our control over ourselves is not so complete that we may not suddenly one day go further than we had intended. In my opinion, therefore, we ought not to give up the neutrality towards the patient, which we have acquired through keeping the counter-transference in check'.[4]

The analyst has a constant battle to wage in his own mind against the forces which seek to drag him down from the analytic

[1] (1912e) 'Recommendations to Physicians Practising Psycho-Analysis', S.E., Vol. 12, p. 114.

[2] ibid., p. 115.

[3] (1915a) 'Observations on Transference Love (Further Recommendations on the Technique of Psycho-Analysis, III)', S.E., Vol. 12, p. 160 f.

[4] ibid., p. 164.

level. It is, therefore, essential that he is as aware as possible of these forces. He knows

'. . . that he is working with highly explosive forces and that he needs to proceed with as much caution and conscientiousness as a chemist. But when have chemists ever been forbidden, because of the danger, from handling explosive substances, which are indispensable, on account of their effects ? . . . Psychoanalysis . . . is . . . not afraid to handle the most dangerous mental impulses and to obtain mastery over them for the benefit of the patient.'[1]

Freud warned analysts that to bring their own conflicts to the knowledge of the patients by giving them intimate information about their own lives was a hindrance to analytic treatment.

'Experience does not speak in favour of an affective technique of this kind. Nor is it hard to see that it involves a departure from psychoanalytic principles and verges upon treatment by suggestion. It may induce the patient to bring forward sooner and with less difficulty things he already knows but would otherwise have kept back for a time through conventional resistances. But this technique achieves nothing towards the uncovering of what is unconscious to the patient. It makes him even more incapable of overcoming his deeper resistances, and in severer cases it invariably fails by encouraging the patient to be insatiable: he would like to reverse the situation, and finds the analysis of the doctor more interesting than his own. The resolution of the transference, too—one of the main tasks of the treatment—is made more difficult by an intimate attitude on the doctor's part, so that any gain there may be at the beginning is more than outweighed at the end. I have no hesitation, therefore, in condemning this kind of technique as incorrect. The doctor should be opaque to his patients and, like a mirror, should show them nothing but what is shown to him.'[2]

By 1912, Freud advocated training analysis to help to achieve this aim; he thought the analysing of one's own dreams was frequently impossible without outside help and that everyone

---

[1] ibid., p. 170 f.
[2] (1912e) 'Recommendations to Physicians Practising Psycho-Analysis', S.E., Vol. 12, p. 118.

wishing to carry out analyses on others should undergo an analysis by someone with expert knowledge.

'Anyone who takes up the work seriously should choose this course, which offers more than one advantage; the sacrifice involved in laying oneself open to another person without being driven to it by illness is amply rewarded. Not only is one's aim of learning to know what is hidden in one's own mind far more rapidly attained and with less expense of affect, but impressions and convictions will be gained in relation to oneself which will be sought in vain from studying books and attending lectures.'[1]

This training analysis must, however, be constantly supplemented by the analyst's continued examination of his own personality and acceptance that within himself as well as in the external world, he must always expect to find something new. The danger of the failure of the analyst to continue this self-analysis lies in his counter-transference projection of some of the peculiarities of his own personality, which he has dimly perceived, on to his patients, and into 'the field of science, as a theory having universal validity'.[2]

Strachey suggests that Freud appreciated that he himself may have found women's psychology more enigmatic than men's out of some peculiarity in his transference-relation with women. 'Perhaps I gained this impression [of the difficulty of grasping the first attachment to the mother] because the women who were in analysis with me were able to cling to the very attachment to the father in which they had taken refuge from the early phase that was in question. . . . Nor have I succeeded in seeing my way through any case completely.'[3]

In 'Analysis Terminable and Interminable' Freud reiterated that the analyst from whom is demanded 'much skill, patience, calm and self-abnegation'[4] must be able to act as a model for his patient in certain analytic situations.

'Ferenczi makes the important point that success [in treatment] depends very largely on the analyst's having learnt sufficiently

[1] (1912e) 'Recommendations to Physicians Practising Psycho-Analysis', S.E., Vol. 12, p. 117.
[2] ibid., p. 117.
[3] (1931b) 'Female Sexuality', S.E., Vol. 21, p. 226 f.
[4] (1926e) The Question of Lay Analysis, S.E., Vol. 20, p. 227.

from his own "errors and mistakes" and having got the better of the "weak points in his own personality".[1]

Freud agreed with the many critics of analysis that the personality of some analysts had not always come up to the standard of psychical normality to which they wish to educate their patients. They are people who have learned to practise a particular art but they are also human beings. But the

'. . . special conditions of analytic work do actually cause the analyst's own defects to interfere with his making a correct assessment of the state of things in his patient and reacting to them in a useful way. It is therefore reasonable to expect of an analyst, as part of his qualifications, a considerable degree of mental normality and correctness'.[2]

Freud warned that:

'It would not be surprising if the effect of a constant preoccupation with all the repressed material which struggles for freedom in the human mind were to stir up in the analyst as well all the instinctual demands which he is otherwise able to keep under suppression. These, too, are "dangers of analysis", though they threaten, not the passive but the active partner in any analytic situation; and we ought not to neglect to meet them.'[3]

The way to guard against these dangers was in an analysis of himself with an expert. Freud considered that 'in self-analysis the danger of incompleteness is particularly great. One is too satisfied with a part explanation behind which resistance may easily be keeping back something that is more important perhaps'.[4] Therefore, a training analysis should be undergone and it will have accomplished its purpose if it gives the learner a firm conviction of the existence of the unconscious, it if enables him, when repressed material emerges, to perceive in himself things which would otherwise be incredible to him, and if it shows him a first sample of the technique which has proved to be the only effective one in analytic work. This alone would not suffice for his instruction; but we

[1] (1937c) 'Analysis Terminable and Interminable', S.E., Vol. 23, p. 247.
[2] ibid., p. 247 f.
[3] ibid., p. 249.
[4] (1935b) 'The Subtleties of a Faulty Action', S.E., Vol. 22, p. 234.

reckon on the stimuli that he has received in his own analysis not ceasing when it ends and on the processes of remodelling the ego continuing spontaneously in the analysed subject and making use of all subsequent experiences in this newly acquired sense. This does in fact happen, and in so far as it happens it makes the analysed subject qualified to be an analyst himself.[1]

There is, however, always the danger that analysts learn to make use of defensive mechanisms which allow them to divert the implications and demands of analysis from themselves (probably by directing them on to other people), so that they themselves remain as they are and are able to withdraw from the critical and corrective influence of analysis. This coupled with the dangers inherent in the handling of the material itself, should be dealt with by 'every analyst periodically—at intervals of five years or so—submit himself to analysis once more, without feeling ashamed of taking this step. This would mean, then, that not only the therapeutic analysis of patients but his own analysis would change from a terminable into an interminable task'.[2]

[1] (1937e) 'Analysis Terminable and Interminable', S.E., Vol. 23, p. 248.
[2] ibid., p. 249.

MASTURBATION

Freud's interest in the subject of masturbation can be traced in his written communications as far back as 1892. At this time he was concerned with such problems as the etiology of neurasthenia, the separation of a special syndrome, that is 'anxiety neurosis' from neurasthenia, etc.

In Draft A[1] ('Extracts from the Fliess Papers') he wondered if masturbation could create a special disposition to later sexual traumas, asking for example if coitus reservatus could act as a noxa in the absence of a previous history of masturbation. He further posed the question as to the existence of an 'innate neurasthenia' based on an innate sexual weakness versus the possibility of its being acquired from nurses or from being masturbated by some one else. He concluded that *neurasthenia in males* was acquired at puberty through sexual exhaustion due to masturbation and that the illness usually made itself manifest in the patient's twenties. He thought too, at this point, that excessive masturbation affected a man's potency.[2] Masturbation was thus the first noxa, with a second noxa *onanismus conjugalis* (coitus interruptus) affecting men at a later age especially if they have been disposed to neurasthenia through early masturbation.[3] He added, that perhaps the neurasthenic's mind is unable to tolerate physical tension, being accustomed as they are to frequent and complete absence of tension through repeated masturbation.[4]

It is interesting to find in Draft G a statement that seems to suggest that melancholia could be considered as a sort of intensification of neurasthenia through excessive masturbation.[5]

Some time later, in December 1897, in a letter to Fliess (Letter 79) Freud established an important parallel between other forms of addiction and masturbation. He wrote: 'It has dawned on me that masturbation is the one major habit, the "primal addiction" and that it is only as a substitute and replacement for it that the other addictions—for alcohol, morphine, tobacco, etc.—come into

---

[1] (1950 [1892–1899]) 'Extracts from the Fliess Papers', S.E., Vol. I, p. 177.
[2] ibid., p. 180.   [3] ibid., p. 181.
[4] ibid., p. 194.   [5] ibid., p. 200.

existence.' He added that this addiction (masturbation) played a large role in hysteria.[1]

In 'The Neuro-Psychoses of Defence' (1894) he referred to a very disturbed girl, suffering from obsessional self-reproaches, where he found that her enormous sense of guilt was related to excessive masturbation, practised for years and always accompanied by violent but ineffective self-reproaches.[2] In 'Obsessions and Phobias' (1895) he gave some more examples of the same type.[3]

In *Studies on Hysteria* (1895) and while explaining how conflicts between irreconcilable ideas can have pathogenic effects, he mentioned that frequently such ideas are connected with the individual's sexual life such as 'masturbation in an adolescent with moral sensibilities'.[4]

In 1895 he remarked on how neurasthenia develops when intercourse is replaced by masturbation.[5] Later on, in this paper, he explained the tendency to anxiety in masturbators who have developed neurasthenia, as due to the fact that they easily develop an 'abstinence' syndrome, after being accustomed to discharge (through excessive masturbation) even the smallest quantities of somatic excitation.[6] Two pages later, struggling with the explanation of what he called 'mixed neurosis' (neurasthenia and anxiety neurosis in different proportions) he thought that a man who has become neurasthenic through masturbation can add to it an anxiety neurosis, if for example, he becomes engaged and is frequently sexually excited by his fiancée without an appropriate resolution of that excitement through sexual intercourse. Similarly, for example, a woman whose husband practices coitus reservatus and who is then compelled to masturbate to terminate her distressing unsatisfied excitation may develop an anxiety neurosis plus symptoms of neurasthenia, the first, through repeated excitations without satisfactory conclusion, and the second, through the excessive masturbation she is forced into.[7]

In 'Heredity and the Aetiology of the Neuroses' (1896) he states categorically that the only specific aetiology of neurasthenia is

[1] (1950 [1892–1899]) 'Extracts from the Fliess Papers', S.E., Vol. 1, p. 272.
[2] (1894a) 'The Neuro-Psychoses of Defence', Freud, S., Vol. 3, p. 55.
[3] (1895c) 'Obsessions and Phobias', Freud, S., Vol. 3, p. 76.
[4] (1895d) *Studies on Hysteria*, Freud, S., Vol. 2, p. 210.
[5] (1895b [1894]) 'On the Grounds for Detaching a Particular Syndrome from Neurasthenia under the Description "Anxiety Neurosis"', S.E., Vol. 3, p. 109.
[6] ibid., p. 111.   [7] ibid., p. 113.

immoderate masturbation or spontaneous emissions for prolonged periods. He mentions that in some neurasthenics he did not find this aetiology but that these cases seem 'to have been endowed by heredity with a sexual constitution analogous to what is brought about in a neurasthenic as a result of masturbation'.[1]

In 'Further Remarks on the Neuro-Psychoses of Defence' (1896) he specifically excluded masturbation in childhood from the etiological factors leading to hysteria. He assumed at this time that they were frequently observed together but not because masturbation led to hysteria but because masturbation was a frequent consequence of the abuse or seduction of children.[2] At this time his theory of the 'defence neuroses'* (hysteria and obsessional neurosis) was the seduction theory. Those who developed obsessional neurosis were active participants in the seductive episode while those developing hysteria were the passive victims of an act of sexual abuse or seduction.

In *Abstracts of the Scientific Works of Sigmund Freud* (1897) Freud stated that while true neurasthenia arises from spontaneous emissions or through 'masturbation, the factors belonging to the aetiology of anxiety neurosis are such as correspond to a holding back of sexual excitation—such as abstinence when libido is present, unconsummated excitation and, above all, coitus interruptus.'[3] The same formula is repeated in the 'Sexuality in the Aetiology of the Neuroses' (1898).[4] Freud was so convinced by now that the aetiology of neurasthenia was free indulgence in masturbation that if he did not find such history in a neurasthenia he was led to explore the possibilities of some other disorder such as progressive paralysis.[5]

Later on, in the same publication Freud remarks on how much more frequent masturbation is in grown-up girls and mature men that is generally assumed. He considered that there existed not only the danger of developing neurasthenia but that the patients were

* The *defence neuroses* that is, hysteria and obsessional neuroses are to be contrasted at this point in the development of Freud's thinking with the *actual neuroses* that is, neurasthenia and anxiety neuroses (as understood at the end of last century).

[1] (1896a) 'Heredity and the Aetiology of the Neuroses', S.E., Vol. 3, p. 150.
[2] (1896b) 'Further Remarks on the Neuro-Psychoses of Defence' (II), S.E., Vol. 3, p. 165.
[3] (1897b [1877–1897]) *Abstracts of the Scientific Works of Sigmund Freud* S.E., Vol. 3, p. 251.
[4] (1898a) 'Sexuality in the Aetiology of the Neuroses', S.E., Vol. 3, p. 268.
[5] ibid., p. 269.

afflicted by what they considered a disgraceful secret. He thought it necessary for a successful treatment to break the habit of masturbating and that like in any other addiction it was necessary to place the patient in an institution under medical supervision. Once the patient had recovered 'his strength' he had to be led to normal intercourse practices.[1]

Talking about the sexual theory of the neuroses he stated: 'The main benefit which we obtain from it for neurasthenics lies in the sphere of prophylaxis. If masturbation is the cause of neurasthenia in youth, and if, later on, it acquires aetiological significance for anxiety neurosis as well, by reason of the reduction of potency which it brings about, then the prevention of masturbation in both sexes is a task that deserves more attention than it has hitherto received. When we reflect upon all the injuries, both the grosser and the finer ones, which proceed from neurasthenia—a disorder which we are told is growing more and more prevalent—we see that it is positively a matter of public interest that men should enter upon sexual relations with full potency. In matters of prophylaxis, however, the individual is relatively helpless.'[2]

In *The Interpretation of Dreams* (1900a) as well as in other works there are several references to the symbolic expression in dreams of conflicts around masturbation, such as dreams 'with a dental stimuli', or 'flying dreams', etc.[3] In the same book, Freud referred to a 12-year-old hysterical patient of his who had difficulty falling asleep because he saw 'green faces with red eyes' that terrified him. This, the patient associated with bad habits in children including masturbation, a practice that he engaged in and felt very reproachful of. His mother had predicted that boys like that grow into idiots, do not learn at school and furthermore die young.[4]

In the *Three Essays on a Theory of Sexuality* (1905d) there are a multiplicity of references to the subject of masturbation. He remarked for example how intercourse *per anum* was not the only practice in homosexuality mentioning that frequently masturbation was their only exclusive aim.[5]

Later on in the book and while referring to the sensual sucking of the infant (not at the service of nourishment) he pointed out the

[1] (1898a) 'Sexuality in the Aetiology of the Neuroses', S.E., Vol. 3, p. 275.
[2] ibid., p. 278.
[3] (1900a) *The Interpretation of Dreams*, S.E., Vol. 5, p. 385.
[4] ibid., p. 544.
[5] (1905d) *Three Essays on the Theory of Sexuality*, S.E., Vol. 7, p. 145.

former is frequently combined with rubbing some sensitive part of the body such as the external genitalia stating: 'Many children proceed by this path from sucking to masturbation.'[1]

Freud used the term masturbation not only to refer to genital masturbation but to anal masturbation as well pointing out how stimulation of the anal zone by the finger is by no means a rare practice among children.[2]

He referred to 'early infantile masturbation' as something 'that scarcely a single individual escapes'. He pointed out at this time that girls frequently masturbated genitally by bringing their thighs together while boys use their hands, a fact that he thought of as the contribution that the instinct of mastery makes to masculine sexual activity. He remarked further that three phases of infantile masturbation were to be distinguished. The first phase belongs to early infancy (second half of the first year of life), a second phase around the fourth year of life and a third phase corresponding to pubertal masturbation. The first phase is short-lived, the second one around the fourth year assumes many different forms but he thought that 'its details leave behind the deepest (unconscious) impressions in the subject's memory, determine the development of its character, if he is to remain healthy, and the symptomatology of his neurosis, if he is to fall ill after puberty'. In footnotes added in 1915 and 1920 to the above paragraph he wondered why the sense of guilt of neurotics is frequently attached to pubertal masturbation concluding that since masturbation represents the executive agency of infantile sexuality, it takes over the sense of guilt corresponding to that infantile sexuality.[3]

Freud explained that children who turn into voyeurs frequently do so once their attention has been directed to their genitals through their masturbation. They then develop a marked interest in their playmate's genitals.[4]

Later on and while explaining that inhibitions of sexuality in the guise of guilt, shame, etc. occurs earlier in girls and in the face of less resistance he stated that so far as autoerotic and masturbatory manifestations are concerned 'we might lay it down that the sexuality of little girls is a wholly masculine character'. He further asserted that libido is 'invariably and necessarily' of a masculine character.[5] He thought too that the main erotogenic zone of little

[1] ibid., p. 180.   [2] ibid., p. 187.   [3] ibid., pp. 188–9.
[4] ibid., p. 192.   [5] ibid., p. 219.

girls (around 3 to 4 years) is the clitoris itself the equivalent of the glans penis and that in his experience masturbation at this age is only clitoridal and never involved other areas of the external genitalia. He thought that not even through seduction could a little girl be led to anything else than clitoridal masturbation.[1]

In the *Three Essays on the Theory of Sexuality* (1905) he still maintained that behind neurasthenia there is regular masturbation (or persistent emissions) while anxiety neurosis is to be blamed on unconsummated excitation (such as coitus interruptus).[2] Yet, he acknowledged his previous mistake in terms of his earlier seduction theory stating that he had since learned to explain a number of the fantasies of seduction in the patients 'as attempts at fending off memories of the subject's *own* sexual activity (infantile masturbation)'.[3]

In 'Fragments of an Analysis of a Case of Hysteria' (1905) and while referring to the Dora case he makes the comment that gastric pains occur frequently in those who masturbate.[4] In this paper he comments that hysterical symptoms hardly ever appear so long as children are masturbating. They tend to appear only after a period of abstinence when they become a substitute for the masturbatory satisfaction. In adults, he thought that masturbation and hysterical symptoms can coincide since a *relative* abstinence (diminution in the amount of masturbation) will have the same effect.[5] In this paper he gives several examples of hysterical symptoms, washing compulsions, etc. whose main determinant had come from the infantile masturbatory practices and the struggles against it.[6] Similarly he established a link between bed-wetting (resulting from a regression after an initial period where control had been established) and masturbation, 'a habit whose importance in the aetiology of bed-wetting is still insufficiently appreciated'.[7] He stated too that leucorrhea in young girls was due to masturbation and that all other causes assigned to the complaint were of less importance, a point of view that he corrected in a footnote in 1923.[8]

He referred as well to many forms of symptomatic acts to be observed in the normal and the neurotic who are frequently symbolic representations of masturbation.[9]

[1] (1950d) *Three Essays on the Theory of Sexuality*, S.E. Vol. 7, p. 220.
[2] ibid., p. 272.   [3] ibid., p. 274.
[4] (1905e [1901]) 'Fragments of an Analysis of a Case of Hysteria', S.E., Vol. 7, p. 78.
[5] ibid., p. 79.   [6] ibid., pp. 25 and 81.   [7] ibid., p. 74.   [8] ibid., p. 76.
[9] ibid., p. 77.

In 'Hysterical Fantasies and their Relation to Bisexuality' (1907) he explained the important connection existing between unconscious fantasies and the subject's sexual life, particularly those accompanying masturbation stating that at that point masturbation (in its widest sense and not only manual friction) was composed of two parts. One the evocation of the fantasy, the other some piece of behaviour aimed at self-gratification at the height of the conscious fantasy. This composite was merely soldered together, in other words to start with masturbation was a purely auto-erotic procedure to obtain some pleasure from a part of the body (an erotogenic zone). Later on this auto-erotic procedure is linked up with a wishful idea from the sphere of object-love serving 'as a partial realization of the situation in which the fantasy culminated'. Still later, when such satisfaction (masturbation plus fantasy) is abandoned, the action is given up but the fantasy becomes unconscious. If no other forms of suitable satisfaction supervenes and/or, if such impulses cannot be sublimated, the unconscious fantasy will proliferate and lead finally to the formation of a pathological symptom. 'In this way, unconscious fantasies are the immediate psychical precursors of a whole number of hysterical symptoms.' Thus, the giving up of masturbation is undone, 'and the purpose of the whole pathological process, which is a restoration of the original, primary sexual satisfaction, is achieved—though never completely, it is true, but always in a sort of approximation'.[1]

In '"Civilized" Sexual Morality and Modern Nervous Illness' (1908), Freud elaborated in great detail his view of the potential dangers of excessive masturbation. Discussing abstinence he remarks that it is not always that a clear distinction is made between abstention from sexual intercourse with the opposite object and abstention from any sexual activity whatsoever. He went on to describe how many people who boast about their abstinence can only do so with the help of masturbation and other similar forms of auto-erotic infantile activities explaining how these substitute practices *are by no means harmless.* They predispose to various neuroses and psychoses 'which are conditional on an involution of sexual life to its infantile forms'. He thought too, that masturbation did not meet the ideal demands of civilized sexual morality (as present at that point) with the consequence that young people find themselves in

[1] (1908a) 'Hysterical Fantasies and their Relation to Bisexuality', S.E., Vol. 9, pp. 161–2.

conflict with the very ideals of education that they hoped to avoid through abstinence. Furthermore, he thought that it vitiates the *character* in more than one way through indulgence. First, 'it teaches people to achieve important aims without taking trouble and by easy paths instead of through an energetic exertion of force —that is, it follows the principle that *sexuality lays down the pattern* of behaviour; secondly, in the fantasies that accompany satisfaction the sexual object is raised to a degree of excellence which is not easily found again in reality'. He mentioned a Viennese witty writer who cynically expressed this truth in reverse by saying: 'Copulation is no more than an unsatisfying substitute for masturbation.'[1]

Later on, still in the same publication Freud stated that men given to masturbatory or perverse sexual practices go into marriage with diminished sexual potency. This is bound to be disruptive, the wife may remain dissatisfied sexually. Even more, some will remain anaesthetic even in those cases where the disposition to frigidity (due to their education) could have been overcome by a powerful sexual experience.[2]

In 'The Sexual Theories of Children' (1908) he referred to that stage in child development where the boy is dominated by excitations in his penis that would naturally lead to his playing with it with his hand which may have led to threats of cutting off his penis, a set of experiences linked with the castration complex.[3]

In 'Some General Remarks on Hysterical Attacks' (1909) he mentions that the investigation of the infantile history of hysteric patients shows the hysterical attack as a substitute of an infantile auto-erotic satisfaction whose practice have been abandoned. In some cases masturbation, by contact or by pressure of the thighs, is present during the attack and while consciousness is deflected.[4]

In 'Analysis of a Phobia in a Five-Year-Old Boy' (1909) Freud mentions how at 3½ the child was found playing with his penis by the mother who threatened him: 'If you do that, I shall send for

[1] (1908a) ' "Civilized" Sexual Morality and Modern Nervous Illness', S.E., Vol. 9, pp. 199, 200.
[2] ibid., p. 201.
[3] (1908c) 'The Sexual Theories of Children', S.E., Vol. 9, p. 217.
[4] (1909a [1908]) 'Some General Remarks on Hysterical Attacks', S.E., Vol. 9, p. 232.

Dr A. to cut off your widdler.'[1] Freud argued that Little Hans' pathological anxiety was not due to the child's masturbation that he had indulged for over a year but to the struggle to break himself from the habit, a fact that according to him fitted better with repression and the generation of anxiety.[2] He mentioned too that what frequently leads children to touch their genitals is a sensation of itching in the glans penis.[3] Freud recounted a masturbatory fantasy of Little Hans. He had woken with a fright about six o'clock, and when asked what has happened, the child said: 'I put my finger to my widdler just a very little (he had been warned many times not to do this by his father and mother). I saw Mummy quite naked in her chemise and she let me see her widdler. I showed Grete, my Grete what Mummy was doing, and showed her my widdler. Then I took my hand away from my widdler quick.'[4]

Later on, he referred to the possible *deferred* effect of threats of castration used earlier on in the life of the child in regard to masturbatory practices. Little Hans' mother uttered the threat to stop him from giving himself pleasure by playing with his penis, when 'the little boy had begun to practice the commonest—and most normal—form of auto-erotic sexual activity'.[5]

In 'Notes Upon a Case of Obsessional Neurosis' (1909) Freud discussed again why it was that neurotic patients were unanimous in blaming their pubertal masturbation for their illness. Doctors, he argued, are either unable to decide or since masturbation during puberty is a typical occurrence will dismiss such a possibility. He argued that masturbation during puberty is no more than a revival of infantile masturbation—usually reaching a climax during the ages of 3 and 5. He concluded that in a disguised way they are blaming their illness in their infantile sexuality. He thought the patients were right since it is in their infantile sexuality that the aetiology of later neuroses must be sought.[6]

He thought it important not to treat masturbation as a clinical unit since it represents a form of discharge for every sort of sexual component instinct and of the fantasies to which they give rise. Similarly he thought, that the injurious effects of masturbation are not due to the masturbatory act *per se* but were 'part and parcel of

---

[1] (1909b) 'Analysis of a Phobia in a Five-Year-Old Boy', S.E., Vol. 10, pp. 7–8.
[2] ibid., p. 27.   [3] ibid., p. 30.   [4] ibid., p. 32.   [5] ibid., pp. 35, 36.
[6] (1909d) 'Notes Upon a Case of Obsessional Neurosis', S.E., Vol. 10, p. 202.

the pathogenic significance of the subject's sexual life as a whole'.[1]

He added further: 'The fact that so many people can tolerate masturbation—that is, a certain amount of it—without injury merely shows that their sexual constitution and the course of development of their sexual life have been such as to allow them to exercise the sexual function within the limits of what is culturally permissible; whereas other people, because their sexual constitution has been less favourable or their development has been disturbed, fall ill as the result of their sexuality—they cannot, that is, achieve the necessary suppression or sublimation of their sexual components without having recourse to inhibitions or substitutes.'[2]

In this same paper he discusses many of the peculiarities of behaviour and compulsive symptoms of the patient in relation to the underlying conflicts around masturbation concluding that 'obsessional acts tend to approximate more and more—and the longer the disorder lasts the more evident does this become—to infantile sexual acts of a masturbatory character'.[3]

In 'A Special Type of Choice of Object Made by Men' (1910) and while discussing how the boy comes under dominance of the oedipus complex he explains how the forbidden impulses towards the possession of the mother can determine fantasies having as their subject the child's mother's sexual activities. The tension thus raised frequently finds relief in masturbation.[4] In the same paper, while discussing the 'family romance' and the *rescue* fantasies characteristic of certain males love life he stated that there 'is no difficulty in assuming that the masturbation assiduously practised in the years of puberty has played its part in the fixation of the fantasies'.[5]

Still later, in the same publication he explained how when the libido is turned away from objects in reality it goes into the patient's fantasy life strengthening the images of the first sexual objects and establishing a fixation to them. Since these are incestuous objects the process takes place in the unconscious (away from consciousness). He thought that nothing is changed by the fact that the miscarried advances in reality to non-incestuous

[1] (1909d) 'Notes Upon a Case of Obsessional Neurosis', S.E., Vol. 10, pp. 202–3.
[2] ibid., p. 203.   [3] ibid., p. 244.
[4] (1910h) 'A Special Type of Choice of Object Made by Men', S.E., Vol. 11, p. 171.
[5] ibid., p. 172.

objects is now completed in fantasy that is, if through a substitution in fantasy the original sexual objects are replaced by others. The fantasies accompanying masturbation are then acceptable in consciousness but no progress whatsoever is made in terms of the allocation of libido in reality and furthermore sensuality in this way remains tied to incestuous objects in the unconscious.[1]

In 'The Psycho-Analytic View of the Psychogenic Disturbances of Vision' (1910), he referred to the talion punishment such as when the fingers of people who had conflicts around masturbation refuse to learn the movements required for learning the piano or the violin.[2]

In the Schreber Case (1911), he made the by now well-known connection between the fear of losing one's reason because of sexual indulgence and especially masturbation. He added of the Schreber's case: 'Considering the enormous number of delusional ideas of a hypochondriacal nature which the patient developed, no great importance should perhaps be attached to the fact that some of them coincide word for word with the hypochondriacal fears of masturbators.'[3]

From November 1911 to April 1912 there were nine evenings devoted by the Vienna Psychoanalytic Society to a discussion on the subject of masturbation. Freud contributed the concluding remarks and when the proceedings of these meetings were published he wrote an introduction to it.

According to Freud there was agreement on:

(a) The importance of the role of fantasies (that either accompany or *represent the act of masturbation*).
(b) The importance of the sense of guilt attached to it.
(c) The impossibility of attaching a qualitative determinant for the injurious effect of masturbation, a point in which agreement was not unanimous.

There were unresolved differences of opinion:

(a) In respect to a denial of a somatic factor in the effects of masturbation.

[1] ibid., p. 182.
[2] (1910i) 'The Psychoanalytic View of the Psychogenic Disturbances of Vision', S.E., Vol. 11, p. 217.
[3] (1911c) 'Psycho-Analytic Notes on an Autobiographical Account of a Case of Paranoia (Dementia Paranoides)', S.E., Vol. 12, p. 57.

(b) In respect to a general denial of the damaging effects of masturbation.
(c) In respect of the origin of the sense of guilt.
(d) In respect of the ubiquity of masturbation in infancy.

Significant uncertainties remained:

(a) As to the mechanism of the damaging effects of masturbation if there were any and
(b) As to the aetiological relationship between masturbation and 'actual neuroses'.

He further pointed out to the convenience of dividing masturbation according to subject's age that is, infants, children and puberty.

He kept to his early views in regards to neurasthenia, similarly defending his concept of anxiety neuroses, adding now hypochondria as the third actual neuroses.

He took a position in regard to the damaging effects of masturbation that was in opposition to Stekel's view that is, that there was no real damage to the practice, only prejudices associated with it. Freud argued that if we admit that the sexual urges can have a pathogenic effect, we should not deny a similar effect to masturbation (which is no more than carrying out such sexual urges). He added: 'Masturbation is not anything ultimate—whether somatic or psychologically—it is not a real "agent", but merely the name for certain activities. Yet, however much we may trace things further back, our judgement on the causation of the illness will nevertheless rightly remain attached to this activity. And do not forget that masturbation is not to be equated with sexual activity in general; it is sexual activity subjected to certain limiting conditions. Thus it also remains possible that it is precisely these peculiarities of masturbatory activity which are the vehicles of its pathogenic effect.

'We are therefore brought back once more from arguments to clinical observation, and we are warned by it not to strike out the heading "Injurious Effects of Masturbation". We are at all events confronted in the neuroses with cases in which masturbation has done damage.'[1]

This damage seems to occur in three different ways:

[1] (1912f) 'Contributions to a Discussion on Masturbation', S.E., Vol. 12, pp. 245–51.

(a) Organic injury taking place by some unknown mechanism . . . excess and inadequate satisfaction being two of the factors to be considered.
(b) The damage may take place through the laying down of a *psychical pattern* according to which no changes in the external world are necessary to satisfy needs.
(c) Through a fixation to infantile sexual aims with a persistence of psychical infantilism which predisposes to the development of neurosis.

He referred to the relation of masturbation and concomitant fantasies to the pleasure principle versus living according to the reality principle. He thought that masturbation makes possible certain sexual developments and sublimations in fantasy but if all remains at that level these are not real advances but injurious compromises. Yet as Stekel's pointed out this kind of compromise can render severe perverse inclinations harmless and avoid some of the consequences of abstinence.[1]

He said too that he could not rule out, on the basis of his medical experience, that a permanent reduction of potency is among the results of excessive masturbation at puberty further elaborating that this may not prove as injurious as it may seem since some reduction in potency and in the brutal aggressiveness associated with it are of help to civilization.[2]

He thought it advantageous to distinguish between *direct* injuries (due to masturbation itself) and *indirect* ones arising from the ego's objection to it.[3]

He went then to discuss under what conditions, in which cases and in what people was masturbation injurious, assuming that it was so. He had no answer here but pointed out to the need to assess the *quantitative* factor, the combined operation of various pathogenic factors, and the individual constitutional dispositions. He acknowledges that the latter factor was very difficult to assess.[4]

His concluding statements concerned the fact that little attention had been paid to unconscious masturbation (during sleep, in hysterical fits, etc.) and finally he referred to 'the therapeutic return of masturbation' by which he meant that the return of masturbation during treatment is for some patients a great step forward

[1] ibid., p. 252.   [2] ibid., p. 252.   [3] ibid., p. 253.   [4] ibid., p. 253.

assuming that they have no intention to make a permanent stop at that infantile halting-place.[1]

In *Totem and Taboo* (1912–13) he again explained the psychical mechanisms behind touching phobias in obsessionals and its relation to the child's conflict about touching his own genitals.[2]

After 'Contributions to a Discussion on Masturbation' Freud's references to this subject are frequently in the context of the castration complex. Thus, in the paper on 'The Unconscious' (1915) he referred to a patient where pressing the content of blackheads was a substitute for masturbation while the cavity left behind represented the female genital that is, the fulfilment of the threat of castration brought about by his symbolic masturbatory activities.[3]

In the *Introductory Lectures on Psycho-Analysis* (1916–17) he gave again some of the common symbols in dreams that stand for masturbation such as all kinds of playing with something, including playing the piano, gliding, sliding, pulling off a branch, etc. while the falling out of a tooth or the pulling out of a tooth (dreams with a dental stimuli) represent castration as a punishment for masturbation.[4]

In the same work he pointed out once more how many obsessional actions can be traced back to masturbation, the obsessional acts being disguised repetitions of the act, etc.[5] A few pages later and while talking of the enormous importance of the breast for the infant, as the first object of his sexual instinct, he explains how that object is replaced by a part of the body (his thumb or his tongue) and in this way makes himself independent of the external world as regards gaining pleasure. Since not all parts of the body are equally excitable, 'it is an important experience when the infant, as Lindner reports, discovers, in the course of feeling around, the specially excitable regions afforded by his genitals and so finds his way from sucking to masturbation'.[6]

He explained that a child's sexual life is made up of the activities of several component instincts looking for gratification indepen-

---

[1] (1912f) 'Contributions to a Discussion on Masturbation', S.E., Vol. 12, pp. 235–4.
[2] (1912–13), *Totem and Taboo*, S.E., Vol. 13, p. 29.
[3] (1915e) 'The Unconscious', S.E., Vol. 14, p. 200.
[4] (1916–17) *Introductory Lectures on Psycho-Analysis*, S.E., Vol. 15, pp. 156 and 190.
[5] ibid., p. 309.   [6] ibid., p. 314.

dently of one another, either through objects or in the subjects own body. The genitals are naturally important and there are people that go without interruption from infantile masturbation 'to the unavoidable masturbation of puberty and persists for an indefinite length of time afterwards'. He added: 'Incidentally, the topic of masturbation is not one that can be so easily disposed of: it is something that calls for examination from many angles.'[1]

It was in the *Introductory Lectures* too that Freud makes the contrast between the development of a proletarian and a middle-class girl that while playing together may have stimulated each other sexually. The comparison is aimed at showing the freer sexual development of the proletarian girl and her greater freedom regarding masturbation while the middle class girl will grow with a sense of having done something wrong, and other moral and social pressures regarding sexual activities that may wreck her sexual life and through guilt, disgust and repression may lead to a neurosis.[2]

He mentioned too that a fantasy of having been seduced when no seduction has taken place usually is used to screen infantile masturbatory practices.[3]

He defended in this work his earlier views regarding neurasthenia and masturbation, as well as the sexual etiology of the actual neurosis.[4]

In 'From the History of an Infantile Neurosis' (1918) and while talking of the attempts at seduction of his patient, by the patient's sister he commented on how the child began to play with his penis in his nurse's (Nanya) presence 'and this, like so many other instances in which children do not conceal their masturbation, must be regarded as an attempt at seduction'.[5] His nurse rejected his seduction adding that boys that play with their penises develop 'a wound' there. He shows in this case how children begin their sexual researches after the first genital excitations and how they hit upon the 'problem of castration' usually through observations of girl's genitals.[6]

He shows too how his patient gave up masturbation after this threat and in so doing the genital zone, that was starting to acquire dominance was thrown back or forced to regress (through this

[1] ibid., pp. 316–17.   [2] ibid., p. 353.   [3] ibid., p. 370.   [4] ibid., p. 386.
[5] (1918b [1914]) 'From the History of an Infantile Neurosis', S.E., Vol. 17, p. 24.
[6] ibid., p. 25.

external obstacle or danger) to an earlier phase of pre-genital organization (in this patient's case the anal-sadistic organization).[1]

In 'A Child is Being Beaten' (1919), he referred to the extraordinary frequency of this type of fantasy that is highly pleasurable and usually accompanied by genital masturbation. He thought that this phenomena usually started not later than the fifth or sixth year of life and stated that all his male patients with such masturbatory fantasies had to be considered masochists in the sense of a sexual perversion.[2]

In 'The Economic Problem of Masochism' (1924) Freud, while discussing the type of feminine masochism in men described how the fantasies of these patients (that are frequently impotent in intercourse) terminate in an act of masturbation.[3]

In 'The Dissolution of the Oedipus Complex' (1924) he explains how when the interest of the male child centres in his genitals this is betrayed by the child's frequent manipulation of his penis and how more or less plainly or even brutally threats of castration are issued in order to stop him from the practice. To start with, the child may take little notice of such threats but it is frequently the sight of the female genital that breaks down his disbelief of the threats.[4] Here again he equated adult emissions with bed-wetting in children saying 'It is an expression of the same excitation of the genitals which has impelled the child to masturbate at this period.'

In the same paper Freud remarks that masturbation does not by any means represent the whole of his sexual life at this age ($2\frac{1}{2}$–5). He is in the middle of his oedipus complex and masturbation is at this point only a genital discharge of the sexual excitation (and active and passive fantasies) belonging to that complex. Throughout his later life masturbation will owe its importance to this relationship.[5]

In 'The Significance of the Anatomical Distinction Between the Sexes' (1925) he came back to the relationship between masturbation and the fantasies associated with the oedipus complex wondering if masturbation had been associated with the oedipus complex in this way from the beginning or whether on the contrary mastur-

[1] (1918b [1914]) 'From the History of an Infantile Neurosis', S.E., Vol. 17, p. 26.
[2] (1919e) 'A Child is Being Beaten', S.E., Vol. 17, p. 179.
[3] (1924c) 'The Economic Problem of Masochism', S.E., Vol. 19, p. 161.
[4] (1924d) 'The Dissolusion of the Oedipus Complex', S.E., Vol., 19 pp. 174–5.
[5] ibid., p. 176.

bation appears first spontaneously as an activity of a bodily organ and only later is brought into relation with the oedipus complex.* He speculated that perhaps the whole sexual development of the child is triggered off by listening, at a tender age, to the noises of parental copulation that may trigger off the first sexual excitations. It is then later on that masturbation and the two attitudes of the oedipus complex (passive and active) are attached to this early experience, 'the child having subsequently interpreted its meaning'. Since he found it impossible to assume that observation of coitus is a universal occurrence he was led to postulate the existence of 'primal fantasies'.[1]

Later, in the same paper and in regard to girls, he referred to the tenacity of the bond with their fathers in certain women, which culminates in the unconscious wish of having a child by him. He said he had good reasons to assume 'that the same wishful fantasy was also the motive force of their infantile masturbation . . .'.[2] A few pages later, he reiterated an earlier statement concerning the 'masculine' character of clitoridal masturbation and of the libido. He added, that the analyses of the remote phallic period in girls has taught him that soon after the first sign of penis envy, 'an intense current of feeling against masturbation makes its appearance, which cannot be attributed exclusively to the educational influence of those in charge of the child'. He thought of it as a developmental force.[3]

As late as 1925, in his *An Autobiographical Study*, he was still defending his early views, (dating from 1895) of the sexual etiology of the actual neuroses (neurasthenia and anxiety neurosis) and the relationship of neurasthenia with excessive masturbation and that of coitus interruptus or any unconsummated form of sexual excitation with anxiety neurosis. Nevertheless, he acknowledged that for many years he had had no opportunity to further study the subject of actual neuroses stating that he considered now his early findings as rough outlines of very complicated matters though on the whole he felt they still held good. He made it clear that he was not denying the existence, in neurasthenia, of mental and neurotic

---

* This seems to imply the possibility of a distinction between a phallic, and a later phallic-oedipal phase that is frequently discussed among child-analysts.

[1] (1925j) 'Some Psychical Consequences of the Anatomical Distinction Between the Sexes', S.E., Vol. 19, p. 250.

[2] ibid., p. 251.   [3] ibid., p. 255.

conflicts and complexes but went on to assert that their symptoms were not mentally determined or removable by analysis. He concluded that they must be regarded as toxic consequences of disturbed chemical processes.[1]

In *Inhibitions, Symptoms and Anxiety* (1926) he describes as one of the main tasks of latency the struggle against the temptation to masturbate. As a result of it symptoms in the nature of ceremonials appear in the most different individuals. 'They tend to become attached [the ceremonials] to activities (which would later be carried out almost automatically) such as going to sleep, washing, dressing and walking about; and they tend to repetition and waste of time.' He thought that the sublimation of anal-erotic components plays a significant part in them but he could not explain why.[2] Later, in the same book, he refers to the phobia of being alone that ultimately is an endeavour to avoid the temptation to masturbate.[3]

In *The Question of Lay Analysis* (1926) Freud discusses the ubiquitous phenomena of infantile masturbation asking what kind of attitude should we assume towards early childhood sexuality stating: 'We know the responsibility we are incurring if we suppress it; but we do not venture to let it take its course without restriction. Among races at a low level of civilization, and among the lower strata of civilized races, the sexuality of children seems to be given free rein. This probably provides a powerful protection against the subsequent development of neuroses in the individual. But does it not at the same time involve an extraordinary loss of the aptitude for cultural achievements? There is a good deal to suggest that here we are faced by a new Scylla and Charybdis.'[4]

In a letter to Reik (1929) concerning 'Dostoevsky and Parricide' (1928) he established a connection between those neuroses accompanied by a severe sense of guilt and the struggles against masturbation further linking masturbation and an addiction to gambling such as that shown by Dostoevsky.[5]

In his paper on 'Female Sexuality' (1931) he stated that little girls discover by themselves their characteristic phallic activity, clitoridal masturbation, an activity that to start with was not

[1] (1925d [1924]) *An Autobiographical Study*, S.E., Vol. 20, p. 25.
[2] (1926d) *Inhibitions, Symptoms and Anxiety*, S.E., Vol. 20, p. 116.
[3] ibid., p. 127.
[4] (1926e) *The Question of Lay Analysis*, S.E., Vol. 20, p. 217.
[5] (1928b) 'Dostoevsky and Parricide', S.E., Vol. 21, pp. 183 and 196.

accompanied by fantasies. He thought that the role of seducer is given to mothers and nurses because they are responsible for the hygienic activities of the nursery. He stated too that a prohibition of masturbation is in itself a form of incentive to give it up but at the same time might become the motive to rebel against those who interfere with this practice and later on with their substitutes, adding that a defiant persistence of masturbation opens the ways to masculinity and other complications of female development. Later he added that girls will attribute the lack of a penis to the fact of castration as a punishment for their masturbation.[1]

He pointed too towards the identity of the phallic attachment to the mother in both boys and girls, the girl abandoning this position by her recognition of her castration (or her dissatisfaction with her clitoris) and with this move she frequently abandons masturbation as well, with a resultant increment in the passive feminine trends.[2] Freud came back to the above subjects explaining in the *New Introductory Lectures*;[3] *Moses and Monotheism*[4] and in *An Outline of Psychoanalysis*[5] the role of masturbation during the phallic-oedipal phase for boys and girls with their similarities and differences as well as the role played by castration anxiety, castration threats and penis envy in the abandonment of masturbation (and concomitant fantasies) and in the further vicissitudes of masculine and feminine development.

In the 'Splitting of the Ego in the Process of Defence' (1940) Freud mentions how some patients can ignore the threat of castration associated with masturbation and reinforced by the sight of the female genital by means of the creation of a fetish. He said: 'So long as he was not obliged to acknowledge that females have lost their penis [by means of creating a substitute for it in the form of the fetish], there was no need for him to believe the threat that had been made against him: he need have no fears for his own penis, so he could proceed with his masturbation undisturbed.'[6]

In some notes written on August 3rd, appearing under 'Shorter

[1] (1931b) 'Female Sexuality', S.E., Vol. 21, pp. 232 and 233.
[2] ibid., pp. 239 and 241.
[3] (1933a) *New Introductory Lectures on Psycho-Analysis*, S.E., Vol. 21, p. 126.
[4] (1939a [1937–39]) *Moses and Monotheism*, S.E., Vol. 23, p. 79.
[5] (1940a [1938]) *An Outline of Psycho-Analysis*, S.E., Vol. 23, pp. 155–189 and 193.
[6] (1940e [1938]) 'Splitting of the Ego in the Process of Defence', S.E., Vol. 23, p. 277.

Writings' (1937–8) in the Standard Edition he had written that behind all intellectual and work inhibitions one finds the inhibition of masturbation in childhood. He added that perhaps the problem went deeper that is, that it was the unsatisfying nature of masturbation at this age (because of the absence of orgasm) that was somehow responsible for this.[1]

[1] (1937–38) 'Shorter Writings', S.E., Vol. 23, p. 300.

INDEX

Bold type indicates main entry

frustration 184, 189

gastric pain and masturbation 212
genetic: points of view 38, 41, **43–6**; psychology 19, 20
genital: masturbation 211; zone activity 151; zones and forepleasure 152
girls and castration anxiety 225
guilt complex 9
guilt, sense of 35

hallucination 161; cathectic process in 93–4
Hartmann, H., 15, 16 'The Development of the Ego Concept in Freud's Work' 16n.
Hartmann H., Kris, E., and Loewenstein, R. M., 'The Function of Theory in Psychoanalysis' 15 and n., 16 and n.
hate 110
homosexuality 106, 107, 132, 138, 194, 210
hostility 184
humour 75
hypercathexes 77, 85, 86, 189

hysteria 46, 49, 74, 99, 117, 125, 137, 170, 198; in masturbation 109, 212

id, the, 21, 31, 32, 38, 40, 41, 42, 46, 71, 72, 73, 75, 82, 95, 105, 161; cathexes in 91, 92
ideational: activity 50; complex 44
identity 157
illusion 74
impulses, affectionate and hostile 130
incest 154
inertia, principle of 66
infantile: amnesia 45; anxiety 154; masturbation 211, 215, 224. See also children; sexuality 43, 45, 139, 149, 150, 151
inferiority complex 9
inhibition 52
instinct for knowledge 151
instincts: and object 20, 27, 65, 132, 141, 142; theory of 64, 68, 108, 109, 110
insusceptibility to excitation of un-cathected systems 68–9
intoxication 36, 75
introversion 124
inversion 144, 154

Jones, E. 200; Freud's letter to 102. See also Sigmund Freud, Life and Work of
judgement, function of 164
Jung, C. G., 113; theory of 60

Kris, E. 15 and n.; 16 and n.

latency of neurosis 45
Least Expenditure of Innervation principle 55–6, 67
leucorrhea 212
libidinal: cathexes 22, 77, 82, 84, 141, 176; components 37; development 43, 117; fixation and regression 126; impulse 106, 128; instincts 65, 110; types 102. See also libido
libido 35, 36, 39, 71, 85, 88, 92, 95, 96, 107, 109, 115, 128, 148, 176, 178, 196, 211; in conflict 98, 99; detachment of the 125; economics of 37; in fixation 113; in illness 118; liberated 126; in neurosis 104; organization of 124; regression of 121, 123, 124, 125; theory 153; in

transference 184, 189; undischarged 127. See also libidinal
life instinct 70, 71. See also Eros
Little Hans, case of, see Freud, Cases of
Loewenstein, R. M. 15 and n., 16 and n.
love 173; and hate 131, 141; instinct and sexual aim 134; and loving 131

masochism 107, 146–7; inherent 76
masturbation 207–26; anal zone 150; and bedwetting 212; and children 211; in concomitant fantasies 219; damaging effects 218; danger of 213–14; feminine 211; hysteria in 109, 212; injuries due to 219; masculine 211; and progressive paralysis 209; sense of guilt 217; and sexual potency 214; substitute for 220; threats used by parents 214–15; treatment for 210; unconscious 219; warning to children 214–15
material reality 104, 105
megalomania dementia praecox 189
melancholia 118, 126, 132, 137, 190
memories, cathectic processes in 93–4
mental apparatus 70, 74; disturbances, mechanism of 39; functioning, principles of 47–76; health, danger areas of 64; processes, differences between 79
metaphysics 23
metapsychology 19–26; points of view in 27
mind, division of 40
mnemic image 54, 55, 93, 94
mobile cathexis 77, 79, 80, 81; energy of 83
mother, effect of absence of 33
mother complex 9
mother-child relationship 134
mother's breast and child 141
motor discharge 63, 83
mourning 35

narcissism 36, 95, 118, 127, 126. See also narcissistic
narcissistic: cathexes 84; disorder 180, 188–90; libidinal cathexes 141; libido 88, 95; neurosis 41, 46, 190. See also narcissism
negative transference 180
neurasthenia 207, 223; and masturbation 208, 221